FOREVER TEXAS

FOREVER TEXAS

TEXAS HISTORY, THE WAY THOSE WHO LIVED IT WROTE IT

Edited by Mike Blakely
and Mary Elizabeth Goldman

A TOM DOHERTY ASSOCIATES BOOK
NEW YORK

PERMISSIONS

The following list of material has been created by Mary Elizabeth Goldman, coeditor of *Forever Texas*, and is being printed in this volume by permission of and special arrangement and understanding with the holders of the respective copyrights. All photos belong to the original copyright holder and are included here with the permission of the copyright holder.

Introduction by David Nevin
"Elmer Kelton Remembers His West Texas Roots"
    by Elmer Kelton
"What Texas Means to Me" by Jory Sherman
"Texas Bound" by Carole Nelson Douglas
"The First Texans"
    by Calvin R. Cummings and Linda Scott Cummings
"Texas—from the Outside" by Bill Groneman
"Facets of the Alamo" by Frank Thompson
"The Misdemeanor Murder Trial" by Gary James
"Texas Style" by James "Mac" McIngvale
"Recollections of Texas" by H. Ross Perot
"Red River Women" by Sherrie S. McLeRoy
"The Wraith Riding Shotgun"
    by Lucia St. Clair Robson
"The Heart of Texas" by Thomas Fleming
"The Time of Her Life" by Bryan Woolley
"The Cowboy's Paradise" by Patrick Dearen
"Living in the Last Frontier" by Craig Carter
"One Riot, One Ranger" by Mike Cox
"Not Afraid to Go to Hell by Himself" by Dale L. Walker
"Frontiers Old and New" by Douglas V. Meed

"Lost and Found in a Border Town"
   by Randy Lee Eickhoff
"Hell and Texas" by Paul Andrew Hutton
"An Expatriate's Lament: A Texas Pilgrim in Arkansas"
   by W. C. Jameson
"No Drugstore Cowboys" by James "Doc" Blakely
"From Havana to Silicon Hills" by Roger J. Pineiro

Taken from public domain with suggestion and express permission from the Governors Office.

"On Family Values" by Governor George Bush

Taken from letters to Goldman in response to query "What Texas Means to Me." Letters responding to query imply and grant permission to use essays and photographs. All original photos belong to the participants. Photographs belonging to the participants are submitted with permission to reproduce in this volume.

"Texan by Choice" by Mayor Lee P. Brown
"My Texas Hero" by John Cornyn III
"A Texas Legacy" by James A. Baker III
"My Trip to Texas" by Brigitta Herfort
"Bandit Queen Belle Starr" by Danny Shirley
"The Spirit of Texas" by Denton A. Cooley, M.D.
"Real Texans" by Dale Evans Rogers
"It Ain't Much to Look At . . ." by Mac Davis
"Patriots" by Captain Burl Terrill, USMC Ret.
"I'll Always be a Texan" by Gale Storm
"Short and Sweet" by Buck Owens
"What Kind of People?" by Senator Phil Gramm
"Forever Texas" by Senator Kay Bailey Hutchison
"On Coming to Texas" by Walter Cronkite
"The Texas Braggadocio" by Stanley Marcus
"100%" by Tom C. Frost
"Ninnie L. Baird, a Texas Legend" by Members of the Baird Family

Taken from taped interview and letters between Goldman and Fess Parker for the express and only purpose of *Forever Texas*.

"An Awareness" by Fess Parker

Taken from interview between Goldman and Charlie Schreiner III for the express and only purpose of *Forever Texas*.

"The YO Ranch and the Texas Legacy" by Charlie Schreiner III

From the archives of American Airlines and written permission to use material and photos furnished by American Airlines C. R. Smith Museum for *Forever Texas*.

"Mr. C. R. and American Airlines"

Contents

10 CONTENTS

MEMORY ONE

MIKE BLAKELY

Think back, if you will. Back into your own past. What stands out as your earliest memory in life? The first thing you clearly recollect?

My dad, Doc Blakely, once asked the same of me, and I got to pondering. Who knows what his reason was for asking? Perhaps curiosity. Perhaps a compulsion to perfect some philosophy. But he was crafty in the way he presented the subject to me and got me interested. What was *my* earliest memory?

I searched the images stored away in the web-cloaked corners of my brain. I talked with my folks about it, trying to sort the vague recollections of my childhood chronologically. I finally isolated my earliest memory.

I was sitting in a plowed field, playing with clods of dirt. I looked up and saw a horse standing broadside some distance away. That was it—my first memory. Dirt clods and horseflesh in an East Texas field.

When I told my father about this, he smiled. The horse's name was Charlie Horse, he said. My parents were running a small farm near Huntsville at the time, while my father went to school at Sam Houston State. This would have been the spring of 1960, but even in that advanced age of the internal combustion engine, Charlie Horse had been trained to pull a plow. With a horsedrawn sodbuster, my dad had turned up the dirt clods I played with in my earliest memory. I was about a year-and-a-half old when this happened.

With that settled, my father proceeded to tell me *his* earliest memory in life. Perhaps this is what he wanted to share all along, and now I was more than willing to listen. His earliest memory goes something like this.

He was standing on a big wooden porch, looking out over a field of tall grass, or wheat, that undulated in the wind. The field was huge in his eyes. It went on forever. A dirt road led from that front porch, through the field, to some far-off place.

As he looked out over this field, his mother came to his side and said, "Look, your daddy's coming home." So he looked, and saw his father walking down that long dirt road that led through the field of waving stalks. He was happy to see his dad coming home.

Now, I don't know if a person's first recollections of life count for much. Who knows why things start to imprint themselves on our brains? A field of clods. A horse. I still like to see a plow turn up rich earth. I still own horses and like to ride. Does any of this mean anything? Why did my father bring all this up in the first place? Apparently, he was just fascinated.

You should understand that Doc Blakely frequently tunes in to the ethereal. One day we crossed Hamilton Creek on our way to my little *ranchito,* the *Rancho Quien Sabe,* and stopped on the old bridge there to watch surging flood waters boil down the usually brooklike creek.

"That's amazing," he said. "Imagine that much water. Where does it all come from?"

"Well," I began, "this creek drains a lot of country. It's steep, rocky country, too. Doesn't soak up the rain like loamy soils on level ground. It runs off. We got a good three-inch downpour in less than an hour, and the ground was already saturated from that rain a few days ago."

I figured he'd appreciate all this, seeing as how he had once run a soils testing laboratory. But instead, he quoted my grandfather in a familiar phrase that always seemed ill-constructed, yet somehow brilliant in its scope:

"Nothin's ass, boy. It's a mystery."

Then I understood. Not every question needs answering, especially by the likes of me. My father had *wanted* to be fascinated by the volume of water swirling under us. It was the same way with his musings about his earliest memory. Perhaps there was no point to it. It was just fascinating somehow. Mysterious. Why would he choose *that* as his first memory? Or, why would it choose him?

A couple of years after my dad and I talked about our earliest memories of life, I went to visit my grandfather, Jim B. Blakely, who at the time was living in Freer, Texas, in his late eighties. Born in 1906 in Indian Territory, the year before it became Oklahoma, he is now ninety-four years old and still ornery as ever.

When I visit my grandfather, I like to get him talking about life in the old days. It usually doesn't take much prompting. He especially likes to talk about the Great Depression, I guess simply because he survived it, and went on to become a wealthy man one of the hardest ways known to man—welding and machine shop owner in the South Texas oil patch. I have no real concept of how bad things got during the Depression, except for the earnest accounts of my grandfather.

Jim B. Blakely left Rush Springs, Oklahoma, about 1935 and drifted south through Texas, looking for work. He had a wife and a year-old son—my father. He worked for a while on the Lake Buchanan Dam, pushing wheelbarrows full of rocks up a board ramp, but got fired by a boss he didn't get along with. He opened a barbecue joint in Burnet for a while, but few people had the money to buy restaurant fare—even barbecue.

He asked a banker in Burnet for a loan so he could go on looking for work, and the banker loaned him fifty dollars. He went back fifty years later, found that retired banker, and thanked him for the loan. According to my grandfather, the first thing the former banker said was, "Did you ever pay me back?"

Anyway, he drifted south, looking for work, and stayed for a while at a place outside of Gonzales, where somebody let him and his wife and son live in an old vacant farmhouse. While living there, he heard of work in San Antonio, and hitchhiked to the Alamo City. Unfortunately, he found no jobs in San Antonio, and had to walk back to Gonzales in defeat.

My grandfather is a good storyteller. Many of his tales I have heard several times. But this memory he told me only once— on that day. As he told me about this experience, he made me feel almost as dejected as he must have felt coming home to a house that wasn't even his, to tell his family that he had failed in finding work.

"There was a big field of wheat in front of that house," he said, "and I hated to have to walk up through that field and tell my wife and kid I hadn't found a job." He paused, his droll Chowtaw mouth pursing as his head shook but once, as if to cast off the clinging remnants of those hard days. "But when they saw me coming," he said, "up that old dirt road, they jumped down off that porch and came running out to meet me in the middle of that wheat field. I had no money. No food. Nothing. And they didn't care. It was sure good to know that somebody loved me, whether I'd found work or not."

Such a moment. To have hung in the memories of two men, in two very different ways, for decades, that both versions should come to my ear, each in its own good time. Seldom have I heard my grandfather talk about love. Yet, much of his life must have hinged upon that moment in the wheat field.

He drifted south with his family, found work in the oil patch, learned to love the blistering days and breezy nights of the chaparral country, and eventually became a self-made millionaire.

My father turned away from the oil field and toward agriculture, earning a Ph.D. in animal sciences. He taught, wrote, then shifted careers into the entertainment field, becoming one of the most successful humorous speakers in the nation. He also plays a darn fine fiddle.

And now I find myself smack dab in the middle of five living generations of Texans. I have suffered through my own miniature versions of the Great Depression, largely of my own making. I have earned and continue to earn the love and respect of those who went before me, and those who follow. The time approaches when I must ask my son to think back. To identify his earliest memory. The time will come for him to ask his daughter—my granddaughter. What will they say?

As for me, I am still a horseman. A man of the land. I still like to look up with a clod of Texas dirt in my hand to see an old sorrel grazing contendedly in the distance.

What is *your* earliest memory? Does it mean anything? Maybe not. Maybe it's just some ordinary, random event that happened to stick. Then again, maybe it's there in your brain for a reason. Maybe it has shaped you more than you know. Maybe it was the first thing you got worth keeping.

In Search of Texans

MARY ELIZABETH GOLDMAN

Admittedly, when I first began this quest for information, I assumed I already had a certain edge on the *real* story behind Texas. I am, after all, a Texan—I know these things. In fact, the blood of some seven generations of Texans runs warm and fast through my veins, and I have lived in Texas all my life. And for those extended times I was away from Texas, I nevertheless retained my status as a registered voter in the state, returning often enough to maintain my residency and keep the lawn mowed.

Today, when apathy is oftentimes more the norm than the exception, the issue of expressing one's opinion where it literally counts, regardless of how mundane that small act of citizenry is today, has always been important to me. *Expression* is the birthright of all Texans. And for Texans, expression is as much an attitude as it is a way of life. And like Texans everywhere, expression varies in method, it changes with time, but the *attitude* endures.

When Mike and I decided to take on this unique project, we broke the task into two parts. Mike would collect the archival material and as one participant to this book put it, I "drew the short straw" and would work with the here and now, the living among us. But truth be told, there were no "short straws" to draw and nobody could have enjoyed the effort more than I, for this has given me wonderful opportunity to meet, and in small ways, get to know some very special Texans. I've always been lucky that way.

I began by gathering an impressive list of notable Texans everywhere. I wrote to many Texans who had made their mark not only in Texas, but in other places as well. On occasion, I was reminded of an old adage, "Never ask a man if he's from Texas. If he is, he'll tell you; if he isn't, don't embarrass him." But that didn't slow me down. Texas and Texans have influenced many throughout the ages, and these people were also my mark. And people everywhere responded to my query, "What does Texas mean to you?" A simple explanation was oftentimes difficult, but not impossible. Given a few minutes to think about it, a Texan, if he's got something to say, will give a straight answer. It's characteristic of the breed. And responses came from the heart and were of the most thoughtful kind. The stories shared here are personal. They are unique. At the same time, the individuals who chose to recall these intimate details of their lives and of their ancestors also reveal and share a theme with each other. Collectively the stories weave a small corner of an incomplete tapestry depicting the colorful history, the excitement of today, and a glimpse of a promising future.

And finally, at the end of this abundant harvesting of Texas anecdotes, and as I realized I knew really very little about the people of Texas, I was once again discussing the book with my father, like I had done many times in the months before.

Sharp as a whip, his mind honed now with almost a century of training, my father can recall the fine details of a multitude of momentous events. My dad, a true twentieth century man, who just by being himself—compassionate without conditions, straightforward without malice, and above all, one who can be depended upon—personifies everyday what the "spirit of Texas" is all about.

But on this particular spring day in Texas as I filled the coffee cups in the kitchen, I told my dad I wanted to ask him a question, and I wanted a "spontaneous" answer. The first thing that came to his mind I said. I should have known better. If I wanted a "quick answer," he warned me, his answer was categorically "Hell, no." He qualified that by adding he could always reconsider and change his mind later. But it's not that kind of question, I countered, it's an important question. "If it's important," he said, "it deserves pondering, not spontaneity." Right again. And so I asked my dad the same question I've asked others: "What does Texas mean to you?" He folded his arms and sat back in the kitchen chair. He pondered as only a ninety-year-old philosopher can. His coffee cooled and I poured myself a second cup before he answered.

"When I was twenty," he said, "for me, I saw it only as a land of great opportunity, and I was eager to make my fortune."

I could see that coming, as I've known this man all my life.

"When I was thirty," he went on, "I was ready to settle down, start a family, and I still had visions of even greater opportunity in Texas and the people. And at fifty, opportunities still were waiting for any man in Texas. By the time I was seventy I could relax and enjoy the benefits of those years of all that opportunity, and yet, there were more and more options and opportunities for anybody here willing to work.

"And now, in my nineties I still see Texas as a land of opportunity for all people. And through all these years, the one thing I've always noticed about Texans is a genuine friendliness, not just for each other because Texans have never been clannish, but there is a real eagerness about Texans. Texans are proud of this land and I think Texans want everybody to experience the spirit of Texas."

All that pondering and he still managed to hit the nail on the head. The people of Texas represent nations everywhere, yet proudly call themselves "Texans." We come to this land for the opportunities to enrich our lives and the lives of our families, for education, for medical treatment, for adventure, to stretch out and kick back. Many return "home" to Texas when other avenues are closed, when there is a need for grounding, and to have the spirit renewed. Many come home to die. And Texans are indeed friendly people, they welcome strangers and encourage all to experience the land, the cultures, and opportunities that abound within the borders.

And so what is the recurring theme among all Texans? Read

between the lines and determine for yourself. It will become as clear to you as it did for me that cool spring afternoon when I had yet another cup of coffee with my dad at the kitchen table.

Introduction

DAVID NEVIN

He was a leathery old fellow, or at least he looked old to me, this in the middle 1950s when I was a young newspaper reporter. The West Texas sun had burned him so long that you knew he would always have that look of the open land. He had had him a little ranch, ran some cows amidst the mesquite and the prickly pear, and then he got old and his limbs got cranky and his missus died and he came to the city and here he was running a cut-rate gas station alone at night. I called him Mister, Mr. Sterling, and I liked him.

He wore a loose shirt with the tails out and under this shirt he had a .45 caliber automatic pistol tucked into his belt. It was chrome-plated and had yellow butt plates and the hammer was reared back on full cock. I asked him if the safety was on and he gave me a look and didn't answer.

"Ain't nobody going to rob me," he said. It was one of those stations likely to have cash on hand and he was alone and no longer young. It seemed he had sold the ranch for a decent sum and was actually quite comfortable; he worked because a man ought to work, that's what God set him on earth to do.

"Man puts a pistol on you," I said, "it'll be pretty late to pull your own."

"Don't care. Man tries anything with me, he'd better be fast and ready."

"And you'll get shot."

"Well, if that happens it'll be for doing the right thing."

"Gee, Mr. Sterling," I said, "the gasoline company, this is one of a hundred or a thousand stations all over everywhere and they have insurance to cover such losses and they wouldn't want you to get killed trying to save a hundred dollars . . .

"Don't matter!" he cried. "What matters is, a man stands up and he does what's right and he lives by that. And ain't nobody going to rob me. That's just flat all there is to it."

"Yes, sir." I said.

Then one day I went by and a stranger was running the station and no one knew where Mr. Sterling had gone. But I was covering the police beat in San Antonio then so I know that no one robbed him and he didn't kill anyone. Not then, anyway. Maybe that shiny .45 glinting under his shirt told any passing bandit to move along. Or maybe it was the glint in his eye.

So the years have passed and looking back now I see Mr. Sterling as a true transitional figure, a man of the soil come to the city in a rapidly urbanizing state, carrying the old virtues and verities from a day gone by and trying to fit them to a crazy quilt of modernity. Few Texans today, I surmise, would prepare to die to save the evening receipts for the company, nor would I, nor doubtless you. But that does Mr. Sterling an injustice, too; if he could look over my shoulder as I write this he might say, "Well, hell, son, I didn't have in mind to save company money—man tries to rob me, that just ain't right and I wouldn't put up with it one minute."

He lives on in my memory, speaking to me of Texas and Texans.

I wrote a book a long time ago called *The Texans* (some years later I wrote a second book published by the same title in the Time-Life Old West series, making me the only author I know with two totally different books bearing the same title, but that's another story). In *The Texans* I argued that the American spirit was heavily influenced by two powerful forces: the nation's proximity to and continuing relationship with its own frontier melded with its wealth and accumulation of capital. Granted, this is a proposition that can be argued in many different ways, but I like my way. I think the old frontier connection accounts for the country's thrust and daring and initiative while the growth of capital as a continent was settled gave it the power to reshape the world.

And Texas, so I argued then, stood as the epitome of this American spirit, intensified by its unique experience. For in the first half of the twentieth century, at least, Texas stood close to its frontier origins with all the take-care-of-yourself outlook full of gumption that drove the frontier. But in that same period the attitude that once had had to do with breaking forty acres to cotton or nursing a little herd through drought with the water holes drying and the grass browning was given vast new power by the discovery of huge pools of capital in the form of oil. Texans already used to doing as they damned pleased had the power to do just that—and do it they did.

Years later a friend told me that Harry Ransom, the great president of the University of Texas, had remarked upon reading *The Texans* that I was a writer to watch. The compliment thrills me to this day because Harry Ransom was a great man. He took that oil money powering the University of Texas and assembled one of the great book collections of the world, rivaling the Bancroft at Berkeley and the Widener at Harvard and the New York Public Library. Clark Kerr, then the towering chancellor of the University of California at Berkeley is said to have remarked that every time he heard of a new collection of important books for sale and hurried there with checkbook in hand he found it all tagged "Sold to Harry Ransom!"

Somehow to this day I don't think of Texas in terms of world class intellectuality, this in spite of Doctors Cooley and De-Bakey swapping hearts around and the M.D. Anderson clinic drawing sufferers from across the world and Baylor's impact on medicine and Texas Instruments and Dell and Compaq creating Silicon Prairie and NASA scientists at Houston lofting men into orbit to say nothing of the moon. I don't think of the air-conditioning that is now pervasive and has changed Texas radically as it has changed all the South or that as a result a great many of the men and women you see in cities today look as if they are strangers to the sun. Maybe I reel back the years in my mind, but what I think of are men and women, leathered from the sun or straight from the counting house but sharing alike that attitude of power, vigor, grit. They are not necessarily charming, kindness is not the first word that comes to mind, but there is a drive-ahead force that is in the air. Not all Texans take part in its profits, which can be bountiful, perhaps relatively few do so, but the air is there for everyone to breathe. Old Sam Houston personified that quality. It's fashionable these days to condemn that great man for reasons I may be too old fashioned to grasp fully, but that's all right. Today's calumniators are nothing in comparison to those who lit into Houston in his own day, and doubtless his name will survive intact when today's denouncers are dead and gone and forgotten, as it survived those of his own day. But to my mind he was another personifier of the Texas spirit, a man of the frontier and a man of power.

Yes, I know he was a ferocious boozer and dashing with women and his first marriage was checkered indeed and he kept slaves and fought Mexicans and wasn't above raising a bit of hell. (Kept slaves, yes, slavery recognized today as the evil it surely was, but he redeemed himself in his long, failing battle to keep Texas from entering the disaster of the Civil War, knowing full well that slavery would not survive that conflict.) But he—and Stephen F. Austin—were men of power. It took such a man to hold the Texans together as Houston did after Santa Anna raped Zacatecas and overran the Alamo. Nowadays Houston's brilliant retreat across Texas is labeled cowardly flight in some quarters, which is nothing much compared to the outrage in Texas at the time over what was called "the runaway scrape." His own people forgave him when he turned suddenly on the plains of San Jacinto and struck the advance contingent of the Mexican army and captured Santa Anna—and really, it seems to me today's calumniators might do the same.

But it was in the time that followed, the Republic years, that Houston demonstrated greatness. Holding his people together through that bitter decade, the threat from Mexico constant, he maneuvering and dickering and playing the British off against the United States, held the fort until James Polk seized opportunity and slid Texas with all its faults into the Union. And the patterns that lasted for the next century were set.

The next century . . . Texas was admitted in 1845, so what of the half-century that followed that next century, the period that brings Texas to our own day? God knows the world has changed, the nation and all its circumstances have changed, and of course Texas has changed with it. Yet I think the voices you will hear in this stalwart collection of Texans and their stories and what mattered to them across history and across their own lives will persuade you that the Texas spirit is real, transmuted in time, perhaps, adjusted to circumstance, but still real. A lot of things about today would puzzle Mr. Sterling and a lot more would outrage him, but scratch down to the core of Texans and Texas and I think he'd be satisfied.

DAVID NEVIN is a Texan. The son of a veterinary officer of the United States Army, he spent his boyhood living on Army posts that had garrisoned Indian-fighting soldiers in the early to mid-1900s. He served in the United States Navy, has worked as a newspaperman in Texas, and became a writer for Life. *He has written for* The Saturday Evening Post *and* McCalls. *He is the author of many books including two by the same title—*The Texans, *one for the Time Life Old West series along with three others for Time Life—*The Soldiers, The Expressmen, *and* The Mexican War. *He is the* New York Times *best-selling author of* 1812, Dream West—*which was made into the acclaimed TV miniseries—and* Louisiana Purchase.

ELMER KELTON REMEMBERS HIS WEST TEXAS ROOTS

BY ELMER KELTON

⭐ If Texas has icons recognizable worldwide, they are probably an oil well and a cowboy on horseback. But these are too simplistic to represent fully a state like ours. One thing that has long impressed me about Texas is its great diversity, due in no small part to its size and the wide variety of terrain, even climate, that exists within its borders. It has piney woods and blacklands on the east, desert and mountains on the west, high plains on the north and chaparral on the south.

Though all are Texas cities, Amarillo has little in common with Brownsville, and El Paso is vastly different from, say, Texarkana. Each has its own distinct character. There is no way to focus on one characteristic and declare that it represents all of Texas, except perhaps the pride we Texans share in our unique heritage.

As an agricultural journalist for forty-two years I came to know all areas of Texas pretty well, though my own roots are in the western part, particularly the ranching and oil-patch communities. Each of us has his or her own *querencia,* the home of the heart. West Texas is mine, though I recognize that it by no means represents all of our Texas heritage.

On my father's side of the family, the Keltons were ranch people from the time my grandfather's parents came out from the East Texas pines through the Cross Timbers to Callahan County with a covered wagon and a string of horses in the 1870s. Two of my great-grandfathers were ranchmen. My father's father was a working cowboy and rancher, and so was my father.

On my mother's side the menfolks usually gravitated into the oil fields at an early age and spent their lives there, mostly on drilling rigs. My maternal grandmother kept a rooming house, first in the boomtown of Pyote and later in Grandfalls, catering to oil-patch families.

I attended school in Crane, an oil town born the same year I was. My schoolmates' fathers for the most part worked for the various oil companies. A large percentage of those first-generation boomers came from farms, ranches, and small towns, so their roots were much the same as my own. Most had the comfort of knowing that if the oil business played out they could go back to the land, an escape no longer viable for their urban-raised descendants.

My cowboy father, Buck Kelton, had a lot of friends in the oil patch. They spoke the same language. A number of the cowboys who worked with him at one time or another wound up in the oil field because its pay scale was much higher than cowpuncher wages. Some switched back and forth, taking to the saddle when the drilling trade slacked off, then returning to the rigs when demand picked up.

McElroy Ranch roundup crew near Crane, Texas, in 1930.
Buck Kelton is at far right. He was Elmer Kelton's father.
PHOTO COURTESY OF ELMER KELTON

There was a certain cosmopolitan aspect to the McElroy Ranch, where I lived. The company bookkeeper was a Norwegian, a man of the world who had come to this country as a youth to seek his fortune. He never found his own, but he helped others make theirs. In a place where Levis and boots were the unofficial uniform, he wore a coat and tie. He was in one sense part of the ranch family but in another always an outsider.

Though I never could make a rope work for me, I grew up in a veritable nest of great ropers, several of whom left their mark in the rodeo world. One of our cowboys, Manerd Gayler, went to England with Tex Austin's rodeo troupe. The whole outfit came home broke. He was a participant in the rodeo cowboys' strike at Boston Garden and was a party to the organizing of what eventually became today's Professional Rodeo Cowboys Association. Later on he acquired a ranch in southern Arizona.

Sometimes on Sunday afternoons several of these calf ropers would practice at the ranch. I put calves in the chute for such people as the late great Toots Mansfield, several times world champion, a real gentleman, and a gentle man.

In later years, as a journalist, I was privileged to interview many oldtimers of widely varied experience. One was Sam Capps of Mason, who participated in some of the late cattle drives. The Associated Press picked up the story, and it ran in many newspapers across the country. He received a lot of mail, including several letters from elderly women proposing marriage. I asked him how he handled those. He said, "I let my wife answer them."

Another, a latter-day trail driver from the same town, was Ervin Ellebracht. In the 1920s, before livestock trucks came into wide use, he would contract to drive ranchers' cattle thirty miles to the railroad, usually a three-day trip. Once three elderly cowboys from the Kansas trail-drive days asked if they could go along for old times' sake, to relive in a small way a high point of their youth. Reluctant to assume the responsibility but unwilling to disappoint them, Ervin agreed.

The drive went smoothly the first two days, and the three old men had a ball. But rain set in on the third day, and the

Llano River was starting to rise. Ervin decided he had better put the herd across right away before the water got even higher. Busy with the crossing, he forgot about the old men until the cattle were on the far side of the river. Then he realized that the old trail drivers were nowhere in sight. Desperate, fearing they had drowned on his watch, he and the others searched downriver on both sides without success. Finally, to everyone's surprise, the old men came riding in. They had gone upriver and crossed over on a bridge.

"That," Ervin said, "is how they got to be *old* trail drivers."

Today a great deal has changed. Oil-field drilling activity has diminished compared to those earlier days because most of the state has been explored and most of its potential oil and gas fields put into production. The production phase of the business does not require as large a labor force. The bustling oil-field towns of my youth have for the most part declined in size and activity. The excitement of the boom days is long gone.

By the same token, ranching has changed. Cowboys are still around; there simply are not nearly so many of them. As an old-timer expressed it, "They are mighty few and thin on the ground." Or as cowboy author John Erickson has said, they are still out there, but you can't see them from the interstate.

High costs of production and chronic low prices for cattle have forced ranch owners to economize wherever possible if they are to survive. Smaller pastures and a variety of labor-saving options allow them to operate with far fewer hands than when I was a lad. Today's cowboy is likely to spend a lot more time in a pickup than on horseback. Some even use a motorbike or a four-wheeler. A horse has to eat whether you use him or not. A pickup or four-wheeler burns fuel only when it is going somewhere, and it gets its rider there a lot faster than a horse.

The use of trailers to haul horses to the job has cut out a lot of riding time. As my old schoolteacher and ex-cowboy friend Paul Patterson has said, "Two things you seldom see anymore are a cowboy riding or a horse walking."

When I was a boy, my father—by then ranch foreman—hauled out the chuckwagon twice a year for roundup. The summer "works" would last a week or so, the winter "works" as long as three weeks. Cowboys ate and slept wherever the wagon camped, usually beside a windmill far from headquarters.

A few years ago the aforementioned Paul Patterson went out to the same ranch to observe the roundup. The hands were mostly townspeople out for a few days' fun while they played at being real cowboys. Many were wearing tennis shoes and "gimme" caps. And he said, "As God is my witness, when noontime came they hauled the whole bunch to the Dairy Queen."

Some would argue that technology and mechanization have taken a lot of the romance out of ranch life. Perhaps so, but some elements in old-time ranching were far from romantic. Most of the complainers never knew or at least have forgotten the thrill of getting up at four-thirty on a bitter winter morning and riding ten miles on horseback with feet frozen in the stirrups before the real cow work even starts.

As a boy I was fortunate that there were still a few old-time cowboys around who in their youth had seen the passing of the open range and had participated in the last trail drives. The first funeral I can remember attending was of a neighbor, a rancher who in his youth had hunted buffalo. I have no idea how many hours I spent listening to cowboy stories told by the men who lived the life. I do not remember the details, but I remember the spirit, the flavor of those stories. They are, to me, an indelible part of my Texas heritage.

When mention is made of the old-time oil-field folks, I think about the late Bill Allman, who came down from Kansas as a very young man, following the oil booms into Texas and winding up in the Crane fields. At a time when rotary rigs took over most drilling operations, he stayed with the older, slower but dependable cable-tool rig to the end of his working days. Every

two years, when Odessa, Texas, had its big oil show, Bill Allman would be a volunteer at the cable-tool exhibit, explaining
its operation. He loved that rig.

One of the last times I saw him he had spent a long, hot
summer day on the derrick floor, patiently demonstrating its
workings over and over to a constantly changing crowd.

He was ninety years old.

Is it any wonder that I cherish my memories of those kinds
of people? Cowboys, ranchers, farmers, merchants, oil field
roughnecks, and drillers . . . they are all part of the Texas heritage.

*ELMER KELTON, of San Angelo, Texas, is one of the most re-
vered western writers in America. With more than thirty-five
novels and six Spur Awards, Kelton has been voted Greatest
Western Writer of All Time in a Western Writers of America
survey of its members.*

WHAT TEXAS MEANS TO ME

BY JORY SHERMAN

☆ The little shack, a bunkhouse for my father, sat on a vast empty prairie that seemed devoid of all life at first glance. My father, Keith Edward Sherman, was a wildcatter during the mid- to late-1930s, drilling for oil on that desolate plain, and he was good at it. He brought the gushers in and loved that moment when, after the nitroglycerin had exploded at the bottom of a shaft, the oil shot upward into the air, coating the derrick, drenching everyone around the drilling site with black gold.

But this was in the 1930s, and oil sold for fifty cents a barrel, so my father did not gain monetary wealth just then. Instead, he was living his dream; the dream that had brought him to Texas as it had so many others before him.

I was perhaps five or six years old when my dad began taking me to his little cabin in the oil fields near Monahans. This was my introduction to the poetry of deserted places as depicted in the paintings of Max Ernst. It did seem desolate and lonesome there, as first, but the experience instilled in me a love of wide-open spaces and a love of all wildlife. At night, I listened to the plaintive songs of coyotes and watched the bats knife through the air at dusk as they fed on insects.

In the deep of those nights in the oil fields, the dark sky was filled with stars and the Milky Way blazed a trail through the vast universe that ignited a small boy's imagination. The stars seemed much closer than they did in Monahans, and more friendly, somehow, although they were still beyond reach of anything but the mind.

In the silence of the night sky, while standing alone in the stillness of that seemingly endless plain, some inner longing stirred timeless, ancient questions, and nurtured the first buds of a love for empty places that would flower into a life-long love of Texas and the West.

I was fascinated by the jackrabbit my father told me about. Every night, after my father had finished work and was alone in his cabin, he would hear a thump on the ground outside the door. When he opened the door, a large male jackrabbit hopped inside where it would spend the night sleeping. It seemed to know that this was a place safe from coyotes and the owls floating overhead on silent pinions.

My father looked forward to these visits and yet the rabbit never came while I was there. But when I went back to town, the rabbit would be at his door on Sunday night. It was as if they had a special rapport with one another, a mysterious bond between a man and nature.

During the week, in Monahans, which was a very small town surrounded by sandhills and loamy soil, I harbored a strong desire to return to my father's lonely cabin, that place where earth and sky seemed to blend together and become one. Monahans was hot and dusty and ramshackle even then. But, for a small boy who was curious, there were many delights. I spent a lot of time carrying around my mother's saltshaker because the old-timers had told me, tongue-in-cheek, that if you could put salt on a bird's tail, you could easily catch it. It took me a while to catch on and to realize the truth in that old saw. Of course, if one got close enough to put salt on a bird's tail, it might be easily caught.

I had the most fun with tarantulas and I teased them to make them jump at me. It was amazing to me how far they could bound and how tolerant they were of my ignorance and youth.

We had moved to Texas from Minnesota, to that desolate town of Monahans, but our stay there marked the onset of my love for Texas and the West.

Over the years, I have come to appreciate that boyhood time when I first felt the powerful and magnetic attraction of Texas, when something of its majesty and allure found harbor in my heart.

Texas is a place where dreamers go, a place where dreamers are born. It is a place where you can find out who you are, where you came from, and where you are going.

Texas was that dream in my father's mind, that same dream that lured men like Richard King, Moses and Stephen Austin, Jim Bowie, and Davy Crockett to set foot on disputed soil and put down roots, men with ideas that continue to inspire those of us who inherited the fruits of the dreams they dreamed, the same dreams that brought men and women to NASA and launched them into space, that frontier beyond the sky I first glimpsed in the oil fields near Monahans, toward those stars that filled the night sky when that small boy looked to the heavens.

Texas is the history of a great nation, of man's eternal quest for spiritual fulfillment, for the destiny he has always sensed was waiting for him in such a land.

Texas is that vast and mysterious country of the mind and heart—the land that drums at your temples like a heartbeat, that sings in your veins and hums in your ear like an ancient song, that whispers like the Gulf of Mexico in a seashell and on the wind that blows across the Monahans plain, with its deserted oil fields, the black sands that still hold my boyhood shadow on the silent dunes.

JORY SHERMAN is the Spur Award winning author of the Song of the Cheyenne *and* Medicine Horn *in addition to his Baron Saga. He is a real cowboy who has lived in Texas for many years and worked the rodeo circuit.*

TEXAS BOUND

BY CAROLE NELSON DOUGLAS

⭐ 1984: Orwellian Boomtime

Why Texas?

If I had a nickel for every time I've heard those two words, I could buy a whole case of Lone Star beer and an armadillo T-shirt.

It started when I announced that I was leaving Minnesota, where I'd been reared, gone to college, and had pursued a journalism career to exhaustion, to move to Texas and write fiction full-time. *Why Texas?* Minnesotans would follow the question with predictions that if the big bugs, frequent tornadoes, and horrible heat in Texas didn't get me, the rednecks sure would.

Some of my most incredulous interrogators were Manhattan publishing types who managed to drip scorn over the phrase. *Why Tex-ass?* To the rarified coastal dweller, east or west, the Midwest—north or south—is comparable to the hole in the donut: it may be essential, but to them it's also essentially irrelevant, immaterial, and invisible.

Why Texas? Whyever not? It's warmer than Minnesota; its real estate is cheaper than California's, and it's a literal melting pot of energetic can-do Midwestern virtues, unlike Florida, which exudes a decadent, indolent air. And Texas is one of the few warm-weather states that have no state income taxes.

These factors make Texas "The State of the Art" for the freelance writer in need of economic mercy and a benign climate in which to unwind one's overwritten mind.

Texas first became the object of my full-time fantasy in 1978, when I had sold my first two novels and was writing my third. In those days, Austin was my Eldorado. Everybody in Texas wants to live in Austin, goes the Texas truism, but there are no jobs there. (Everybody in Texas, in fact; would like to live somewhere else in Texas, which I discovered as I explored relocation possibilities—the Rio Grande River Valley if the economy were better; Galveston if prices and winds were lower; San Antonio if it weren't so big—but the greener grass is always in Texas.) That's another Texas attraction: so much of it was once under the rule of the famous six flags that it offers a nation's worth of cultural and geographical variety within one state border.

There are "no jobs" in Austin because the University of Texas at Austin pumps 40,000-some student workers into the local economy to provide cheap labor. So what? Full-time freelance writers don't need jobs; that's the whole idea of being a writer, isn't it? And Austin is a scenic city, big enough to be the state capital, small enough to be laid-back, yet booming.

Every "boom" environment has its flip side, but so far Texas remains a state brimming with optimism and opportunity. It reminds me of California forty years ago before everybody went there and spoiled it. The Texas urban landscape even offers the same vaguely Mediterranean profusion of flowering bushes and manicured shrubs, not to mention such exotica as palms and cacti.

Like California, Texas had already "boomed" past my capacity to cope with its more obviously desirable parts. Austin developed into the Silicon Hill Country, housing prices escalated; traffic clogged. In the Orwellian year of 1984, knowing almost no one in the state, I found myself relocating to Fort Worth, an unassuming city that shelters a graceful quality of life under the shadowing scorn of neighboring Dallasites, who call it Cowtown. Fort Worth calls itself Cowtown, but that's a brag, not a putdown. Many Texans were appalled that I was snubbing Dallas. (*Why Fort Worth?* was the second question I could have parlayed from nickels into dollars.) All I could cite in my defense was the Jimmy Buffet song that says folks in Dallas are callous, and, besides, any city with more Cadillacs per capita than the Arab emirates is no place for a struggling writer. Besides, Fort Worth boasts world-class museums and the Fabulous Bass Brothers who are busy transforming its "inner city" into a downtown arts and dining mecca.

Whatever part of Texas you pick, it remains the State of the Art for writers, a sort of Twilight Zone on the Trinity or Brazos or Rio Grande. (Pick your river; Texas has scads.) I've not only been welcomed by Texas-sized enclaves of writers and readers, but have observed the native population, which faces extinction from the steady infusion of exotic outlanders like myself. Yankees, some say. I find it refreshing to be called something, which never happened in bland, Nordic, and relentlessly civil Minnesota.

When I refer to aliens, I am not thinking of the illegal kind, but the native fauna. Texas is the only state, for instance, where your freeway-barreling car can crush an armored tropical-zone mammal with a name out of Edgar Rice Burroughs. The armored and innocuous armadillo acts as Texas's informal state mascot and is usually, and sadly, seen in a crushed condition on farm-to-market roads. (As are empty beer cans.)

Then there are Texas "bugs." Reared in the north where winter is nature's way of telling insects to slow down, I suffer from a cultural antipathy to anything bigger than an ant. Dubious Minnesotans I left behind so terrified me with stories of such Texas-size monsters as tarantulas that I retaliated with my own Texas tall tale: I told them that I'd open a fast-food franchise down here and was wealthy on Texas's famed rich natural resources. I'd call my franchise "Tarantula Rancher"—heck, there are so many of the fuzzy little buggers down here that you can just run 'em over in your driveway and harvest a fresh batch daily. Think what Colonel Sanders could have done with eight drumsticks to a bird!

Other than one indistinct furry form the size of a runt cat scurrying across the access road to Ridgmar Mall on errands of a peculiarly repellent nature that have nothing to do (I hope) with Neiman-Marcus, I haven't seen a one. I have seen, however, things I'd only dreamed of in Minnesota, generally in nightmares: a toad, a shake, a praying mantis, three scorpions, and a lizard on a fence post. I've also sighted a rich assortment of "big bugs," flying and otherwise. Instead of retreating, I've gone out to study them. Now we view each other with wary appreciation. If I ever need to dream up insectoid aliens for a science fiction novel, all the raw material cavorts daily in my own back yard.

Some would maintain that space, the last frontier, is a state of mind especially to be savored in Texas. Montana is known as Big Sky country, but it doesn't have a thing on Texas. The stars at night are indeed bigger here, especially in the treeless new suburb I inhabit, where Orion strides across my rooftop nightly and the Big Dipper pours its bounty down over the neighbor's shingles. I have seen a shooting star, which I hadn't in elm tree-obscured Minnesota skies.

Vacant Texas heavens demand that one look up; chronically windy weather produces high-flying kites and the silent ballet of hot-air balloons. The sky teems with airplanes, private and military. It is ripe for speculation and UFOs. It's no accident that I didn't dream up my science fiction novel *Probe,* which involves a close encounter (in Minnesota—but one must write what one knows), until I'd visited the Dallas Market Center in 1980. And some would say the aliens have already landed, especially when seeing a battered pickup escalate onto the freeway at 85 mph, its otherwise empty bed rattling to the music of used beer cans. I couldn't believe my eyes the first time I saw a good ol' boy tilting his Lone Star to his lips while switching lanes on I-30. Imbibing beer while driving is not illegal here.

That probably will change soon, as will much that is charming or cheap about Texas, now that outlanders like me have discovered it. When stereotypes collide, new life forms emerge. Texas won't change as much as other similarly beset states, because this is Texas and we're pretty independent people. Alamo and all that, you know.

In the meantime, sit back and enjoy it. You know you're in Texas when you can buy jalapeno-flavored bread, jalapeno mustard, and even jalapeno Bloody Mary mix. You know you're in Texas when you run to the curb mailbox in high summer and find you've developed a tan George Hamilton would envy. You know you're in Texas when native twangs mix with Midwestern mush and every franchise restaurant serves "chicken-fried steak." You know you're in Texas when folks are friendly, think writers are wonderful, and make everyone feel right at home.

So have a good time, y'all, and don't take too much sun or jalapeno joy juice. And watch out for pickup trucks and house-sized tarantulas on the highway. I think we've all seen that movie before.

2000: MILLENNIUM UPDATE

After sixteen years of residency, I've marked more purely Texas Firsts: Forget falling stars, I saw my first space shuttle heading to Florida like a long, slow comet crossing the dimming, big Texas sky. Shortly after arriving, I was thrilled to waltz to the health club door one day to find it occupied by a fully accoutered horse. A cowboy member had brought in the critter for show-and-tell.

In an empty meadow behind the last row of houses near our block and across the street from a strip shopping center, a few head of horses used to munch and run. When a big FOR SALE sign sprung up like a literate weed one day, the horses disappeared. The undeveloped land ever has, and I wish I still, had horses so close to home. I did spot a rider and horse on the local park green space one day, probably playing hooky from the riding stable ten minutes away by car. I'm sure there's a law against these ghosts of Texas's past crossing paths with me and my car, but I wish it would happen again.

I've never developed a Texas accent. Soon after I'd moved to the state, a Tennessee western writer I'd never met who needed information on a convention called, and I gave him an insider's perspective. Grateful, he finished by saying, "Now I am not familiar with that 817 area code. Just where are you located?" "Foat Wurth, Texas," I said in my best drawl, used at no other time in the conversation. "Well now, ma'am," he drawled back in courtly compliment, "I jest knew that someone so nice couldn't be a *Yankee*." Oops. Yankees can be nice, but we never *sound* as nice as Texans. I've driven across Texas from Texarkana to El Paso, from the Oklahoma border to South Padre Island. I have found the land and people, even its dull parts, always warm and intriguing. What I most like about the state is that it encompasses bayous, treed hill country, badlands, piney woods, tropical gardens, desert scrub, and seashore. Like the oil that brought its first boom, you can find the refined and the crude, and all degrees of character, class, and idiosyncrasy. The round fifties condominium building I saw in Corpus Christi has relocated to Las Vegas for one of my mystery series. Las Vegas readers tell me they know just the building I mean. The elderly lady, whose condo was crowded with wigs and photos of her dancing with cruise-ship gigolos, had escaped a lost Tennessee Williams play to put down what straggly bleached roots she could in Texas. She hasn't made it into a novel yet, but she will.

Texas is always full of surprises, like climate. I explain the climate to nonresidents by saying you can leave the house on a February morning with the heater on, and return from an hour appointment with the air conditioner on. Our second year in Texas, my husband and I drove all day from Fort Worth to Van Horn one Halloween, en route to Tucson. I was anticipating laps in the outdoor motel pool at journey's end: hardy ex-Minnesotans can swim outside in Texas's mild autumns. But a Blue Norther blew in and by evening the temperature had plunged. Stubborn, I visited the deserted pool and stuck in a toe to make sure it was too icy to use. It was, and by morning our Blazer hood was dusted with white stuff, the first slap across the face from snow we or our virgin vehicle had encountered in the Lone Star State.

We couldn't complain. We knew we were in the right state at the first Fort Worth bank we visited, when we explained our relocation to the customer-service woman with tales of hoisting the snow blower atop our Minnesota roof to remove the winter drifts. She listened wide-eyed, then asked, "What's a snow blower?"

In my case, happily, history. And that's why Texas.

CAROLE NELSON DOUGLAS is a Fort Worth resident and a former award-winning Minnesota journalist and the author of thirty-eight novels, including the Midnight Louie and Irene Adler mystery series.

Carole Nelson Douglas with the Midnight Louie shoes.
PHOTO COURTESY OF SAM DOUGLAS.

The Journey of Alvar Núñez Cabeza de Vaca

⭐ Close to shore a wave took us and hurled the barge a horse's length out of water. With the violent shock nearly all the people who lay in the boat like dead came to themselves, and, seeing we were close to land, began to crawl out on all fours. As they took to some rocks, we built a fire and toasted some of our maize. We found rainwater, and with the warmth of the fire, people revived and began to cheer up. The day we arrived there was the sixth of the month of November (1528).

AFTER THE PEOPLE had eaten I sent Lope de Oviedo, who was the strongest and heartiest of all, to go to some trees nearby and climb to the top of one, and examine the surroundings and the country in which we were. He did so and found we were on an island, and that the ground was hollowed out, as if cattle had gone over it, from which it seemed to him that the land belonged to Christians, and so he told us. I sent him again to look and examine more closely if there were any worn trails, and not to go too far so as not to run into danger. He went, found a footpath, followed it for about one-half league, and saw several Indian huts which stood empty because the Indians had gone out into the field.

He took away a cooking pot, a little dag, and a few ruffs and turned back, but as he seemed to delay I sent two other Christians to look for him and find out what had happened.

They met him nearby and saw that three Indians, with bows and arrows, were following and calling to him, while he did the same to them by signs. So he came to where we were, the Indians remaining behind, seated on the beach. Half an hour after a hundred Indian archers joined them, and our fright was such that, whether tall or little, it made them appear giants to us. They stood still close to the first ones, near where we were.

We could not defend ourselves, as there were scarcely three of us who could stand on their feet. The inspector and I stepped forward and called them. They came, and we tried to quiet them the best we could and save ourselves, giving them beads and bells. Each one of them gave me an arrow in token of friendship, and by signs they gave us to understand that on the following morning they would come back with food, as then they had none.

THE NEXT DAY, at sunrise, which was the hour the Indians had given us to understand, they came as promised and brought us plenty of fish and some roots which they eat that taste like nuts, some bigger, some smaller, most of which are taken out of the water with much trouble.

In the evening they returned and brought us more fish and some of the same roots, and they brought their women and children to look at us. They thought themselves very rich with the little bells and beads we gave them, and thereafter visited us daily with the same things as before. As we saw ourselves provided with fish, roots, water, and the other things we had asked for, we concluded to embark again and continue our voyage.

We lifted the barge out of the sand into which it had sunk (for which purpose we all had to take off our clothes) and had great work to set her afloat, as our condition was such that much lighter things would have given us trouble.

Then we embarked. Two crossbow shots from shore a wave swept over us, we all got wet, and being naked and the cold very great, the oars dropped out of our hands. The next wave overturned the barge. The inspector and two others clung to her to save themselves, but the contrary happened; they got underneath the barge and were drowned.

The shore being very rough, the sea took the others and thrust them, half dead, on the beach of the same island again, less the three that had perished underneath the barge.

The rest of us, as naked as we had been born, had lost everything, and while it was not worth much, to us it meant a great deal. It was in November, bitterly cold, and we in such a state that every bone could easily be counted, and we looked like death itself. Of myself I can say that since the month of May I had not tasted anything but toasted maize, and even sometimes had been obliged to eat it raw. Although the horses were killed during the time the barges were built. I never could eat of them, and not ten times did I taste fish. This I say in order to explain and that anyone might guess how we were off. On top of all this, a north wind arose, so that we were nearer death than life. It pleased Our Lord that, searching for the remnants of our former fire, we found wood with which we built big fires and then with many tears begged Our Lord for mercy and forgiveness of our sins. Every one of us pitied not only himself, but all the others whom he saw in the same condition.

At sunset the Indians, thinking we had not left, came to bring us food, but when they saw us in such a different attire from before and so strange-looking, they were so frightened as to turn back. I went to call them, and in great fear they came. I then gave them to understand by signs how we had lost a barge and three of our men had been drowned, while before them there lay two of our men dead, with the others about to go the same way.

Upon seeing the disaster we had suffered, our misery and distress, the Indians sat down with us and all began to weep out of compassion for our misfortune, and for more than half an hour they wept so loud and so sincerely that it could be heard far away.

Verily, to see beings so devoid of reason, untutored, so like unto brutes, yet so deeply moved by pity for us, it increased my feelings and those of others in my company for our own misfortune. When the lament was over, I spoke to the Christians and asked them if they would like me to beg the Indians to take us to their homes. Some of the men, who had been to New Spain, answered that it would be unwise, as, once at their abode, they might sacrifice us to their idols.

Still, seeing there was no remedy and that in any other way death was surer and nearer, I did not mind what they said, but begged the Indians to take us to their dwellings, at which they showed great pleasure, telling us to tarry yet a little, but that they would do what we wished. Soon thirty of them loaded themselves with firewood and went to their lodges, which were far away, while we stayed with the others until it was almost dark. Then they took hold of us and carried us along hurriedly to where they lived.

Against the cold, and lest on the way some one of us might faint or die, they had provided four or five big fires on the road, at each one of which they warmed us. As soon as they saw we had regained a little warmth and strength they would carry us to the next fire with such haste that our feet barely touched the ground.

So we got to their dwellings, where we saw they had built a hut for us with many fires in it. About one hour after our arrival they began to dance and to make a great celebration (which lasted the whole night), although there was neither pleasure, feast, nor sleep in it for us, since we expected to be sacrificed. In the morning they again gave us fish and roots, and treated us so well that we became reassured, losing somewhat our apprehension of being butchered.

THAT SAME DAY I saw on one of the Indians a trinket he had not gotten from us, and asking from where they had obtained it they answered, by signs, that other men like ourselves and who were still in our rear, had given it to them. Hearing this, I sent two Christians with two Indians to guide them to those people. Very nearby they met them, and they also were looking for us, as the Indians had told them of our presence in the neighborhood. These were the Captains Andrés Dorantes and Alonso del Castillo, with all of their crew. When they came near us they were much frightened at our appearance and grieved at being unable to give us anything, since they had nothing but their clothes. And they stayed with us there, telling how, on the fifth of that same month, their barge stranded a league and a half from there, and they escaped without anything being lost.

All together, we agreed upon repairing their barge, and that those who had strength and inclination should proceed in it, while the others should remain until completely restored and then go as best they could along the coast, following it till God would be pleased to get us all together to a land of Christians.

So we set to work, but ere the barge was afloat, Tavera, a gentleman in our company, died, while the barge proved not to be seaworthy and soon sank. Now, being in the condition which I have stated—that is, most of us naked and the weather so unfavorable for walking and for swimming across rivers and coves, and we had neither food nor any way to carry it, we determined upon submitting to necessity and upon wintering there, and we also agreed that four men, who were the most able-bodied, should go to Pánuco, which we believed to be nearby, and that, if it was God, Our Lord's will to take them there, they should tell of our remaining on the island and of our distress. One of them was a Portuguese, called Alvaro Fernandez, a carpenter and sailor; the second was Mendez; the third, Figueroa, a native of Toledo; the fourth, Astudillo, from Zafra. They were all good swimmers and took with them an Indian from the island.

A FEW DAYS after these four Christians had left, the weather became so cold and tempestuous that the Indians could no longer pull roots, and the canebrake in which they used to fish yielded nothing more. As the lodges afforded so little shelter, people began to die, and five Christians, quartered on the coast, were driven to such an extremity that they ate each other up until but one remained, who being left alone, there was nobody to eat him. Their names are: Sierra, Diego, Lopez, Corral, Palacios, and Gonzalo Ruiz. At this the Indians were so startled, and there was such an uproar among them, that I verily believe if they had seen this at the beginning they would have killed them, and we all would have been in great danger. After a very short time, out of eighty men who had come there in our two parties only fifteen remained alive.

Then the natives fell sick from the stomach, so that half of them died also, and they, believing we had killed them, and holding it to be certain, they agreed among themselves to kill those of us who survived.

But when they came to execute it an Indian who kept me told them not to believe we were the cause of their dying, for if we had so much power we would not have suffered so many of our own people to perish without being able to remedy it ourselves. He also told them there remained but very few of us, and none of them did any harm or injury, so that the best was to let us alone. It pleased Our Lord they should listen to his advice and counsel and give up their idea.

To this island we gave the name of the *Island of Ill Fate* . . .

ON THE ISLAND I have spoken of they wanted to make medicine men of us without any examination or asking for our diplomas, because they cure diseases by breathing on the sick, and with that breath and their hands they drive the ailment away. So they summoned us to do the same in order to be at least of some use. We laughed, taking it for a jest, and said that we did not understand how to cure.

Thereupon they withheld our food to compel us to do what they wanted.

At last we found ourselves in such stress as to have to do it, without risking any punishment.

The way we treated the sick was to make over them the sign of the cross while breathing on them, recite a Pater noster and Ave Maria, and pray to God. Our Lord, as best we could to give them good health and inspire them to do us some favors. Thanks to His will and the mercy He had upon us, all those for whom we prayed, as soon as we crossed them, told the others that they were cured and felt well again. For this they gave us good cheer, and would rather be without food themselves so as to give it to us, and they gave us hides and other small things. So great was the lack of food then that I often remained without eating anything whatsoever for three days, and they were in the same plight, so that it seemed to me impossible for life to last, although I afterwards suffered still greater privations and much more distress, as I shall tell further on.

The Indians that kept Alonso del Castillo, Andrés Dorantes, and the others, who were still alive, being of another language and stock, had gone to feed on oysters at another point of the mainland where they remained until the first day of the month of April. Then they came back to the island, which was from there nearly two leagues off, where the channel is broadest. The island is half a league wide and five long.

AFTER DORANTES AND Castillo had come back to the island, they gathered together all the Christians, who were somewhat scattered, and there were in all fourteen. I, as told, was in another place, on the mainland, whither my Indians had taken me and where I suffered from such a severe illness that, although I might otherwise have entertained some hope for life, this was enough to take it away from me completely. When the Christians learned of it they gave an Indian the robe of marten we had taken from the cacique, as stated, in order that he should guide them to where I was, to see me, and so twelve of them came, two having become so feeble that they did not dare to take them along.

The names of those who came are: Alonso del Castillo, Andrés Dorantes and Diego Dorantes, Valdivieso, Estrada, Tostado, Chaves, Gutierrez, an Asturian priest; Diego de Huelva, Estevanico, the negro Benitez, and as they reached the mainland they found still another of our men named Francisco de Léon, and the thirteen went along the coast. After they had gone by, the Indians with whom I was told me of it, and how Hiéronimo de Alaniz and Lope de Oviedo had been left on the island.

My sickness prevented me from following or seeing them. I had to remain with those same Indians of the island for more than one year, and as they made me work so much and treated me so badly I determined to flee and go to those who live in the woods on the mainland, and who are called those from Charruco.

I could no longer stand the life I was compelled to lead. Among many other troubles I had to pull the eatable roots out of the water and from among the canes where they were buried in the ground, and from this my fingers had become so tender that the mere touch of a straw caused them to bleed. The reeds would cut me in many places, because many were broken and I had to go in among them with the clothing I had on, of which I have told. This is why I went to work and joined the other Indians. Among these I improved my condition a little by becoming a trader, doing the best in it I could, and they gave me food and treated me well.

They entreated me to go about from one part to another to get the things they needed, as on account of constant warfare there is neither travel nor barter in the land.

So, trading along with my wares I penetrated inland as far as I cared to go and along the coast as much as forty or fifty leagues. My stock consisted mainly of pieces of seashells and cockles, and shells with which they cut a fruit which is like a bean, used by them for healing and in their dances and feasts. This is of greatest value among them, besides shell-beads and other objects. These things I carried inland, and in exchange brought back hides and red ocher with which they rub and dye their faces and hair; flint for arrow points, glue and hard canes wherewith to make them, and tassels made of the hair of deer, which they dye red. This trade suited me well because it gave me liberty to go wherever I pleased; I was not bound to do anything and no longer a slave. Wherever I went they treated me well, and gave me to eat for the sake of my wares. My principal object in doing it, however, was to find out in what manner I might get further away. I became well known among them; they rejoiced greatly when seeing me and I would bring them what they needed, and those who did not know me would desire and endeavor to meet me for the sake of my fame.

1540: The Expedition of Coronado

BY PEDRO DE CASTAÑEDA OF NAJERA

☆ Now we will speak of the plains. The country is spacious and level, and is more than 400 leagues wide in the part between the two mountain ranges—one, that which Francisco Vazquez Coronado crossed, and the other that which the force under Don Fernando de Soto crossed, near the North Sea, entering the country from Florida. No settlements were seen anywhere on these plains.

In traversing 250 leagues, the other mountain range was not seen, nor a hill nor a hillock which was three times as high as a man. Several lakes were found at intervals; they were round as plates, a stone's throw or more across, some fresh and some salt. The grass grows tall near these lakes; away from them it is very short, a span or less. The country is like a bowl, so that when a man sits down, the horizon surrounds him all around at the distance of a musket shot. There are no groves of trees except at the rivers, which flow at the bottom of some ravines where the trees grow so thick that they were not noticed until one was right on the edge of them. They are of dead earth. There are paths down into these, made by the cows when they go to the water, which is essential throughout these plains. As I have related in the first part, people follow the cows, hunting them and tanning the skins to take to the settlements in the winter to sell, since they go there to pass the winter, each company going to those which are nearest, some to the settlements at Cicuye, others toward Quivira, and others to the settlements which are situated in the direction of Florida. These people are called Querechos and Teyas. They described some large settlements, and judging from what was seen of these people and from the accounts they gave of other places, there are a good many more of these people than there are of those at the settlements. They have better figures, are better warriors, and are more feared. They travel like the Arabs, with their tents and troops of dogs loaded with poles and having Moorish packsaddles with girths. When the load gets disarranged, the dogs howl, calling someone to fix them right. These people eat raw flesh and drink blood. They do not eat human flesh. They are a kind people and not cruel. They are faithful friends. They are able to make themselves very well understood by means of signs. They dry the flesh in the sun, cutting it thin like a leaf, and when dry they grind it like meal to keep it and make a sort of sea soup of it to eat. A handful thrown into a pot swells up so as to increase very much. They season it with fat, which they always try to secure when they kill a cow. They empty a large gut and fill it with blood, and carry this around the neck to drink when they are thirsty. When they open the belly of a cow, they squeeze out the chewed grass and drink the juice that remains behind, because they say that this contains the essence of the stomach. They cut the hide open at the back and pull it off at the joints, using a flint as large as a finger, tied in a little stick, with as much ease as if working with a good iron tool. They give it an edge with their own teeth. The quickness with which they do this is something worth seeing and noting.

There are very great numbers of wolves on these plains, which go around with the cows. They have white skins. The deer are pied with white. Their skin is loose, so that when they are killed it can be pulled off with the hand while warm, coming off like pigskin. The rabbits, which are very numerous, are so foolish that those on horseback killed them with their lances. This is when they are mounted among the cows. They fly from a person on foot.

PEDRO DE CASTAÑEDA of Najera was a member of Coronado's expedition through Texas in 1541.

Into North America

BY HENRI JOUTEL

☆ Having hitherto said Nothing of the Situation of our Dwelling of St. *Lewis,* nor of the Nature of the Country we were in, I will here venture upon a plain but true Description.

We were in about the 27th Degree of North Latitude, two Leagues up the Country, near the Bay of St. *Lewis* and the Bank of the River *aux Bœufs,* on a little Hillock, whence we discover'd vast and beautiful Plains, extending very far to the Westward, all level and full of Greens, which afford Pasture to an infinite Number of Beeves and other Creatures.

Turning from the West to the Southward, there appear'd other Plains adorn'd with several little Woods of several Sorts of Trees. Towards the South and East was the Bay, and the Plains that hem it in from the East; to the Northward, was the River running along by a little Hill, beyond which there were other large Plains, with some little Tufts of Wood at small Distances, terminating in a Border of Wood, which seem'd to us to be very high.

Between that little Hill and our Dwelling, was a Sort of Marsh, and in it Abundance of wild Foul, as Curlies, Water-Hens, and other Sorts. In the Marsh there were little Pools full of Fish. We had also an infinite Number of Beeves, wild Goats, Rabbits, Turkeys, Bustards, Geese, Swans, Feldifares, Plovers, Teal, Partridges, and many other Sorts of Fowl fit to eat, and among them one call'd *le grand Gosier,* or, the great Gullet, because it has a very large one; another as big and Fleshy as a Pullet, which we called the *Spatula,* because its Beak is shap'd like one, and the Feathers of it being of a pale Red, are very beautiful.

As for Fish, we had several Sorts in the River and in the

Lakes I have mention'd. The River afforded a Sort of Barbles, differing from ours in Roundness, in their having three Bones sticking out, one on the Back, the others on each Side of the Head, and in the Flesh, which is like Cod, and without Scales. The River supply'd us with Abundance of other Fishes, whose Names we know not. The Sea afforded us Oysters, Eeles, Trouts, a Sort of red Fishes, and others whose long, sharp, and hard Beak tore all our Nets.

We had Plenty both of Land and Sea Tortoises, whose Eggs serv'd to season our Sauces. The Land Tortoises differ from those of the Sea, as being smaller, round, and their Shell more beautiful. They hide themselves in Holes they find or make in the Earth. It was looking for these Tortoises, that one of our Surgeons, thrust his Arm into a Hole, and was hit by some venomous Creature, which we suppos'd to be a Sort of Toad, having four Feet, the Top of his Back sharp and very hard, with a little Tail. Whether it was this Creature, or a Snake, his Arm swelled very much, however he was cured by such Applications as were made Use of; but it cost him a Finger was cut off.

Among the venomous Sorts of Snakes, as Vipers, Asps, and others, whereof there are many, those call'd Rattle-Snakes are the most common. They generally lye among the Brambles, where they make a Noise by the Motion of two Scales they have at the End of their Tail, which is heard at a considerable Distance, and therefore they are call'd Rattle-Snakes. Some of our Men had eaten of them and found their Flesh was not amiss, and when we had kill'd any of them, our Swine made a good Meal.

There are also many Alligators in the Rivers, some of them of a frightful Magnitude and Bulk. I kill'd one that was between four and five Foot about, and twenty Foot in Length, on which our Swine feasted. This Creature has very short Legs, insomuch that it rather drags along than walks, and it is easy to follow the Tract of it, either among the Weeds or on the Sands, where it has been. It is very ravenous, and attacks either

Men or Beasts, when they are within Reach in the River, and
comes also ashore to seek for Food. It has this particular Quality, that it flies from such as pursue, and pursues those who fly
from it. I have shot many of them dead.

The Woods are composed of Trees of several Sorts. There
are Oaks, some of them ever green and never without Leaves;
others like ours in *Europe,* bearing a Fruit much like our Galls,
and lose their Leaves in Winter, and another Sort not unlike
ours in *France,* but the Bark of them thicker, these as well as
the second Sort bear an Acorn, differing from ours both in
Taste and Bigness.

There is a Sort of Tree, which bears small Berries, which,
when ripe, are red, and indifferent pleasant. It bears twice a
Year, but the second Crop never ripens. There is another Tree,
bearing a Fruit not unlike *Cassia,* in Taste and Virtue.

There are others of the Sort I had seen in the Islands, whose
Leaves are like Rackets, whence the Tree bears the Name. The
Blossoms grow out about the Leaves, and of them comes a
Fruit somewhat resembling Figs, but the Leaves and the Fruit
are full of Prickles, which must be carefully rubb'd and taken
off, before it is eaten, else they dangerously inflame the Mouth
and the Throat, and may prove mortal, as happen'd to one of
our Soldiers, who had eaten of them too greedily, and without
that Precaution.

I have seen some Trees resembling the Palm, whose lofty and
long Branches spread like that call'd the *Latanier,* bearing a
Fruit, said to be indifferent good. Others the same Sort, but
whose Leaves are like Gutters, harsh and so sharp pointed, that
they will pierce the thickest Stuffs. This Tree has a Sprout on
the Top, which shoots out Flowers in the Shape of a Nosegay,
of a whitish yellow, and some of them at the Top of that Sprout
have sixty or eighty Flowers hanging down, not unlike the
Flower de Luce, and after those Flowers follows a Fruit as long
as a Man's Finger, and thicker than the Thumb, full of little
Seeds, so that there is scarce any Thing but the Rhind fit to eat,
the Taste whereof is sweet and delicate.

There are Abundance of creeping Vines and others, that run up the Bodies and to the Tops of Trees, which bear plenty of Grapes, fleshy and sharp, not to compare to the Delicacy of ours in *Europe;* but we made Verjuice of them, which was very good in Sauce. Mulberry Trees are numerous along the Rivers, their Fruit is smaller, but sweeter and more delicious than ours; their Leaves are beautiful and large, which would be of good Use for feeding of Silkworms. The Plains are strew'd with a Sort of small Sorrel, the Leaf whereof is like Trefoil, and the Taste of it sharp like ours. There are Abundance of small Onions, no bigger than the Top of a Man's Finger, but very well tasted, and when the Heat has scorch'd up the Plains, that Plant shoots out first, and produces Flowers which look like an agreeable Enamel. Nothing is more beautiful than to behold those vast Plains, when the Blossoms appear; a thousand Sorts of different Colours, whereof many have an agreeable Scent, adorn those Fields, and afford a most charming Object to the Eye. I have observed some that smell like a Tuberose, but the Leaf resembles our Borage. I have seen Primroses, having a Scent like ours, *African* Gilliflowers, and a Sort of purple wind Flowers. The Autumn Flowers are almost all of them yellow, so that the Plains look all of that Colour.

The Climate is mild and temperate, tho' we were in about 27 Degrees of North Latitude, and yet the Seeds I caused to be sow'd did not thrive; whether it was because they had been soak'd in the Sea Water, or for any other Reason. Some came up pretty well, as Pompions, Melons, Parsnips, and Endive; but the Beasts and the Insects left us not much.

HENRI JOUTEL came to Matagorda Bay in 1685 as a member of the last expedition of the great French explorer René Robert Cavelier, Sieur de La Salle.

The First Texans

BY CALVIN R. CUMMINGS AND LINDA SCOTT CUMMINGS

☆ New Years Day 1966 dawned with the continuation of an arctic storm sweeping the Texas Panhandle. Under a dark and dull leaden sky, the landscape lay blanketed in white, the freezing north wind piling up huge drifts. I could believe the local saying that the only thing between the North Pole and the Texas Panhandle is a drift-fence—and it's down. That also being the day I arrived in Texas. In the little town of Fritch, 35 miles north of Amarillo, I reported for duty as the first National Park Service employee assigned to Alibates Flint Quarries. The United States Congress had authorized the Alibates Flint Quarries National Monument in August of 1965, and my new job as archaeologist included providing immediate protection and starting the planning and interpretation process for the new national monument.

Standing on the cold windswept blufftop, in the brakes of the South Canadian River, my first view of the quarries reminded me of a place where an artillery battle had been fought. Individual quarries pockmarked the ridges and hillsides. Hundreds upon hundreds of pits spread before me where various Indian cultures had mined the beautiful multicolored chert over the past 12,000 years. Over the centuries those ancient people had removed tons of stone. Names paraded through my mind: Clovis, Folsum, Midland, Plainview, Meserve, Milnsand, Scottsbluff, Eden, Angostura, Agate Basin, and others—names given these prehistoric cultures by the archaeologists who study them. The names derived from the locations where the different cultures had first been discovered, a number of them in Texas. The oldest of these prehistoric peoples are collectively called Paleo-Indians. Oldest of them all are the people of the Clovis culture, hunters of extinct megafauna like the Columbian mammoth and the giant *Bison antiquus*.

What knowledge existed of these ancient people from thousands of years in the distant past? The remains of their labor lay before me, scattered in millions of bits of colorful stone. The ground beneath my feet lay paved with flakes, chunks, and bits of multicolored chert. Such beautiful colors— each little piece vying for the attention of my eye. Deep reds, blue with purple speckles, alternating red and white bands, white streaked with brown—it seemed that every color and combination in the rainbow had painted this material. Mixed in with all the chert debris lay broken prehistoric tools, half a knife blade here, a scraper there. Without metal picks and chisels, how could the prehistoric people have possibly mined such large quantities of chert to leave these huge pits? What flint-napping techniques did they use to turn this colorful stone into their expertly crafted chipped tools? Once manufactured, how did the people of the distant past use those chipped chert tools—the spear points, arrowheads, knives, scrapers, and drills?

What of the people, from Clovis and Folsum to Comanche and Kiowa, who quarried here over the past 12,000 years? What kind of lives did they lead? Of all those ancient societies, the people of the Clovis culture intrigued me most. I could not begin to imagine what it would be like killing a mammoth using only a wooden shaft with a piece of chipped stone on the end.

So began my search for information about the Clovis people, the first Texans, and my professional archaeological association with Texas over the next three and a half decades.

FAR IN THE past, between 10,000 to 14,000 years ago, the last North American Ice Age, the Wisconsin Glaciation, was ending. The massive ice sheet that had blanketed much of North America, reaching a maximum extent 18,000 to 22,000 years ago, was now receding. When the ice sheets receded, the climate changed dramatically. The ancient pollen record indicates this to be a period of climatic deterioration, bringing great changes to the environment and vegetation of Texas. The face of Texas at that time had a look that no current resident would recognize today. During the height of the glaciation, vast forests, differing by region, covered all of Texas.

Between 10,000 to 14,000 years ago the vast pine, spruce, and fir forests in West Texas gave way to open grasslands, leaving only protected stands of conifers at lower elevations. At the elevations above 6,000 feet, like the Guadalupe Mountains, the conifer forests of pine, spruce, and Douglas fir remained stable. The climate for the region became drier than it had been during the height of the Wisconsin Glaciation, and summers became warmer. However, the overall climate appears to be moister and cooler than today.

In Southwest Texas, scrub grasslands with mixed hackberry, oak, locust, and plum replace the pinon-juniper forests. In the Chisos Mountains pine, spruce, and Douglas fir remain.

The Central Texas deciduous woodlands gradually changed over to grasslands and oak savannas. Willow, ash, and birch decreased markedly and hazelnut, waxmyrtle, basswood, and maple completely disappeared. On the coast, the forest extended a hundred miles out on the continental shelf, the sea level lowered by the ocean waters locked in the glacial ice sheets.

The deciduous forests in East Texas changed the least of all the environments in Texas. Pine, sweetgum, and oak increased and spruce, birch, and maple disappeared or became less abundant.

ABOUT 11,500 YEARS ago, large expanses of grass stretch across most of West Texas, with clusters of remnant pine parklands making islands in this grassy sea. Forest-lined stream channels periodically slice through the landscape. Lakes, playas, and springs dot the savanna, surrounded by wooded and marshy areas that teem with wildlife. Great size is the most striking aspect of many of these animals; some are half again to twice the size of similar modern animals. The most powerful Pleistocene predator, the shortfaced bear (*Arctodus simus*), stood as large as the Alaskan brown bear. In the Great Lakes area lived a giant beaver (*Castoroides*) the size of a black bear. Bison (*Bison antiquus*) are half again bigger than modern bison and the Columbian mammoth (*Mammuthus columbi*) stood 3.2 to 3.4 meters high at shoulders.

Scattered across the vast green grasslands are great herds of grazing bison. A pack of timber wolves (*Canis lupus*) circles a bison herd, waiting for a stray to leave the protection of the herd. Flocks of insect-eating birds follow in the wake of the grazing bison, snatching up bugs disturbed by the passing herd. Interspersed among the bison are clusters of smaller grazing animals, camels (*Camelops hesternus*), the diminutive pronghorn (*Caprameryx minor*), Stock's pronghorn (*Antilocapra stockoceros*), and several species of horse. Browsing in a tree grove are a troop of giant Columbian mammoth, their great curved tusks gleaming in the bright sunlight.

At another place in the savanna, a band of stilt-legged horse (*Equus scotti*) grazes near a group of pronghorn (*Antilocapra americana*). A pride of American lions (*Panthera leo atrox*) rests in the shade of a stand of trees. A pair of dire wolves slinks across the grassland, getting ever closer to a band of grazing camels. Overhead a golden eagle rides the air currents on wide-spread wings.

Near a small wooded playa, a pair of sabertoothed cats feasts on a horse they have just killed. Several species of vultures and condors circle overhead, waiting their turn at the remains. On the waters of the playa swim ducks, momentarily safe from the predators. Near the edge of the woods a coyote chases a black-tailed jackrabbit (*Lepus californicus*) while a band of curious mule deer watch the chase.

A forested valley cuts across the grasslands, the stream in the bottom draining from the Llano Estacado to the Gulf of Mexico. Birds of many varieties flit back and forth through the branches, and a herd of white-tailed deer browse in the shady forest. On the valley floor a kit fox pursues the plains pocket gopher and the prairie vole. Further downstream a small band of flat-headed peccary, the size of European wild boars, root for tubers. A flock of turkey (*Meleagrididae*) moves cautiously among the trees.

Muskrats live in marshy areas along streams and around lakes, while frogs croak in the reeds. Catfish swim in the lakes. These waters are also home to numerous species of turtles: carolina box turtle (*Terrapene carolina*), ornate box turtle, box turtle, yellow mud turtle (*Kinosternon flavescens*), elegant slider turtle, and soft-shelled turtle.

THE FIRST TEXANS

Into this sylvan scene comes a new and deadly predator—humans. About 11,500 years ago groups of Clovis people, specialized megafauna hunters, first arrived in what is now Texas. Evidence indicates that at this time the Clovis culture suddenly appears all across the North American continent not covered by the ice sheets.

Traveling in small bands, accompanied by domesticated dogs (*Canis familiaris*), each group might have been an extended family. Hunters of great skill, these nomadic people stalked and killed the peccary, the camel, the pronghorn, the horse, the deer, and the great bison. While the Clovis people appear to specialize in hunting large animals, undoubtedly they utilized all the resources in their environment. Fish, rabbits, squirrels, and rodents, as well as roots, leaves, seeds, nuts, fruits, and berries likely made up a significant part of their diet. Turtle carapaces are almost always found in mammoth kill sites; the common occurrence and abundance indicates these people ate them on a regular basis. Perhaps they had a fondness for turtle soup? The most fascinating thing about the Clovis people, an aspect that sets them apart from all other humans in North America, is the fact that they hunted the giant Columbian mammoth. Armed only with chipped-stone-tipped spears and darts, these people sought out the mightiest beast on the landscape.

IN THE GRASSLAND sits a lake, surrounded by a thick wooded area. Assorted wildlife regularly come for water, carving established trails through the trees to the water's edge. Constantly sniffing the air for signs of danger, a lone bull mammoth moves cautiously down the trail toward the lake. During part of the year the bulls leave the cows and calves to become solitary wanderers. A half-dozen Clovis hunters wait in ambush. One hunter takes a pinch of dust from a leather bag and drops it, testing the air currents to be sure the hunters are still downwind. A mammoth's eyesight is not good, but its sense of smell is acute. As the bull reaches the lake's edge, the hunters rush out of hiding, striving for a quick kill. Sharp, stone-pointed darts, hurled with great force from their atlatls, plunge deep into the sides of the startled mammoth.

With bellows of anger and pain, the bull rushes at the tiny creatures who bring the pain, trying to trample them under his massive feet, swinging mighty tusks to impale these puny antagonists. The hunters have chosen their ambush site well, keeping the mammoth's movements restricted by thick trees on one side and a low earth bank on the other. The bull throws back his head to trumpet and a hunter hurls a dart that rips through the mammoth's throat and lodges in a vertebra.

Carefully keeping their distance, the hunters ring the bull, keeping him hemmed in against the trees and bank. The mammoth stands now, weak and no longer charging, his great head swinging tusks and trunk back and forth. Now and then, a dart glances off a rib, but many well-aimed darts drive between the ribs to penetrate deep into the lungs, where hemorrhaging will kill within just a few hours. Each breath and each movement causes the sharp stone points to cut and slice more, increasing the bleeding. The heart is buried too far inside the body to reach, and if wounded only in the stomach and intestines a mammoth will live for days. Finally the bull stumbles and goes down and a great cry goes up from the hunters. The Clovis people will feast tonight.

While one of the hunters goes to get the women and children who waited some distance away, the other hunters begin the butchering. Each of those butchering has preferred tools. Some knock off long flakes from a chert cobble, and use these razor-sharp blades to slice through the thick mammoth hide. The skin is so tough a new blade must be struck for every foot of cut, the hide rapidly dulling the razor-sharp edge. Other hunters prefer to work with finely flaked chert knives, which are retouched with fresh chipping when dulled.

The huge belly is sliced open and the intestines and stomach are pulled out. Some of the intestines will be cleaned and used as containers, perhaps some as canteens to carry water as the group travels. Other intestine portions, the ends tied closed, might be filled with water, chunks of meat, roots and tubers, and perhaps leafy greens and herbs, and then placed to simmer in the campfire coals. The rest of the intestine is destined to be eaten.

With the intestines removed, a hunter crawls into the body cavity to retrieve the lungs and heart. The inside is like a dark, warm cave, the great ribs stretching overhead clearly visible.

Women and children arrive; the air echoes with shouts and squeals of glee. Everyone has assigned tasks and quickly pitches in, the women joining in dismembering and butchering. Older children set about gathering deadwood and limbs from the forest, and soon fires are blazing. Smaller children scout the margins of the lake hunting for turtles. Nearby, a hunter stands guard with atlatl and darts ready, for the smell of the dead mammoth will soon draw the predators and scavengers. Between chores, the children crowd around the working adults seeking tidbits to eat. Dogs rush in to grab scraps, then retreat elsewhere to consume the bounty.

Mammoth skin peels away from the carcass easily and segments are cut into pieces to be cleaned and processed, and later made into boots, clothes, bags, and other needful items. One woman takes a section of hide and stakes it out flat on the ground with wooden pegs, hair side down. The remaining flesh and fat are scraped from the inside using a fist-sized stone with flakes removed from one end to leave a steep-faced plane.

One hunter cuts open one of the legs and starts stripping the flesh away. Unlike most other animals, a mammoth has only a few large ligaments holding the leg bones together, thus when the flesh and ligaments are cut, the leg bones just fall out. Another hunter removes the skin and flesh from the head, then smashes open the skull with a hammerstone to obtain the brains.

A rack is fashioned of poles near a fire, and strips of meat are hung on the rack. The dried meat will sustain the band until the next kill is made. Other strips of meat are skewered on poles and set over the fire to cook. Pits are dug in the soil near the fire, lined with hide and filled with water. Pottery had not been invented that far back in time. Stones are heated superhot in the fire, lifted with poles, and dropped into the hide-lined basins, quickly bringing the water to a boil. Meat and vegetables are added—stew is cooking.

When the Clovis people depart, only the bare bones of the mammoth remain. Most of the skeleton remains where the bull died, hide and meat stripped away, the great rib cage stands like a forest of dead trees. The massive legbones, too large to move or crush, lay where they fell. Lodged in a neck vertebra is a fluted point. Under the bones lay several more fluted points trampled into the dirt by the mammoth. Scattered around the abandoned campsite are small bones, broken tools, dulled flakes, and stone chips. Fire-cracked rock rests in charcoal from burned-out fires. Time passes and all becomes buried, to lie for thousands of years until uncovered by archaeologists.

Of course, the scene of our mammoth hunt and butchering is but an educated reconstruction. Remains from archaeological mammoth kill-sites give only clues about the activities engaged in by the Clovis people. Information on mammoth butchering comes from several archaeologists who have butchered modern elephants with prehistoric tools. Much of the butchering and cooking description is from practices followed by today's Stone Age societies.

INFORMATION ABOUT THE Clovis culture is sparse, coming from buried mammoth kill sites scattered across North America. Their remains are always recognized by their distinctive fluted points. What these people looked like is unknown, since no human remains, positively identified as Clovis, have yet been found. With origins in Asia, they most likely had Mongoloid features similar to today's American Indian populations. However, they might possibly have been Caucasoid instead, related to the Ainu of Japan.

The passing of ten thousand years has reduced all of the leather, hides, fiber, and other perishable materials of the Clovis culture to dust. Studies of Stone Age societies around the world today show that more than 70 percent of the things manufactured and used are from perishable materials. Undoubtedly these people wore clothing of leather and dressed animal skins, sewn together with sinew and rawhide. Animals skins, perhaps cured with animal brains and camp fire ash, became beds and probably capes used in bad weather.

Likewise, no evidence remains of whatever shelter these people might have constructed. It is possible that they simply moved from kill site to kill site, having no need of shelters most of the time and constructing temporary brush and hide huts only in bad weather. Then again, they might have maintained a base camp in some protected location, with pole and skin lodges, foraging from there into the countryside on hunting expeditions. However, no such camps have been discovered to date.

The passage of time has left the expertly crafted stone tools made by the Clovis culture. These people prized superior quality stones for their tools, often ignoring lesser quality local material to use the best material from distant sources. Beauty in the selected stones appears to be important for their fluted points. Several Clovis points from one mammoth kill site had been crafted from clear quartz crystal, a very difficult material to work. West Texas has a number of excellent sources of superior quality stone for making points and chipped-stone tools: the multicolored Alibates chert, the yellow and red Tecovas chert, and the gray and blue-gray Edwards Plateau chert. The Clovis people frequently used all of these materials to manufacture their chipped-stone tools.

The most diagnostic Clovis tools are the distinctive, masterfully crafted fluted points. Clovis points are works of art, each a gem of great beauty. In spite of their beautiful appearance, the designed purpose of the Clovis point is lethal and deadly. This lance-shaped point is made specifically for hunting mammoth and other large animals. Its sharp tip ensures penetration of the hide and the sharp edges cut an opening large enough for the shaft to penetrate far into the body cavity. The razor-sharp edges cause massive bleeding. The point narrows slightly at the base to allow for a pitch and sinew binding that will not impede entry. The flutes, starting at the base and extending partway up the center of the point, provide thinning to fit the nock in long, cylindrical wood, bone, or ivory foreshafts. The finished point and foreshaft was then attached to darts—short spears that are thrown with a spear thrower called an atlatl. The atlatl increases the length of the throwing arm, providing increased leverage, and propels the dart with tremendous force. The Clovis points also might have been attached to spears as a close-in defense against predators.

The Clovis people manufactured many other kinds of chipped-stone tools, flaked knives and blades for butchering, and various types of scrapers for both butchering and processing skins and hides. Small flakes with manufactured sharp points might have been used for engraving wood, bone, and ivory objects.

Other Clovis tools include grinding stones, which indicate

they processed plant materials, perhaps seeds, to eat with mammoth and other meat. Undoubtedly, they gathered nuts, berries, and fruits in season, and likely harvested roots, tubers, seeds, and greens to supplement their meat diet. Studies of today's Stone Age societies around the world show a remarkable knowledge of medicinal plants, and the Clovis people probably developed their own natural plant pharmacy.

Hammerstones, fist-sized rocks with battered surfaces, are commonly found at kill sites. These all-purpose tools might be used to break bones for marrow and to smash skulls to obtain brains, or to knock flakes and blades from a chunk of chert.

Animal bones provided the Clovis people with additional material to make tools. Mammoth kill sites have yielded such items as a mammoth-bone spear-shaft straightener, bone and ivory foreshafts, and scrapers and awls manufactured from mammoth and bison bone. Deer antlers might have been utilized for chipping points and knives.

The Clovis culture lasted less than 500 years. After appearing suddenly about 11,500 years ago, the Clovis tool kit is gone by 11,000 years ago—gone from Texas, and gone from the North American continent. Some archaeologists theorize that the Clovis people adapted to the loss of megafauna and the drastically changing environment at the end of the Wisconsin Glaciation, their decedents becoming the Folsom culture, which followed the Clovis in time. The Folsom people are the only other prehistoric culture known to use fluted points.

Pieces of a Puzzle

Great debates rage today over the origins of the Clovis culture and their impact on the megafauna 11,500 years ago. Geologists, biologists, anthropologists, and archaeologists have formulated many theories, often conflicting, to explain the origin of these people, the role they might have played in megafauna extinction, and the disappearance of Clovis culture.

The first irrefutable proof of the first people in North America is of the Clovis culture. The remains of these people are located in the oldest soil strata of archaeological sites and almost always are associated with mammoth bones. While there is some evidence that other people moved from Asia into the New World before the Clovis culture, the evidence to prove their existence is still being gathered. Some scientists argue that Clovis people are decedents of these earlier people, while others contend that Clovis people entered the North American midcontinent through the ice-free corridor.

Shortly after the arrival of the Clovis people, many of the Ice Age animals disappeared from North America and Texas. Megafauna (mammoth, camel, pronghorn, and horse) present in Texas 11,500 years ago might well have been hunted to extinction by these people. Many giant predators, the sabertoothed cat, American lion and cheetah, and dire wolf also became extinct at this same time, perhaps due to the disappearance of the mammoth and other prey. Many scavenger birds (eagles, condors, and vultures) also disappear. Are the Clovis people responsible for these massive extinctions? Did the drastically changing environment and climate bring about their disappearance? In all likelihood a combination of many factors, including hunting by Clovis people, caused these extinctions.

There are so many unanswered questions about the Clovis culture and the changing environment at the end of the Ice Age. Theories have been generated, but the evidence to provide answers often remains hidden. But this, after all, is the nature of archaeology. Each new find adds another small piece to the puzzle. Slowly the pieces come together to form a picture of life and people in the far distant past.

Acknowledgments

The authors wish to thank Dr. Pegi Jodry, archaeologist at the Smithsonian Institution and Dr. George Frison, archaeologist emeritus, at the University of Wyoming for freely sharing their knowledge of Clovis people and their experience in butchering elephants. Thanks also to Mike and Kathy Gear, and especially to Bob Gleason at Tor-Forge Books, for this opportunity.

CALVIN R. CUMMINGS retired as the National Park Services senior archaeologist. He and his, wife, Linda reside in Golden, Colorado, where Cal writes, sculpts, and landscapes.

LINDA SCOTT CUMMINGS is the founder, owner, and director of Paleo Research, a thirty-year-old archaeobotanic company in Golden, Colorado, that studies plants (examining pollen, phytoliths, starch, seeds, fibers, wood, charcoal, and protein residue) used by prehistoric and historic peoples, and reconstructing past environments.

TEXAS—FROM THE OUTSIDE

BY BILL GRONEMAN

⭐ I am not a Texan. I was born and raised in New York City. My interest in Texas and Texans stems from the early influences of television in the mid to late 1950s when every other show was a Western. Some of these shows were set in Texas or had episodes that featured Texas or Texan characters. My main interest in Texas revolves around the battle of the Alamo. This also came about through the childhood influence of Walt Disney's *Adventures of Davy Crockett* series starring Texan Fess Parker. While growing up I was always alert for any mention of Texas because there may have been some reference to the Alamo connected with it.

My interest solidified in later years as I began to read the many books about the battle. One of the earliest was *Remember the Alamo* by Robert Penn Warren. I remember my frustration when I walked to my local library in Howard Beach and discovered New Yorker Walter Lord's landmark book on the Alamo *A Time to Stand*. I was not allowed to withdraw the book since it was in the adult section and I only had a child's library card. I promptly returned with my father and circumvented the bureaucracy. I was fascinated by the fact that so many books could tell the story of the Alamo in so many different ways and interpretations. I became interested in the personnel of the Alamo when I read *A Time to Stand*. This book, considered the best among Alamo aficionados, featured an alphabetical list of all of those who died at the Alamo along with their birthplaces or places of residence before coming to Texas. The names had been listed at other times and in earlier works, but this marked the first time that I had seen such a list. It was a revelation since I had looked on the majority of the men of the Alamo as nameless, faceless individuals who died in the battle and were forever lost to history. Here was a list of real names of real people who had faces, families, and backgrounds. The names were not so very different from those of people I knew or went to school with. Another fact that struck me in seeing this list was that the vast majority of the men who died at the Alamo were from someplace other than Texas.

The Alamo that had existed only as a thing in the hazy past began to take shape and form for me. I knew that I would travel to Texas someday and see the real thing. I finally did this in 1975 and I am one of the few visitors who was not disappointed by the size and shape to the modern Alamo. I have been linked to the Alamo and Texas ever since, by way of the fact that I have been lucky enough to have written and published a few books on the Alamo and also one on Texas battlefields.

As a native New Yorker I can only write about Texas as an outsider. I never try to or claim to do it as anything else. I know I'm not a Texan and occasionally I am reminded. Once I received a card from a Texan telling me, "People from New York got *no* place writing about the Alamo—which place is truely [sic] the cradle of Texas liberty."

As a non-Texan who visits the Lone Star State fairly frequently I can appreciate the allure that it holds for newcomers. The sheer size of the state imparts a feeling of limitless freedom. Every sun-washed morning feels like a new beginning full of opportunity.

How much more so would these feelings have been to the men who ventured to Texas in the 1830s? Texas had been opened to colonization by the Mexican government and thousands of restless Americans flocked to its vast expanse. Some sought land. Others longed for a new beginning after suffering some failure or loss back home. When the Texas Revolution against the government of Antonio Lopez de Santa Anna broke out in 1835 the emigrants still came. The newer ones traveled to the new land with the full knowledge that they would be going in harm's way before they could stake any claim to Texas.

Texas worked its spell on these emigrants. Not only did they enjoy a new beginning, but many went through a virtual rebirth. They were reborn—as *Texans*. Micajah Autry, a lawyer and shopkeeper from Jackson, Tennessee, felt this rejuvenation. He wrote to his wife that "I feel more energy than I ever did in anything I have undertaken. I am determined to provide for you a home or perish." He later wrote to her that he had ". . . become one of the most thoroughgoing men you ever heard of . . ." since coming to Texas. A washed-up Tennessee politician named David Crockett also felt it. He wrote to his children, "I am blessed with excellent health, and am in high spirits, although I have had many difficulties to encounter." He added that he ". . . would rather be in my present situation than to be elected to a seat in Congress for life." David Cummings, a twenty-seven-year old surveyor from Lewiston, Pennsylvania wrote ". . . I have been very healthy since I have been here and am improving. . . ."

What brought about this rebirth?—The land itself. Within days of setting foot on Texas soil these men became converts. Autry described that there was ". . . not so fair a portion of the earth's surface warmed by the sun." He was convinced that it was prime "cotton country." Crockett felt it was ". . . the garden spot of the world . . . [with] . . . the best land and best prospects for health I ever saw." He favored the Bodark or Chocktaw Bayou of the Red River, and had no doubt that it was ". . . the richest country in the world, good land, plenty of timber, and the best springs, and good mill streams, good range, clear water and every appearance of health—game aplenty." Cummings felt the pull of the land. He wrote ". . . I have the satisfaction of beholding one of the finest countries in the world and have fully determined to locate myself in Texas." He also cast a professional eye on the land: "As I will most likely be engaged in surveying of public lands I might be of

service to some of our friends in procuring disirable [sic] or
choice locations."

Once they had their minds set on Texas these men were not to
be deterred. Cummings walked from New Orleans to reach
Gonzales, Texas, and sold his best rifle for thirty dollars in order
to have enough money to complete his trek. Crockett traded his
gold watch for a silver one and a balance of thirty dollars while
on his way to Texas. Twenty-four-year-old lawyer Daniel W.
Cloud of Kentucky traveled through Illinois, Missouri, Arkansas, and Louisiana on his way to Texas. He felt that some places
in Arkansas were ". . . rich, well watered, and healthy and [the]
society tolerably good." He believed that ". . . had we chosen to
locate in Ark. we would have made money rapidly, if blessed
with health and life. Dockets and Fees being large." He and his
companions blew right by these opportunities to get to Texas—
and war. Autry feared starvation in Natchitoches, Louisiana
for, as he explained ". . . the impulse to Texas both as to soldiers and moving families exceeds anything I have ever
known." Smallpox broke out in Natchitoches while he was
there, but he stated ". . . I fear the Tavern bill a great deal
worse." He finally reached Nacogdoches, Texas after what he
described as ". . . many hardships and privations," including a
hundred fifteen-mile walk through ". . . torrents of rain, mud,
and water." Still, he and all of the others continued on. Texas
was a goal worth all of the trouble and risk.

Once under the spell of the land the newcomers became instant ambassadors for Texas. They wanted everyone they knew
to follow them there. Autry wrote to his wife, "Tell Mr. Smith
not to think of remaining where he is but to be ready to come
to this country at the very moment the government shall be
settled . . . Tell brother Jack to think of nothing but coming
here with us; that if he knew as much about this country as I
already do he would not be kept from it." Cummings wrote,
". . . I say come on, there is a fine field open to you all no
matter how you are situated or what may be your circumstances. At least come and see the country, as a farmer, me-

chanic, or a Soldier [sic] you will do well—I believe no country offers such strong inducements to Emmigration [sic], affording all the conviences [sic] of life that man can devise. . . ." Crockett wrote to his children that "I have great hope of getting the agency to settle that country and I would be glad to see every friend I have settle there, it would be a fortune for them all."

The desire for new lands and new beginnings fueled a feverish patriotism and spirit of self-sacrifice in these newcomers. Twenty-seven-year-old John C. Goodrich used his family's acquaintance with Sam Houston to secure a place in Texas's struggle for freedom. He wrote,

> I have left my own dear, native land, my relations and friend, the companions of my early years, and every thing that I held dear and valuable to come to Texas to seek an establishment and home for myself . . . I feel a great desire to render some service to this country of my adoption in her struggle for freedom . . .

James Butler Bonham, a young firebrand lawyer from South Carolina and later Alabama is said to have volunteered his services in the cause of Texas ". . . without conditions. I shall receive nothing, either in the form of service pay, or land or rations." Twenty-three-year old John M. Thurston of Pennsylvania and later Kentucky expressed his wish to ". . . remain in the cause of Texas until the termination of her struggle." Autry wrote that "I go the whole Hog in the cause of Texas. I expect to help them gain their independence and also to form their civil government, for it is worth risking many lives for." Cloud outdid them all. He wrote,

> If we succeed the Country is ours. It is immense in extent, and fertile in its soil, and will amply reward all our toil. If we fail, death in the cause of liberty and humanity is not a cause for shuddering. . . .

Later he wrote,

> If we succeed a fertile region and a grateful people will be
> for us our home and secure to us our reward. If we fail,
> death in defense of so just and so good a cause need not
> excite a shudder or a team . . . When Texas becomes free
> I see in prospective a charming picture . . . opulence, se-
> curity, intelligence, religious and moral excellence, and so-
> cial happiness and refinement . . . The prospect is grand,
> too much so for my feeble power of description to com-
> pass.

Cloud wrote his outpourings of sacrifice in the cause of
Texas from Natchitoches, Louisiana. He had not even set foot
in Texas yet!

So they came. Outsiders from Tennessee, Missouri, Pennsylvania, South Carolina, Kentucky, New York, New Jersey, Mas-
sachusetts, England, Scotland, Germany, Ireland, and elsewhere,
all dedicated to the cause of Texas and the desire to be Texans.
The hopes, aspirations, and predictions about Texas by the
newcomers proved to be true, but not necessarily for themselves. Like Moses upon Mount Nebo they were permitted to
view the new land but not partake in its bounty. Instead men
like Autry, Bonham, Cloud, Crockett, Cummings, and Goodrich were inducted into a very elite fraternity. They, along with
approximately two hundred fifty others, became the men of the
Alamo. On the morning of March 6, 1836, they gave their lives
on behalf of Texas and thus irrevocably linked themselves to
the land of their adoption in a way none of them could have
imagined. They came to Texas as emigrants—outsiders. They
gambled everything they had for a stake in Texas, and sacrificed themselves on the altar of Texas liberty—as Texans.

BILL GRONEMAN is a long-time student of the Alamo battle and author of Defense of a Legend: Crockett and the de la Pena Diary, Roll Call at the Alamo, Alamo Defenders, *and* Eyewitness to the Alamo, *as well as numerous articles for the revision of* The Handbook of Texas. *He is a member of the Alamo Society, the Texas State Historical Association, the John Steinbeck Society, and the Western Writers of America. His most recent book is* The Death of a Legend *published by Republic of Texas Press.*

An Escape from Goliad

BY J. C. DUVAL

☆ On the morning of the 27th of March, a Mexican officer came to us and ordered us to get ready for a march. He told us we were to be liberated on "parole," and that arrangements had been made to send us to New Orleans on board vessels then at Copano. This, you may be sure, was joyful news to us, and we lost no time in making preparations to leave our uncomfortable quarters. When all was ready we were formed into three divisions and marched out under a strong guard. As we passed by some Mexican women who were standing near the main entrance to the fort, I heard them say "pobrecitos" (poor fellows), but the incident at the time made but little impression on my mind.

One of our divisions was taken down the road leading to the lower ford of the river, one upon the road to San Patricio and the division to which my company was attached along the road leading to San Antonio. A strong guard accompanied us, marching in double files on both sides of our column. It occurred to me that this division of our men into three squads and marching us off in three directions was rather a singular maneuver, but still I had no suspicion of the foul play intended us. When about half a mile above town, a halt was made and the guard on the side next the river filed around to the opposite side. Hardly had this maneuver been executed, when I heard a heavy firing of musketry in the directions taken by the other two divisions. Someone near me exclaimed, "Boys! they are going to shoot us!" and at the same instant I heard the clicking of musket locks all along the Mexican line. I turned to look, and as I did so the Mexicans fired upon us, killing probably one hundred out of the one hundred and fifty men in the division. We were in double file, and I was in the rear rank. The man in front of me was shot dead, and in falling he knocked me down. I did not get up for a moment, and when I rose to my feet I found that the whole Mexican line had charged over me, and were in hot pursuit of those who had not been shot and who were fleeing toward the river about five hundred yards distant. I followed on after them, for I knew that escape in any other direction (all open prairie) would be impossible, and I had nearly reached the river before it became necessary to make my way through the Mexican line ahead. As I did so, one of the soldiers charged upon me with his bayonet (his gun, I suppose, being empty). As he drew his musket back to make a lunge at me, one of our men coming from another direction, ran between us, and the bayonet was driven through his body. The blow was given with such force that in falling the man probably wrenched or twisted the bayonet in such a way as to prevent the Mexican from withdrawing it immediately. I saw him put his foot upon the man, and make an ineffectual attempt to extricate the bayonet from his body, but one look satisfied me, as I was somewhat in a hurry just then, and I hastened to the bank of the river and plunged in. The river at that point was deep and swift, but not wide, and being a good swimmer, I soon gained the opposite bank untouched by any of the bullets that were pattering in the water around my head. But here I met with an unexpected difficulty. The bank on that side was so steep I found it was impossible to climb it, and I continued to swim down the river until I came to where a grapevine hung from the bough of a leaning tree nearly to the surface of the water. This I caught hold of and was climbing up it hand over hand, sailor fashion, when a Mexican on the opposite bank fired at me with his escopeta, and with so true an aim that he cut the vine in two just above by head, and down I came into the water again. I then swam on about a hundred yards further, when I came to a place where the bank was not quite so steep, and with some difficulty I managed to clamber up.

THE RIVER ON the north side was bordered by timber several hundred yards in width, through which I quickly passed, and I was just about to leave it and strike out into the open prairie when I discovered a party of lancers nearly in front of me sitting on their horses, and evidently stationed there to intercept anyone who should attempt to escape in that direction. I halted at once under cover of the timber, through which I could see the lancers in the open prairie, but which hid me entirely from their view.

Whilst I was thus waiting and undecided as to the best course to pursue under the circumstances, I saw a young man by the name of Holliday, one of my own messmates, passing through the timber above me in a course that would have taken him out at the point directly opposite to which the lancers were stationed. I called to him as loudly as I dared and fortunately, being on the "qui vive," he heard me, and stopped far enough within the timber to prevent the lancers from discovering him. I then pulled off a fur cap I had on and beckoned to him with it. This finally drew his attention to me, and as soon as he saw me he came to where I was standing, from whence, without being visible to them, the lancers could be plainly seen.

A few moments afterward we were joined by a young man by the name of Brown, from Georgia, who had just swam the river, and had accidentally stumbled on the place where Holliday and I were holding a "council of war" as to what was the best course to pursue. Holliday, though a brave man, was very much excited, and had lost to some extent his presence of mind, for he proposed we should leave the timber at once and take the chances of evading the lancers we saw on the prairie. I reasoned with him on the folly of such a proceeding, and told him it would be impossible for us to escape in the open prairie from a dozen men on horseback. "But," said Holliday, "the Mexicans are crossing the river behind us, and they will soon be here." "That may be," I replied, "but they are not here yet, and in the meantime something may turn up to favor our escape." Brown took the same view of the case I did, and Holliday's wild proposition to banter a dozen mounted men for a race on the open prairie was "laid upon the table."

Whilst we were debating this (to us) momentous question, some four or five of our men passed out of the timber before we saw them into the open prairie, and when they discovered the lancers it was too late. The lancers charged upon them at once, speared them to death, and then dismounted, and robbed them of such things as they had upon their persons. From where we stood the whole proceeding was plainly visible to us, and as may be imagined, it was not calculated to encourage any hopes we might have had of making our escape. However, after the lancers had plundered the men they had just murdered, they remounted, and in a few moments set off in a rapid gallop down the river to where it is probable they had discovered other fugitives coming out of the timber. We at once seized the opportunity thus afforded us to leave the strip of timber, which we knew could give us shelter but for a few moments longer, and started out, taking advantage of a shallow ravine which partially hid us from view. We had scarcely gone two hundred yards from the timber when we saw the lancers gallop back and take up their position at the same place they had previously occupied. Strange to say, however, they never observed us, although we were in plain view of them for more than a quarter of a mile, without a single brush or tree to screen us.

We traveled about five or six miles and stopped in a thick grove to rest ourselves, where we stayed until night. All day long we heard at intervals irregular discharges of musketry in the distance, indicating, as we supposed, where fugitives from the massacre were overtaken and shot by the pursuing parties of Mexicans.

As the undergrowth was pretty dense in the grove where we had stopped, we concluded the chances of being picked up by one of these pursuing parties would be greater if we traveled on than if we remained where we were, and we determined to "lie by" until night. In talking the matter over and reflecting upon the many narrow risks we had run in making our escape, we came to the conclusion that in all probability we were the only survivors of the hundreds who had that morning been led out to slaughter; although in fact, as we subsequently learned, twenty-five or thirty of our men eventually reached the settlements on the Brazos.

AS SOON AS it was dark we left our hiding place and set out in a northeasterly direction, as nearly as we could determine, and traveled until daylight, when we stopped an hour or so in a grove to rest. We then proceeded on our course again till near sunset, when we encamped in a thick "mot" of timber without water. An unusually cold norther for the season of the year was blowing, and a steady drizzling rain was falling when we stopped. Brown, who had pulled off his coat and shoes before he swam the San Antonio River, suffered severely, and I was apprehensive, should we be exposed all night to such weather without a fire, that he would freeze to death. I had a little tinderbox in my pocket containing a flint and steel, but all the tinder there was in it a small piece not much larger than a pinhead.

This I carefully placed on a batch of cotton taken from the lining of my fur cap, and after many unsuccessful efforts I managed at last to ignite it. With this we started a fire, and then the first thing I did was to tear off a portion from my drawers which I partially burned, thus securing a good supply of tinder for future use. Before going to sleep we collected fuel enough to last until daylight, with which we occasionally replenished the fire so that we passed the night in tolerable comfort.

The next morning Brown, found himself so sore and crippled he was unable to travel. The prairie we had passed over the day before had been recently burned off and the sharp points of the stubble had lacerated his naked feet dreadfully. It was evident he could not go on without some sort of covering for his feet. I cut off the legs of my boots, and with a pair of scissors which he happened to have in his pocket and some twine I contrived to make him a pair of sandals, such as I had seen worn by Mexican soldiers. After thus shoeing him (by way of remuneration, I suppose), Brown separated the two blades of the scissors and gave me one of them, which was of great service to me, for by whetting it on stones I gave it an edge, and it answered pretty well in place of a knife.

The next morning we set out, as we supposed, in the direction we had traveled the day before, and in about one hour we came to some timber bordering upon what I thought was one of the branches of the Coletto Creek. Here we laid ourselves down on the grass to rest for a few moments, and scarcely had we done so when a party of ten Mexican lancers made their appearance, riding along a trail that ran within fifty yards of where we were lying. As luck would have it, just as they came opposite to where we were, they met another soldier and stopped to have a talk with him. For nearly an hour, it seemed to me, but in fact I suppose for only a few minutes, they sat on their horses conversing together within a few paces of where we were lying, and without a single bush or tree intervening to hide us from their view, but fortunately they never looked toward us or we would inevitably have been discovered. At length they rode on and we were very glad when we lost sight of them behind a point of timber.

THE NEXT MORNING we again took our course across the prairie, but owing to the rank growth of grass with which in many parts it was covered, and our increasing weakness, our progress was slow and painful. On the way Holliday found about a dozen wild onions, which he divided with Brown and myself, but the quantity for each was so small that it seemed only to aggravate the pangs of hunger. During the day we saw in the distance several parties of Mexicans or Indians, we could not tell which, as they only came near enough for us to see that they were men on horseback.

The evening of the fifth day after leaving Goliad, we descried a long line of timber ahead of us, and just before sunset we came to a large stream which from my knowledge of the geography of the country I was sure must be the Guadalupe. At the point where we struck it, the prairie extended up to the bank, which was high and very steep. A few hundred yards above us we saw a cow and her calf grazing near the edge of the bluff, and approaching them cautiously we attempted to drive them over it, hoping that one or the other would be disabled or killed by the fall, but after several ineffectual efforts to force them to take the leap, they finally broke through our line and made their way to the prairie, taking with them some steaks we stood very much in need of.

Completely exhausted by our exertions, and suffering extremely from hunger, we looked around for a suitable place to camp, as it was now nearly night, and coming to a pit or sink twelve or fourteen feet deep, which would protect us from the cold wind blowing at the time, we built a fire at the bottom, laid down upon the leaves, and in a little while we all went to sleep. How long I had slept I do not know, but I was at length aroused from my slumbers by a rattling among the sticks and dry leaves above me, and looking up I discovered a wild sow with her litter of pigs coming down the almost perpendicular bank of the sink. I silently grasped a billet of wood lying near me, and awaited their approach. The old sow came on, totally unsuspicious that three ravenous chaps were occupying her bed at the bottom (for by this time our fire had burnt out), and when she and her pigs were in striking distance I suddenly sprang up and began a vigorous assault upon the pigs. The noise aroused Brown and Holliday, and comprehending at once the state of affairs they sprang to my assistance, and before the sow and her pigs could make their escape up the steep sides of the pit we had "bagged" five of the latter. We made a desperate attack on the old sow, also, but weak as we were from starvation, and with our inefficient weapons, she routed us completely, leaving us, however, in possession of the field and the "spoils of war." We immediately started our fire again, and with no other preparation than a slight roasting on the coals, enough to singe off their hair, we very expediously disposed of the five pigs we had killed—nearly a pig and a half for each one, but then you must remember that they were small sucking pigs, and that we had not had a mouthful to eat for five days except a handful of wild onions. Greatly refreshed by our supper of scorched pig, we laid down again upon the leaves at the bottom of the sink and slept soundly until the sun was an hour or so high.

As soon as we awoke we left the sink and went out to make a reconnoissance of the river, to see what the chances were for crossing it. Though not very wide at that point, we soon perceived we had a difficult job to undertake, for the river was much swollen by recent rains, and its turbid waters were rushing along at a rapid rate. Holliday and I were both good swimmers, and I felt sure we could reach the opposite bank safely; but I had my doubts about Brown. He was a poor swimmer, and consequently was timid in water. However, there was no alternative but to make the attempt, and we therefore stripped off our clothes, tied them in a bundle on our heads to keep them as dry as possible, and plunged in the turbid flood. Holliday and I soon reached the opposite bank, but hardly had we done so when I heard Brown cry out for help, and looking back I saw that he was still some distance from the shore, and evidently just on the eve of going under. At the very point where I landed there happened to be a slab of dry timber lying near the water, which I instantly seized, and swimming with it to the place where Brown was struggling to keep his head above the surface, I pushed the end of the slab to him, which he grasped and to which he held on with the usual tenacity of a drowning man, and with the assistance of Holliday I at last got him to the shore and dragged him out of the water. It was fortunate for Brown that Holliday and I, between us, had taken his clothes, as otherwise no doubt he would have lost them all.

Continuing our course, we passed through a heavily timbered bottom more than a mile wide, and then came to a large prairie in which we saw many herds of deer and some antelopes.

We also saw today a party of Indians on horses, but we eluded them by concealing ourselves in some tall grass that grew in the bottom of a ravine. About dusk we came to the timber on the farther side of the prairie, in which we encamped under the spreading branches of a live oak tree.

Whilst collecting a supply of fuel for the night I came upon a heap of brush and leaves, and scraping off the top to see what was beneath I discovered about half the carcass of a deer which apparently had been recently killed and partly eaten by a panther or Mexican lion, and the remainder "cached" in this heap for future use. Of course, under the circumstances, I had no scruples about appropriating the venison, and calling Brown and Holliday to my assistance we carried it to camp, where, after cutting off the ragged and torn portions of the meat, we soon had the balance spitted before a blazing fire. After making a hearty supper on our stolen venison, we raked a quantity of dry leaves close to the fire and "turned into bed."

During the night, at various times, we heard the roaring of a Mexican lion (very probably the lawful owner of the larder that had supplied us with supper), and for fear he might be disposed to make a meal of one of us in place of venison, we took good care not to let our fire burn down too low.

After escaping the Goliad Massacre, J. C. DUVAL wrote about Texas and Texans. He was the last survivor of Fannin's Army. He died in 1897.

...STEPHEN F. AUSTIN

CIRCULAR

From the Committee of safety of the jurisdiction of Austin. All are aware of the present movements of volunteers toward the western frontiers. For the information of every one this Committee deem it proper to state as briefly as possible the leading facts which have given rise to this excitement. When the circular of this Committee, under date of the 19th ult. was issued, information of an unquestionable character had been received here, as to the marching of soldiers from Bexar, in some short period, within the limits of the colonies. The object appeared to be the apprehension of certain citizens, among them Don Lorenzo de Zavala, now a citizen of Texas, was particularly designated and aimed at. This gentleman had come to Texas, as to an asylum from the persecution of the present administration of Mexico. His offense we know not, except that he is the known friend of free institutions. This distinguished man, the authorities of Texas have been arbitrarily required by military mandate to surrender into the hands of General Cos, who, in his zeal to secure the person of this patriotic and virtuous citizen, actually issued an order some time since, addressed to Colonel Ugartechea, commandant at Bexar, to march into the colonies and *take him,* at the risk of losing all the force he should employ. The mere intimation of such an order would be an evident disrespect to the citizens of Texas, but the issuing of it, with the correspondent threats of Colonel Ugartechea of putting it into execution, is at once an open outrage upon the civil authorities of Texas, and upon the Constitution. But what is of most importance, such proceedings serve plainly to show us all, what *kind of government* the present reformers in Mexico are aiming to subject us to—which is the *government of the bayonet,* and the regulation of all the affairs of Texas by military power, regardless of the Constitution, of the civil authority, and of all the legally vested, equitable, and natural rights of the people of Texas.

That such is the real and ultimate object of the military power now reigning in Mexico, and that the reasons assigned for the present hostile movements are nothing but mere pretexts to cover the main objects, and thus fill the country with troops, is clear and evident; but should there still remain doubts on the mind of any person, let him weigh and maturely consider the following facts, and draw his own conclusions.

The Constitutional Governor of the State, Viesca, and also another governor, Falcon, who had been constitutionally installed to succeed Viesca, have been deposed by the military at Monclova. The state authorities were imprisoned, and a governor appointed by the acting president of the general government of Mexico. This is evidently an act of military usurpation and despotism, and the state of Coahuila and Texas is at this time without any constitutional or legal government at all, and the people of every part of the state, and those of Texas in particular, are left at full liberty to provide for themselves as they may deem best.

But a more general, though succinct view of matters, is necessary for a full and proper understanding of this subject.

A disastrous and ruinous civil war was kindled in 1832, by means of an insurrection against the Bustamante administration, and General Santa Anna was placed at its head. The avowed object of this insurrection was to *protect the federal system, and sustain the Constitution of* 1824, which, it was *then* alleged, was attacked and endangered by the measures and projects of the Bustamante administration. On this principle the people of Texas supported General Santa Anna to defend the Constitution of 1824, and the federal system. This general was enthusiastically supported by every liberal and free Mexican, and by the friends of the federal system in every part of the nation. With this support he triumphed. He became the man of the people—the protector of the federal system—the oracle of public opinion—the arbiter of the nation's political destinies. How has he used this power, *thus acquired?* Let the military despotism now enthroned in Mexico upon the ruins of the federal system—let the friends of this system, who are now groaning in prisons or wandering in exile—let the Constitution of 1824, which still raises its dying voice from beneath the feet of military usurpation—let the free and impartial in Mexico and in the whole civilized world give the reply. They all say, he used it to *destroy* what he avowed he had taken up arms to protect; he used the federal party as blind instruments to destroy the federal system; he abandoned his federal friends who had given him power, and united with the military, ecclesiastical and central party, against whom he took up arms in 1832. The same party is now governing in Mexico, and they say to the people of Texas, in the language of friendship and persuasion—in that of *sugarplums and honey,* that in the new Constitution, or central government that is organizing in Mexico, guarantees shall be given to the people of Texas, their rights shall be protected and secured, and they are told that the government expects from their "docility" a *submission to all the reforms and alterations that may be agreed to by the majority of the nation.* But who compose, and what is this majority of the nation spoken of by the minister, and how are these reforms to be effected? It is composed of the same military power before spoken of, who have assumed the voice of the nation, and have suppressed, by military influence, the expression of public opinion; and the reforms are to be effected by *unconstitutional means;* a sufficient proof of which is, that the present Congress in Mexico, who was elected with constitutional powers alone, have, by their own act, declared themselves to be invested with the powers of a national convention, to frame a new constitution, or reform that of 1824 as they think proper.

What is here meant by *"reforming"* the Constitution of 1824, may be clearly deduced by the "reform" of the militia made by this same general Congress. This "reform" reduced the militia of the States to *one militiaman* for every five hun-

dred inhabitants, and disarmed all the rest. The people of Zacatecas resisted this iniquitous law, but were unfortunate and
compelled, for the time being, to submit to the military power
of the reformer: so that, in fact, "reform" means destruction.

From this condensed view of the past let every impartial man
judge for himself what degree of faith or credit ought to be
given to the professions of the present government of Mexico,
and ask himself whether a subtle poison may not be concealed
in the *sugar-plums,* or a sting in the *honey,* that is now offered
to the "docile," people of Texas.

But, in addition to this general view of matters, information
of the most positive and unquestionable character is in the possession of this Committee, that every possible effort is making
by the government in Mexico to raise troops, money, and resources to fit out an expedition—*an army of invasion* against
Texas. Infantry, artillery, and cavalry have been ordered from
San Luis Potosi, Saltillo, and Tamaulipas; and all the disposable
infantry at Campeche has also been ordered on to Texas by
water, as it was supposed they would stand the climate better
than other troops. Magazines of arms and ammunition are
forming at Matamoras, Goliad, and Bexar, and the old bar-
racks and fortifications at the latter place are repairing to receive a large force, In short, the common talk all over Mexico
among the military is the *invasion* of Texas.

Now, if the present government of Mexico is sincere in its
profession of liberal guarantees for Texas, why all this preparation for a military invasion? Why has General Cos marched
with all the disposable force at Matamoras (about four hundred men) to Bexar, where he now is, according to last accounts? Can it be that the government, in its fatherly care for
Texas, fears that there are servile slaves in this country, who
will oppose *liberal guarantees*? Or is it that the promised guarantees, are only a cover and a false show, to quiet Texas until
the general Government is prepared to give to it a military government.

It is well known to all that the reforms spoken of by the

minister, and now being made in Mexico, contemplate the abolition of the whole federal system, the establishment of a central or consolidated government, which is to absorb and swallow up all the powers and authorities of the nation: military commandancies will supply the place of the state governments, and the vested rights of Texas under the constitution and law of May 7, 1824, are to be disregarded and violated. Ought, or can, or will the people of Texas submit to all this? Let each man study the subject, and answer for himself. If he will submit, let him go to the military power and prostrate himself. If he will not submit, let him give his answer from the mouth of his rifle!

In regard to the present movements of the military, the letter from Gonzales, and extracts from other letters of unquestionable faith will inform the public. By these letters the people of Texas are informed that their fellow citizens at Gonzales *have been attacked—the war has commenced!* They will also perceive that General Cos has arrived with reinforcement of troops, and is preparing for a campaign of extermination against the people of Texas.

The head quarters of the ARMY OF THE PEOPLE for the present is at Gonzales. It is already respectable in numbers, and invincible in spirit.

This Committee exhorts every citizen who is yet at home, to march as soon as possible to the assistance of his countrymen now in the field. The campaign is opened. Texas must be freed from military despots before it is closed.

STEPHEN F. AUSTIN
*Chairman of the Committee
of the Jurisdiction of Austin.*

STEPHEN F. AUSTIN, "the Father of Texas," was a colonizer, diplomat, leader, and statesman. He settled the first Anglo-American colony in Texas.

I SHALL NEVER SURRENDER OR RETREAT

BY WILLIAM BARRET TRAVIS

COMMANDANCY OF THE ALAMO,
BEJAR, FEB'Y 24TH, 1836.

To the People of Texas and all Americans in the World.

FELLOW CITIZENS AND COMPATRIOTS—I am besieged, by a thousand or more of the Mexicans under Santa Anna. I have sustained a continual Bombardment and cannonade for 24 hours and have not lost a man. The enemy has demanded a surrender at discretion, otherwise, the garrison are to be put to the sword, if the fort is taken. I have answered the demand with a cannon shot, and our flag still waves proudly from the walls. *I shall never surrender or retreat.* Then, I call on you in the name of Liberty, of patriotism and everything dear to the American character, to come to our aid with all dispatch. The enemy is receiving reinforcements daily and will no doubt increase to three or four thousand in four or five days. If this call is neglected, I am determined to sustain myself as long as possible and die like a soldier who never forgets what is due to his own honor and that of his country. VICTORY OR DEATH.

WILLIAM BARRET TRAVIS,
LT. COL. COMDT.

P.S. The Lord is on our side. When the enemy appeared in sight we had not three bushels of corn. We have since found in deserted houses 80 or 90 bushels and got into the walls 20 or 30 head of Beeves.

TRAVIS.

WILLIAM BARRET TRAVIS (1809–1836) came to Texas as a lawyer in 1831 and quickly rose to leadership among Texans who resisted Mexican authority. He commanded the Texas force at the Alamo, and died in battle there on March 6, 1836.

Facets of the Alamo

BY FRANK THOMPSON

⭐ The first time I saw the Alamo it was sparkling like a diamond. It was June, 1963. My family and I had been traveling by car for two days from South Carolina and were welcomed to the outskirts of San Antonio by a blinding Texas thunderstorm; the rain came down in curtains so opaque and powerful that we had to pull over to the side of the road twice to wait until visibility returned.

Even under the circumstances, it was no problem to find the Alamo. Huge signs with arrows kept us on track and my heart pounded with the idea that we were really there, that I would finally stand on the sacred ground I had dreamed of for so long. As we turned right from Commerce Street onto Alamo Street, the rain suddenly stopped. Within seconds, a brilliant late afternoon sun broke through the clouds. We pulled up to the curb in front of the ancient limestone church and as I sprang from the car, the sunlight glanced off the wet walls and sidewalk puddles, creating a light show of electric rainbow colors so vivid that I had to take a second to allow my eyes to become used to it. The Alamo was alive with light, shimmering and golden.

I was already as well read on the subject as an eleven-year-old could be, having devoured those crucial books by Lon Tinkle, John Myers Myers, William Weber Johnson, and Robert Penn Warren. I had virtually memorized Walter Lord's *A Time to Stand*—indeed, I *had* memorized the list of Alamo defenders in the book's appendix. And I had, like most boys and girls of my generation, immersed myself in the mythic Alamo visions of John Wayne and Fess Parker.

But even at that age, I had an intuition of the separation

between the bloody battle that had been fought there on March 6, 1836—the event that had turned it into the "Shrine of Texas Liberty"—and the place itself. The battle was one reason I found the Alamo interesting, but it wasn't the only reason. It wasn't even the most important one.

In those days, the saga of the Alamo seemed to be pretty simple. A small, beleaguered band of American patriots—maybe as many as a hundred eighty-three—defended the ruined old mission against thousands and thousands of savage Mexican soldiers, led by a heartless, sneering dictator/monster named Santa Anna. Proclaiming that right was on their side, these brave Texans held to their posts through almost two weeks of horrifying siege. And when their young commander, William Barret Travis, drew a line in the dirt and offered them a chance to die with him, or to leave the fort with honor, they all crossed the line happily— eager to perish for Texas.

And perish they did. On the morning of March 6, Santa Anna's cruel hordes attacked. Although each Texan defender personally killed twenty or thirty of the enemy, they were finally overcome. The Alamo had fallen.

Today, the tale isn't nearly so black and white. Few historians today believe the story of Travis's line in the dirt; in fact, it now appears that the men of the Alamo were confident until the day they died that reinforcements were on the way. The number of Alamo defenders might have been as high as two hundred fifty, and Santa Anna's attacking force probably didn't exceed 1,500, many of whom were woefully inexperienced and under trained in the art of war. Even so, their death toll didn't number in the thousands, but in the low hundreds.

And where earlier generations had the men of the Alamo standing resolute and stalwart on the walls until they were cut down, the real struggle was a nightmare of terror and pain, conducted in a hellish confusion of darkness and agonizing death. Many now believe that some seventy men rushed in panic from the fort and were cut down by Mexican lancers; a smaller group of survivors was executed after the battle. Debate still rages with surprising bitterness as to whether they actually surrendered, and whether the Honorable ex-Congressman David Crockett was among them.

The myth of the Alamo is in an almost constant state of revision. We now see the battle with different eyes than we did only a few decades ago. We now question everything, argue every interpretation, fight to establish—or discredit—every new detail or idea. But the Alamo itself remains, both a part of, and apart from, its bloody past. Its benign but mesmerizing face has looked upon horror and triumph, and gazes back at us with all the holy power of the Sphinx.

It is a shrine and a tomb, a source of ethnic bitterness and a wellspring of patriotic pride. It is also a jewel that still glistens and sparkles as it did to me on that afternoon in 1963. Look at the jewel this way and one facet will shine; turn it and another will glimmer. There are facets beyond number, more than we can ever fully understand, perhaps more than we can ever know. But look long enough and you'll discover a facet that reflects an image of who we are, what we think of our past, and what we dream for our future.

FRANK THOMPSON is a filmmaker and film historian, as well as the author of numerous books, including American Movie Classics' Great Christmas Movies, I Was That Masked Man *(with Clayton Moore),* Lost Films, The Star Film Ranch, Los Angeles Uncovered, *and* Abraham Lincoln: Twentieth Century Popular Portrayals. *A contributor to several film encyclopedias, he has also written for* American Cinematographer, Film Comment, *and many other publications. Thompson wrote and directed* The Great American Christmas Movies *for American Movie Classics, served as associate producer and historical consultant for* Wild Bill: Hollywood Maverick, *and wrote and co-produced* Frank Capra: A Personal Remembrance *and* The Making of "It's a Wonderful Life." *He lives in Burbank, California, but openly admits a desire to move to Texas!*

A Mexican's Story of San Jacinto

BY PEDRO DELGADO (1836)

☆ At daybreak on the 21st, His Excellency [Santa Anna] ordered a breastwork to be erected for the cannon. It was constructed with pack-saddles, sacks of hard bread, baggage, etc. A trifling barricade of branches ran along its front and right.

At nine o'clock A.M. General Cos came in with a reinforcement of about 500 men. His arrival was greeted with the roll of drums and with joyful shouts. As it was represented to His Excellency that these men had not slept the night before, he instructed them to stack their arms, to remove their accoutrements, and to go to sleep quietly in the adjoining grove.

No important incident took place until 4:30 P.M. At this fatal moment, the bugler on our right signaled the advance of the enemy upon that wing. His Excellency and staff were asleep; the greater number of the men were also sleeping; of the rest, some were eating, others were scattered in the woods in search of boughs to prepare shelter. Our line was composed of musket stacks. Our cavalry were riding, bareback, to and from water.

I stepped upon some ammunition boxes, the better to observe the movements of the enemy. I saw that their formation was a mere line in one rank, and very extended. In their center was the Texas flag; on both wings, they had two light cannons, well manned. Their cavalry was opposite our front, overlapping our left.

In this disposition, yelling furiously, with a brisk fire of grape, muskets, and rifles, they advanced resolutely upon our camp. There the utmost confusion prevailed. General Castrillon shouted on one side: on another Colonel Almonte was giving orders; some cried out to commence firing; others to lie down to avoid grape shots. Among the latter was His Excellency.

Then, already, I saw our men flying in small groups, terrified, and sheltering themselves behind large trees. I endeavored to force some of them to fight, but all efforts were in vain—the evil was beyond remedy; they were a bewildered and panic stricken herd.

Then I saw His Excellency running about in the utmost excitement, wringing his hands, and unable to give an order. General Castrillon was stretched on the ground, wounded in the leg. Colonel Trevino was killed, and Colonel Marcial Aguirre was severely injured. I saw also the enemy reaching the ordnance train, and killing a corporal and two gunners who had been detailed to repair cartridges which had been damaged on the previous evening.

Everything being lost, I went—leading my horse, which I could not mount, because the firing had rendered him restless and fractious—to join our men, still hoping that we might be able to defend ourselves, or to retire under the shelter of night. This, however, could not be done. It is a known fact that Mexican soldiers, once demoralized, can not be controlled, unless they are thoroughly inured to war.

On the left, and about a musket-shot distance from our camp, was a small grove on the bay shore. Our disbanded herd rushed for it, to obtain shelter from the horrid slaughter carried on all over the prairie by the bloodthirsty usurpers. Unfortunately, we met on our way an obstacle difficult to overcome. It was a bayou, not very wide, but rather deep. The men, on reaching it, would helplessly crowd together, and were shot down by the enemy, who was close enough not to miss his aim. It was there that the greatest carnage took place.

Upon reaching that spot, I saw Colonel Almonte swimming across the bayou with his left hand, and holding up his right, which grasped his sword.

I stated before that I was leading my horse, but, in this critical situation, I vaulted on him, and, with two leaps, he landed me on the opposite bank of the bayou. To my sorrow I had to leave the noble animal, mired, at that place, and to part with him, probably forever. As I dismounted, I sank in the mire waist-deep, and I had the greatest trouble to get out of it, by taking hold of the grass. Both my shoes remained in the bayou. I made an effort to recover them, but I soon came to the conclusion that, did I tarry there, a rifle shot would certainly make an outlet for my soul, as had happened to many a poor fellow around me. Thus I made for the grove, barefooted.

There I met a number of other officers, with whom I wandered at random, buried in gloomy thoughts upon our tragic disaster. We still entertained a hope of rallying some of our men, but it was impossible.

The enemy's cavalry surrounded the grove, while his infantry penetrated it, pursuing us with fierce and blood-thirsty feelings. Thence they marched us to their camp. I was bare-footed; the prairie had recently been burnt up, and the blades of grass, hardened by fire, penetrated like needles the soles of my feet, so that I could hardly walk.

After having kept us sitting in camp about an hour and a half, they marched us into the woods, where we saw an immense fire. I and several of my companions were silly enough to believe that we were about to be burnt alive, in retaliation for those who had been burnt in the Alamo. We should have considered it an act of mercy to be shot first. Oh! the bitter and cruel moment! However, we felt considerably relieved when they placed us around the fire to warm ourselves and to dry our wet clothes.

We were surrounded by twenty-five or thirty sentinels. You should have seen those men, or, rather, phantoms, converted into moving armories. Some wore two, three, and even four brace of pistols; a cloth bag of very respectable size filled with bullets, a powder horn, a saber or a bowie knife, besides a rifle, musket, or carbine.

Was this display intended to prevent us from attempting to escape? The fools! Where could we go in that vast country, unknown to us, intersected by large rivers and forests, where wild beasts and hunger, and where they themselves would destroy us?

PEDRO DELGADO served as a colonel in the Mexican Army under General Santa Anna.

The Misdemeanor Murder Trial

BY GARY JAMES

⭐ For a short balding man who has spent a lifetime as a photojournalist for a Houston TV station, the *Texas Mystique* can best be described in a story I covered back in the sixties.

I was a greenhorn reporter for KPRC AM/TV back in those days staying busy mostly doing radio newscasts and covering breaking news stories in the city. My boss, Ray Miller, came to me one Saturday morning with the opportunity all reporters dream of. A famous murder trial that had its roots in Houston but its conclusions in Miami, Florida, was about to get underway in Miami on Monday. That was two days away. The assigned reporter came down with a toothache and couldn't go, so Ray asked me if I would like to spend a few days in Florida covering the jury selection process in the Candace Mossler/Melvin Lane Powers murder trial. Candace was a well-known socialite living in the upscale River Oaks section of Houston at the time. Her late husband was a banker. Candace and Mel, her nephew, were accused of plotting to kill Jacque Mossler, and then carrying it out in a condo on Key Biscayne in the late 1960s.

Ray offered to fly me to Florida for the assignment, but I chose to take the company car instead. I couldn't stand the thought of not having transportation once I got to Florida, so I drove an old company station wagon with the station call letters and the words HOUSTON, TEXAS brightly displayed on the side. The few old veterans I spoke to before I left on the trip all warned me of how rude most of the people were in Florida, especially in Miami. But when I got to Miami, I was received warmly. That may have been because of my warm and wonderful personality, but I suspect it was because my car had HOUSTON, TEXAS written on the side. Wherever I drove there were Floridians screaming "Hey, Texas," and anxious to exchange friendly words with me.

Being from Texas was the best thing about the trip, which incidentally lasted not a week but sixty-four days. Ray left me there for the entire trial because I did such a good job. Being from Texas assisted me in my work and play. For the first two weeks I played cat and mouse with literally hundreds of reporters who were there from all over the world covering the trial. It was a big trial. One of the defense attorneys was about the most famous attorney of them all—Percy Foreman. Percy had built a reputation as a great defense lawyer in his time. He represented several famous and notorious figures of that day, including Jack Ruby, the man who killed the man who killed President Kennedy. All the reporters crowded around Foreman constantly, trying to get an edge on the others. Every morning and afternoon, for the first couple of weeks, I fought my way through the crowds trying to get Percy's attention, so that I could perhaps get some comment from him about the trial that none else could use on the evening news. But try as I may I just couldn't get his attention.

At the close of the fifteenth day of the trial, I had packed up my gear and was leaving the Dade County Courthouse parking lot in my Channel 2 station wagon heading back toward my lonely motel room when this big voice from the direction of the courthouse yelled out "Hey, Texas." I looked around and it was Percy Foreman walking toward me from the day's session. I stopped and waved back and he came over to the car and said "Are you from Texas?" I replied, "Yes sir, Mr. Foreman. I'm Gary James from KPRC-TV in Houston and I've been sent her by Ray Miller to cover this trial." From that day on Percy took this cub reporter under his wing and led me through the legal proceedings . . . feeding me exclusive information about the ins and outs of the trial daily. All this made my stories more interesting and my job a lot easier.

I'd like to think it was my pleasing disposition and my warm personality and my journalistic knowledge that won me several state and national awards for my coverage of the famous Mossler Murder Trial, but the truth is I suspect it was because I was at the right place at the right time—and—because I emulated a little bit of that thing we call *"Texas mystique."*

GARY JAMES, *a forty-four-year veteran of radio/television broadcasting, has gained regional fame for his creative work at KPRC Channel 2 in Houston, Texas. As producer of* Eyes of Texas *he has traveled the state for more than 30 years developing stories for the award-winning show. For his work on this and other KPRC-TV features, he has won numerous awards both in writing and photography, including two Emmys for investigative documentaries, and is the recipient of a Peabody Award for distinguished journalism. Gary James is the author of six travel books on Texas. His newest book,* The Texas Guide: The Definitive Guide to the Lone Star State, *was published by Fulcrum Publishing.*

Gary James "On the Road" for KPRC-TV Houston.
PHOTO COURTESY OF GARY JAMES.

MR. C. R. AND AMERICAN AIRLINES

☆ An aviation pioneer, Cyrus Rowlett Smith entered the airline business in the days of open-cockpit biplanes. A combination of destiny, daring, and "can-do" determination put him—a man born of the humblest beginnings, who, as a boy, picked cotton and worked as a field hand in West Texas, and, who, as a young man lacked a high school diploma—at the helm of an infant industry, destined to change the world.

In 1934, C. R. Smith wrote the following autobiographical accounting of his outstanding career:

Born Minerva, Milam County, Texas, on September 9, 1899. That date being the ninth day of the ninth month of the ninety-ninth year of the century, it is supposed to mean something by the standards of the stargazers. It would be much more practical, if it could be arranged, to have it mean that sets of fours would occur during my life with some frequency in my poker hands. Perhaps that might be what it is, for I have always had pretty good luck with poker.

I am not sure about the details of the first eight years. During those years we lived in Minerva and Dallas, Texas, Hodge and Ruston, Louisiana. We moved to Amarillo in the early part of 1909.

Amarillo was at that time a town of 12,000 to 15,000 people, the center of the Panhandle cattle country. Even at that late date most of the prairie land was not fenced and you could ride for miles across the country and see neither a fence nor a house. Today Amarillo is a city of some 50,000 people.

We lived in Amarillo on the North Side of town, which was not the best social side of the city. It was on the wrong side of the Fort Worth and Denver tracks. The reason was, naturally, that our finances did not permit living on the other side.

Amarillo was still at that time in a sparsely settled section and many nights you could hear the coyotes whining and crying at the edge of the city limits.

In Amarillo, at the age of nine, I secured my first job, office boy to C. T. Herring, one of the well-known big cattlemen of West Texas. Through him I met Lee Bivins, C. P. Smith, and Mr. Fuqua, all well-known cattlemen of that time. My principal job was to run errands and to keep people out of Mr. Herring's office when he was talking with the cowboys who came in from the ranches. Prior to the time that I began working for Mr. Herring, I had sold *Saturday Evening Post* on the north side of Amarillo.

Between jobs in Amarillo I went to school at the public schools in Amarillo.

We moved to Whitney, Texas, in 1910 and lived there until 1916. I went to school in Whitney between jobs.

During the summer of the early years in Whitney I worked on a good many farms and ranches. I chopped cotton, picked cotton, and ran a disc in connection with the planting of wheat. On a ranch operated then by a gentleman by the name of Bob Rhea I first learned to ride a horse.

The standard wage, at that time, for farm and ranch work was one dollar a day and you furnish your own lunch and transportation. Cotton picking was fifty cents per cwt. And you had to be pretty good to go over two hundred pounds per day. I finally achieved the high water mark on my cotton-picking career with two hundred fifty pounds in one day.

Cotton picking was pretty tough work for you had to kneel in order to pick the cotton. You wore leather pads on both of your knees and you spent most of the time either on your knees or stooping over. Pretty hard both on the knees and the back.

About 1913 I secured a job as a store clerk and delivery boy for a grocery store operated by Mr. E. H. McCown. The pay to start with was twenty dollars a month. I worked there about two years and ended up with twenty-eight dollars per month. The hours usually ran from sunup to sundown, and until about 9:00 P.M. on Saturday nights. We had to have the store swept out by the time the morning train came through, which was about 6:30 A.M. There was no especial significance to the train except that that was a good mark to go by.

I worked in the First National Bank of Whitney for about a year, perhaps a bit more. I started out as bookkeeper and later became bookkeeper and spare teller, waiting on the window when the assistant cashier and the other officials were busy. We kept the books in longhand and it often took until late in the night to get the books balanced. The village electric light plant went off at either 10:30 or 11:00 P.M. and if we had not completed our work by that time we worked by the light of oil lamps. I started out in the bank at a figure something like thirty dollars per month. By the time I had been there a year I was getting forty per month.

We left Whitney and moved to Hillsboro. I secured a job with the Hillsboro Cotton Mills as bookkeeper, the only bookkeeper they had. Later the office manager went into the army and he was not replaced. I took over both jobs, bookkeeper and office manager. The job of office manager involved keeping up with production figures, cotton on hand, some selling work by letter; also making the payroll and paying off each two weeks.

The cotton mills produced principally cotton duck and a coarser cotton fabric used in making sugar sacks. I forget what my pay was at the beginning, probably a hundred to a hundred twenty-five dollars per month. I was making two hundred a month at the time I left.

From Hillsboro we went to Austin, where Governor Pat N. Neff had promised me a job in the capital. I went to work in the office of the Secretary of State and had charge of the Franchise Tax Department. After I had been there for about a year I decided to go to the University of Texas.

I had to secure special permission to enter the university on account of the fact that I did not have the proper high school credits, not having graduated from high school. I secured that permission and entered the university. I took nearly all of the subjects offered by the School of Business Administration, a course in public speaking, some courses in economics, and a couple of courses in law.

I was a member of the Kappa Sigma social fraternity, president of my class in the School of Business Administration in my junior year, president of Speakers Club, a public speaking organization, and member of two honorary societies, one in public speaking and one in business administration. I was president of the honorary society in business administration during one year.

While in the university I had a part-time job with the Federal Reserve Bank, paying $62.50 per month, the work being the examination of reports made by state bank examiners on state banks and the rendition of a summarized report to the Federal Reserve Bank at Dallas.

I also conducted an advertising agency under the name of C. R. Smith & Company. Most of the early income of the agency, which was a one-man organization, came from the sale of stockholders lists to investment firms. I would go through the records of the corporations at the capital and make lists of stockholders and sell those lists to investment firms located throughout the country.

The biggest source of income came from a list of new mothers and fathers. When a baby was born it along with the names and addresses of its parents would be listed in the vital statistics records of the State Health Department. I would make lists of the mothers, with the addresses, and sell the lists to baby buggy companies, baby food companies, baby magazines, etc.

I lost this source of income late in my college life due to an unfortunate accident. The Health Department had no objections to my securing the names for it seemed to them to be a legitimate undertaking. Later along some gentleman with low moral character started getting a list of the deaths and then going around to the family of the deceased with a Bible lettered in gold with the story that the deceased had ordered the Bible before his or her death. The name of the deceased would be on the Bible in gold letters and naturally the family would be reluctant not to take the volume, their father or mother having ordered it before death. The Bible would cost a couple of bucks and the agent would sell it for around ten dollars. When the details of this transaction came out the Health Department shut down on all lists [obtained] from the vital statistics. I then secured the names from the county clerks of the 248 counties in Texas but that proved much more expensive and the days of good profits were over.

When I left school I was making around $300 a month. I took a job in Dallas at $150 for I figured that I could not stay in school forever.

I worked for Peat, Marwick, Mitchell & Co. in Dallas for one season as a junior accountant. When the rush season was over I was out of work temporarily and I went back to Austin for about six months. I worked in Austin for the State Banking Department as an auditor and bank examiner in the bank liquidating department. Our job was to go over the books of busted banks and endeavor to find out what made them go bust.

I then went back to Dallas, with Peat, Marwick, Mitchell & Co. again. I became senior accountant and later spe-

Later along we established the first passenger route between Dallas and El Paso, using for that purpose Fokker Super-Universal planes powered with Pratt & Whitney Wasp 425 hp engines.

Aviation Corporation, a 35 million dollar aviation holding company, was formed in New York in 1929. In 1930 the Aviation Corporation bought control of Southern Air Transport, Inc. from Barrett and our operation became a subsidiary of Aviation Corporation. In 1930 American Airways, Inc. was formed, a wholly owned subsidiary of Aviation Corporation, and our operation became the Southern Division of American Airways, Inc. I was vice president of American Airways, Inc., in charge of the Southern Division.

At the time of the purchase of Southern Air, Graham B. Grosvenor was president of Aviation Corp. He was succeeded by a gentleman by the name of Hamilton, who was succeeded by F. G. Coburn. Mr. Coburn was later succeeded by Mr. La Motte T. Cohu.

Cohu became President of Aviation Corporation, and American Airways, Inc., in, I believe, 1931. Under his management the operation of the different divisions were consolidated into one operation, headed up at St. Louis, one at Cincinnati and one at Fort Worth. I was made vice president for operations, with headquarters in St. Louis, and had charge of operation for the entire company.

E. L. Cord became a large stockholder in Aviation Corporation in, I believe, 1932. He and Cohu could not agree upon company policies and an open fight for proxies and for control of the company took place.

This is where Mr. Smith's personally written diary ends so the details of that struggle for control are not revealed here. However, in April 1934, American Airways became American Airlines and Cyrus Rowlett Smith was elected president of the newly consolidated company. In an age and industry now

Southern Air Transport Offices, Love Field, 1928.
PHOTO COURTESY OF THE AMERICAN AIRLINES C. R. SMITH MUSEUM.

primed for "takeoff," American Airlines was on the veritable runway of expansion and opportunity; but in an industry that had little past experience to draw upon, Smith was faced with the enormous challenges of the moment. He began at once to establish a more integrated route structure and standardizing aircraft and procedures through the system.

One of the early achievements was to develop an air traffic control system that would later be adopted by all airlines and administered by the U.S. Government. Smith recognized that the future of aviation lay in the development of passenger business, and in that same formative year he introduced one of the industry's first sales promotion tools, the Air Travel Plan. This evolved into the Universal Air Travel Plan. American introduced "Advantage" in 1981, the first bonus program to reward frequent flyers for their loyalty.

When the United States entered World War II, C. R. Smith joined the Army Air Force as a colonel to help organize the Air Transport Command. Colonel Smith soon became General Smith and then major general, serving as Deputy Commander of the Air Transport Command, when the war ended. In 1945 "Mr. C. R." returned to American Airlines. With the introduction of the first transcontinental jet service on January 25, 1959, C. R. Smith brought American Airlines into the Jet Age.

To all members of the American Airlines organization, C. R. Smith was "Mr. C. R." or simply, "C. R."

In 1968, "Mr. C. R." retired as chief executive of American Airlines when his longtime friend, President Lyndon B. Johnson, appointed him Secretary of Commerce. He was a member of the Cabinet during the last year of President Johnson's administration. In 1973, American's board of directors asked "Mr. C. R." to return as interim chairman while they searched for a permanent CEO.

Following his second retirement, C. R. Smith remained active in civic affairs in Washington, D.C. He died on April 4, 1990 at the age of 90 and was buried at Arlington National Cemetery.

THE TEXAS BRAGGADOCIO

BY STANLEY MARCUS

☆ Texans have suffered from "overpride," if I may create a new word to describe the exaggerated boastfulness that Texans indulged in during the 1930s. This was about the time that books like *Texas Brags* were on the bestseller lists in the local bookstores.

In their wild enthusiasm, thousands of my fellow citizens sent this book as Christmas gifts to those unlucky inhabitants of the other forty-eight states who were less fortunate in the possession of natural resources than we were.

We boasted about our size gleefully, telling tales of the distance from Texarkana to El Paso, the record-sized potatoes, watermelons, onions, and pumpkins that were larger than any grown elsewhere.

The discovery of oil in East Texas and the record-breaking formation of new fortunes added to our "overpride."

This commentary is not to belittle our achievements and the benefits of the natural resources we enjoy, but to point out that this braggadocio has offended many citizens of our neighboring states as well as the residents of both New York and California.

The strange thing is that some of these big brags are true, but outsiders tend to be irritated by our brashness. Texas has a lot to be proud of, but it is unnecessary to be immodest.

I must admit my sins, for I think I was instrumental in exaggerating emphasis on the exotic as I influenced the choice of some items that brought fame to the Neiman-Marcus Christmas catalogue. An occasional bit of exoticism is all right, but too much is too bad.

On the positive side, Texans have a wonderful quality of "can do." They are not intimidated by obstacles, but take them as a matter of course and succeed more often than not. The tradition of the frontier taught us resourcefulness; the barrenness of the earth and the clarity of our skies (except in Dallas and Houston) help maintain our enthusiasm.

STANLEY MARCUS is a Texas icon on many levels but is prominently associated with the famous Neiman Marcus emporium of international distinction. Now ninety-five years old, Mr. Marcus is still making headlines. He continues to serve as trustee at Southern Methodist University and is a board member of the Georgia O'Keefe Museum in Santa Fe, New Mexico; the board of governors of the Dallas Symphony; and a board member of the Dallas Museum of Art. His former offices and affiliates with business and civic organizations, as well as his earned honors, are numerous. He is the author of hundreds of articles in magazines including Fortune, Atlantic Monthly, *and* Architectural Digest. *He co-edited* American Greats *with Robert A. Wilson in 1999. In spite of a demanding schedule and fast-paced lifestyle, he took time to respond to my question on what Texas meant to him and to explain his thoughts, now tempered by time and experience, on the Texas "braggadocio."*

TEXAS STYLE

BY JAMES "MAC" McINGVALE

☆ A big part of the "Texas Mystique" over the world is that Texans always seem to do things in a BIG way! Texas culture has taught me that you can do big things, in big ways, if you have the heart and the dedication to real hard WORK! I've learned from great people like my father who taught me diligence, constancy of purpose, giving back to the community, and the importance of helping others reach their own dreams and goals. This "Texas-style" work ethic is a big part of my philosophy of business: "Late to bed, early to rise, work like hell . . . and Advertise!"

JAMES "Mac" McINGVALE is founder and co-owner with his wife, Linda, of Gallery Furniture in Houston, Texas. The success of Gallery Furniture is representative of who "Mac" really is. He is dedicated to his customers, his employees, and to his family. Mac knows no boundaries in regard to hard work. His vision is clear. His generous dedication to area youth is abundant. He stresses the importance of staying in school, getting a good education, believing in the family structure, and the importance of just saying "no" to drugs and "yes" to hard work and dedication.

He is a big supporter of the Houston Livestock Show & Rodeo, Black Heritage Day at the HLS&R, Chuck Norris's "Kick Drugs Out of America" Foundation, and makes numerous contributions for the purchase of new equipment and other learning tools for Houston's inner-city schools.

RECOLLECTIONS OF TEXAS

BY H. ROSS PEROT

⭐ I was born on June 27, 1930, in Texarkana, Texas. The temperature that day was 117 degrees. Dr. Kittrell, my mother's doctor, had gout and no fans were allowed in the hospital room. My mother never forgot that experience.

My father, Gabriel Ross Perot, grew up in New Boston, a small town in the northeast corner of Texas. His family had emigrated from France through New Orleans. They worked their way up the Red River establishing trading posts along the river. My grandfather established a trading post in New Boston, near the Red River, which later evolved into a general store. My grandfather's gold pocket watch with a Knights of Columbus watch fob is in my office next to pictures of my father.

My dad's father passed away while Dad was in high school. Although my father was a good student, he had to drop out of high school and work to support his mother. He initially worked as a Texas cowboy and later learned to be a cotton broker, buying cotton from the farmers and selling it to the mills.

My mother's, Lulu May Ray's, ancestors came from Tennessee in covered wagons and settled in Atlanta, Texas. Her dad's father fought in the Civil War, and was captured during the war. He was kept in a prison on the Great Lakes and had to eat rats to survive. He died shortly after my mother's father, Henry Ray, was born. One of my treasured possessions is a small gold wedding ring he made for my great-grandmother from a gold coin while he was a prisoner of war. I keep it in my office near my desk. It was obviously a labor of love created during extremely difficult times.

I GREW UP during the Depression. We did not have a washing machine, so my mother washed all of our clothes by scrubbing them on a washboard. Our food was kept cool in an icebox with blocks of ice that were periodically delivered to our house. My dad worked, saved his money, and bought the house only when he could pay cash for it. Throughout my childhood, he taught me never to buy anything on credit. His words were, "Figure out what you want. Save your money, and when you can afford it, buy it." He emphasized that looking forward to buying something was as much fun, if not more fun, than actually owning it. I later found this to be true, and this lesson has become a part of my business philosophy.

Since it was so hot in the summer, Dad built a small sleeping porch in our backyard, about fifty feet away from our house. On hot summer nights, we could take advantage of the breezes and the lower temperatures outside the house. The sleeping porch had a canvas top, screened sides, and a rough wooden floor.

We slept in that one room, and it was really fun. It was even more fun when it rained, unless the wind was blowing and water came through the screened sides. There were several occasions when we got very wet. But this wasn't a major problem; it doesn't rain much in Texas!

MY MOTHER'S PARENTS, Henry and Elizabeth Ray, lived in Texarkana, and we adored both of them. Grandmother Ray had very strong convictions about morality and behavior. "How Great Thou Art," sung by George Beverly Shea, was her favorite hymn. She felt very strongly that people should not smoke, and she often said, "If God had intended us to smoke, he would have put chimneys on our head."

In her later years, *The Lawrence Welk Show* was one of her favorite television programs. For much of the second half of the fifties, my sister Bette and I knew that we could always find Grandmother at home on Saturday night, watching Lawrence

Welk. But one Saturday night we stopped by and the television was turned off.

We said, "Grandmother, you're not watching Lawrence Welk."

She said, "I don't watch it anymore."

We said, "But Grandmother, this is your favorite program."

She said, "I do not watch that program anymore."

And we said, "Why?"

She said, "I just heard that he is playing champagne music and you know how I feel about drinking."

Years later, I had the privilege of meeting Lawrence Welk, I told him this story, and he loved it.

WE RARELY TOOK trips when I was growing up, but in 1936, Texas was celebrating its centennial. My parents wanted Bette and me to understand Texas history and attend the Texas Centennial in Dallas.

We stayed at the Adolphus Hotel. There was no air-conditioning, and it was brutally hot. In the middle of the night, when Bette and I could not sleep because of the heat, my dad took the top sheet off the bed, soaked it in cold water, and laid it over us—a standard Texas technique for getting through a hot night in the thirties.

The next day, we went to the state fair, and we savored every minute of it. My most vivid memory is of seeing all the new cars, and my dream, as we left Dallas, was that someday I would be able to have a car. In the early 1900s, my grandfather Gabriel Perot, who owned the general store in New Boston, sold cars. They were shipped to his store in a box. There were no mechanics, so the local blacksmith, who shod horses, assembled and repaired them. Little did I know that in this great country I would one day become the largest individual stockholder of General Motors—only in America!

HUMOR WAS IMPORTANT in getting Texans through the Depression. For example, my dad had a good friend who owned

a Greek restaurant. One day, he lost his arm in a serious accident. My dad immediately rushed to the hospital to donate
blood. The Greek restaurant owner recovered, and for years he
would tell his friends that ever since he had Gabe Perot's blood
in him, all he wanted to do was try to trade cotton!

On another occasion, a farmer, Joe Paup, was in the hospital. He was very depressed and thought he was going to die.
The doctor said he wasn't and asked my dad to try to cheer
him up. Dad went to Joe's hospital room and talked with him
for a few minutes. Joe was still very depressed and crying. My
father went into the closet, took Joe's coat out, and was trying
it on in front of the mirror. Joe sat up in bed and said, "Gabe,
what are you doing?" Dad said, "Joe, I'm trying on your coat
because you're not going to need it if you die." At that point,
Joe Paup jumped out of bed and chased my dad out of the
hospital, then got in his truck and went home. Another case of
Texas humor.

SOME OF MY most poignant childhood memories are of standing at the edge of the water as it [the Red River during a flood]
raced across the farmland. The barns had been destroyed, mules
and cattle had been swept away, the crops had been destroyed
for the year, and yet the farmers and their families were standing
there stoically. Nobody complained—nobody cried—this was
just nature. They knew the river would go down and they would
farm again. I also remember neighbors helping neighbors re-
build the barns and put things back together when the river
went down. This was America at its very finest.

IN HIGH SCHOOL I was focused on working and learning to be
a businessman. I was not preoccupied with being an honor student, and yet all of my friends, Paul Young, Richard Russell,
Bill Wright, Jim Morriss, John Carnahan, and others were
honor students.

A turning point in my life occurred one day in high school
when a great English teacher named Mrs. Grady Duck asked

me to stay after class. She looked me squarely in the eye and said, "Ross, why aren't you smart like your friends?"

My response was, "Mrs. Duck, I'm as smart as they are, but they study all the time. I have other interests."

She said, "Ross, talk is cheap. If you are as smart as they are, let me see some results."

I took the challenge, and studied night and day. On the next report card, I had excellent grades. Mrs. Duck gave me the incentive to create an academic record that allowed me to get an appointment to the Naval Academy. She changed my life.

A few years later, at the end of my freshman year at the Naval Academy, I had excellent grades in English. I felt a strong obligation to thank Mrs. Duck, so when I arrived in Texarkana that summer, I went to her home and thanked her. She expressed genuine surprise that I could do that well. This was consistent with the way she had always motivated me.

She then said, "Ross, why didn't you just write me a letter?"

I replied, "Mrs. Duck, every paper I ever turned in to you came back circled with red notes about how I could make it better. I knew I couldn't write a letter that didn't have mistakes in it, and I thought I would be better off to personally thank you."

Without laughing or smiling, she said, "Ross, you're probably right." She kept the pressure on. I owe her a debt I can never repay.

H. ROSS PEROT is the kind of Texan with whom all proud and independent-thinking Texans can relate. His story of growing up in a modest family who instilled hard work, sacrifices, love, and respect for family members and neighbors is not unlike Texans of any generation. While circumstances—like the weather in Texas—constantly change, Ross Perot continues to speak "squarely" for familial values and unconditional beliefs in what is right and what is wrong, on the worthiness of education, and the courage to stand firm for those virtues, and to consistently resist the sway of popular pressures. He is a man of principle.

As always, he possesses a good sense of humor and a humility about his outstanding professional achievements, giving credit to his good luck and, more importantly, to those who were responsible for his opportunities and subsequent successes in life.

Today, Mr. Perot is a man content with the way he has used his time and talent and continues to, and will forever, speak out with "unembarrassed pride of God, country, and parents."

Red River Women

BY SHERRIE S. McLEROY

☆ Here in the far north of Texas; along the bawdy, brawling Red River, lived some of the damnedest women you'll ever encounter. They left behind relatively safe and genteel lives "back East" to carve new lives on the edge of civilization. And the Red River region was just that in the nineteenth century: the first line of settlement to creep westward from the ancient Spanish towns.

This frontier threw every obstacle in the way of those who tried to break it: Indians, heat, blue northers, bugs, a seemingly endless wind, tearing isolation, and violence. Some women met that challenge, countless others withered and died in the trying.

And some took the challenge and flung it back in Texas's teeth.

Sophie Porter outlived four husbands (only one of whom died peacefully) and a harlot's reputation to become an important land developer. The story of the night she got religion while wearing an orange satin dress still leaves people laughing. Mary Elizabeth Lease cared for four children and took in washing while she studied law; toughened by Texas, she moved on to Kansas to exhort farmers to "raise less corn and more hell."

From the Red River came several of Texas's most important educators. Ela Hockaday founded what is now the largest girls preparatory school in the country. And Lucy Kidd-Key built a major women's college and the state's first music conservatory from an abandoned, weed-grown campus. One of her graduates, Evorie Dillingham, started the first public school cafeteria in Texas; another, Mary Winn Smoots, established the state's first newspaper for women.

Edna Gladney transformed a hand-to-mouth orphanage into

a pioneering adoption agency and championed the rights of illegitimate and adopted children. Olive Ann Oatman Fairchild survived the horrors of Indian captivity and the massacre of her family to also work with orphans.

Lydia McPherson lived and worked quietly, without fanfare, the first woman newspaper publisher in the Southwest. But "flamboyant" better describes Lucy Holcombe Pickens, who set a czar's court on its ears and carried on an outrageous social catfight with several divas of the Confederacy. Enid Justin had to borrow money to open her first factory, determined to carry on her father's boot making legacy. The fiesty "Miss Enid" as she was known once threatened her husband's girlfriend with a lead weight, but was beloved by most people especially the local children.

These are only a few of the defiant women bred by the North Texas frontier; it would take volumes to tell all their stories. Red River women were tough, they were survivors.

They had to be.

SHERRIE S. MCLEROY is the author of several books on Texas women including Red River Women *and* Daughter of Fortune: the Bettie Brown Story, *both published by the Republic of Texas Press. She continues to marvel at the wonders and to appreciate the uniqueness and absurdities of Texas and Texans, and has written* First in the Lone Star State, *published by the Republic of Texas Press. Her newest book is a biography of Thomas Voleny Munson for the Wine Appreciation Guild in California and will be released in hardcover in the spring of 2001. Sherrie now resides in Fort Worth, Texas, with her husband and young daughter.*

Dia de San Jose

BY MARY A. MAVERICK

⭐ On Tuesday, the nineteenth of March, 1840, "dia de San Jose" sixty-five Comanches came into town to make a treaty of peace. They brought with them, and reluctantly gave up, Matilda Lockhart, whom they had captured with her younger sister in December 1838, after killing two other children of her family. The Indian chiefs and men met in council at the Court House, with our city and military authorities. The calaboose or jail then occupied the corner formed by the east line of Main Plaza and the north line of Calabosa (now Market) Street, and the Court House was north of and adjoining the jail. The Court House yard, back of the Court House, was what is now the city market on Market Street. The Court House and jail were of stone, one story, flat roofed, and floored with dirt. Captain Tom Howard's Company was at first in the Court House yard, where the Indian women and boys came and remained during the powwow. The young Indians amused themselves shooting arrows at pieces of money put up by some of the Americans; and Mrs. Higginbotham and myself amused ourselves looking through the picket fence at them.

This was the third time these Indians had come for a talk, pretending to seek peace, and trying to get ransom money for their American and Mexican captives. Their proposition now was that they should be paid a great price for Matilda Lockhart, and a Mexican they had just given up, and that traders be sent with paint, powder, flannel, blankets, and such other articles as they should name, to ransom the other captives. This course had once before been asked and carried out, but the smallpox breaking out, the Indians killed the traders and kept the goods—believing the traders had made the smallpox to kill

them. Now the Americans, mindful of the treachery of the Comanches, answered them as follows: "We will according to a
former agreement, keep four or five of your chiefs, whilst the
others of your people go to your nation and bring all the captives, and then we will pay all you ask for them. Meanwhile,
these chiefs we hold we will treat as brothers and 'not one hair
of their heads shall be injured.' This we have determined, and,
if you try to fight, our soldiers will shoot you down."

This being interpreted, the Comanches instantly, with one
accord raised a terrific war whoop, drew their arrows, and
commenced firing with deadly effect, at the same time making
efforts to break out of the council hall. The order "fire" was
given by Captain Howard, and the soldiers fired into the midst
of the crowd, the first volley killing several Indians and two of
our own people. All soon rushed out into the public square,
the civilians to procure arms, the Indians to flee, and the soldiers in pursuit. The Indians generally made for the river—they
ran up Soledad, east on Commerce Street and for the bend,
now known as Bowen's, southeast, below the square. Citizens
and soldiers pursued and overtook them at all points, shot
some swimming in the river, had desperate fights in the
streets—and hand to hand encounters after firearms had been
exhausted. Some Indians took refuge in stone houses and fastened the doors. Not one of the sixty-five Indians escaped—
thirty-three were killed and thirty-two were taken prisoners. Six
Americans and one Mexican were killed and ten Americans
wounded.

When the deafening war whoop sounded in the court room,
it was so loud, so shrill and so inexpressibly horrible and suddenly raised, that we women looking through the fence at the
women's and boys' markmanship for a moment could not com-
prehend its purport. The Indians however knew the first note
and instantly shot their arrows into the bodies of Judge Thompson and the other gentleman near by, instantly killing Judge
Thompson. We fled into Mrs. Higginbotham's house and I,
across the street to my Commerce Street door.

Two Indians ran past me on the street and one reached my
door as I got in. He turned to raise his hand to push it just as
I beat down the heavy bar; then he ran on. I ran in the north
room and saw my husband and brother Andrew sitting calmly
at a table inspecting some plats of surveys—they had heard
nothing. I soon gave them the alarm, and hurried on to look
for my boys. Mr. Maverick and Andrew seized their arms, always ready—Mr. Maverick rushed into the street, and Andrew
into the backyard where I was shouting at the top of my voice
"Here are Indians!" "Here are Indians!" Three Indians had
gotten in through the gate on Soledad Street and were making
direct for the river! One had paused near Jinny Anderson, our
cook, who stood bravely in front of the children, mine and
hers, with a great rock lifted in both hands above her head,
and I heard her cry out to the Indian "If you don't go 'way
from here I'll mash your head with this rock!" The Indian
seemed regretful that he hadn't time to dispatch Jinny and her
brood, but his time was short, and pausing but a moment, he
dashed down the bank into the river and struck out for the
opposite shore.

As the Indian hurried down the bank and into the river Andrew shot and killed him, and shot another as he gained and
rose on the opposite bank,—then he ran off up Soledad Street
looking for more Indians.

I housed my little ones, and then looked out of the Soledad
Street door. Nearby was stretched an Indian, wounded and dying. A large man, journey-apprentice to Mr. Higginbotham,
came up just then and aimed a pistol at the Indian's head. I
called out, "Oh, don't he is dying," and the big American
laughed and said, "To please you, I won't, but it would put
him out of his misery." Then I saw two others lying dead
near by.

Captain Lysander Wells, about this time, passed by riding
north on Soledad Street. He was elegantly dressed and mounted
on a gaily caparisoned Mexican horse with silver-mounted saddle and bridle—which outfit he had secured to take back to his

native state, on a visit to his mother. As he reached the Veri-
mendi House, an Indian who had escaped detection, sprang up
behind him, clasped Wells's arms in his and tried to catch hold
of the bridle reins. Wells was fearless and active. They struggled
for some time, bent back and forward, swayed from side to
side, till at last Wells held the Indian's wrists with his left hand,
drew his pistol from the holster, partly turned, and fired into
the Indian's body—a moment more and the Indian rolled off
and dropped dead to the ground. Wells then put spurs to his
horse which had stood almost still during the struggle, dashed
up the street and did good service in the pursuit. I had become
so fascinated by this struggle that I had gone into the street
almost breathless, and wholly unconscious of where I was, till
recalled by the voice of Lieutenant Chavallier who said, "Are
you crazy? Go in or you will be killed." I went in but without
feeling any fear, though the street was almost deserted and my
husband and brother both gone in the fight. I then looked out
on Commerce Street and saw four or five dead Indians. I was
just twenty-two then, and was endowed with a fair share of
curiosity.

Not till dark did all our men get back, and I was grateful to
God, indeed, to see my husband and brother back alive and
not wounded.

*Immigrating from Alabama, MARY A. MAVERICK was an early
Anglo settler in the San Antonio region of Texas.*

CAPTURED BY COMANCHES

BY REBECCA J. GILLELAND FISHER

☆ My parents, Johnstone and Mary Barbour Gilleland, were living in Pennsylvania, surrounded with everything to make life pleasant, when they became so enthusiastic over the encouraging reports from Texas that they concluded to join the excited throng and wend their way to this, the supposed "Eldorado of the West." They hastily, and at great sacrifice, disposed of their property, and, leaving their home near Philadelphia, set sail for Gálveston with their three children. Not being used to the hardships and privations of frontier life, they were ill prepared for the trials which awaited them. I know not the date of their arrival. They moved to Refugio county, near Don Carlos Ranch, which proved to be their last earthly habitation.

My father belonged to Captain Tumlinson's company for some months, and when not in active warfare was engaged in protecting his own and other families, removing them from place to place for safety. They frequently had to flee through blinding storms, cold and hungry, to escape Indians and Mexicans. The whole country was in a state of excitement. Families were in constant danger and had to be ready at any moment to flee for their lives.

The day my parents were murdered was one of those days which youth and old age so much enjoy. It was in strange contrast to the tragedy at its close. We were only a few rods from the house. Suddenly the war whoop of the Comanche burst upon our ears, sending terror to all hearts. My father, in trying to reach the house for weapons, was shot down, and near him my mother, clinging to her children and praying God to spare them, was also murdered. As she pressed us to her heart we were baptized in her precious blood. We were torn from her dying embrace and hurried off into captivity, the chief's wife dragging me to her horse and clinging to me with a tenacious grip. She was at first savage and vicious looking, but from some cause her wicked nature soon relaxed, and folding me in her arms, she gently smoothed back my hair, indicating that she was very proud of her suffering victim. A white man with all the cruel instincts of the savage was with them. Several times they threatened to cut off our hands and feet if we did not stop crying. Then the woman, in savage tones and gestures, would scold, and they would cease their cruel threats. We were captured just as the sun was setting and were rescued the next morning.

During the few hours we were their prisoners, the Indians never stopped. Slowly and stealthily they pushed their way through the settlement to avoid detection, and just as they halted for the first time the soldiers suddenly came upon them, and firing commenced. As the battle raged, the Indians were forced to take flight. Thereupon they pierced my little brother through the body, and, striking me with some sharp instrument on the side of the head, they left us for dead, but we soon recovered sufficiently to find ourselves alone in that dark, dense forest, wounded and covered with blood.

Having been taught to ask God for all things, we prayed to our Heavenly Father to take care of us and direct us out of that lonely place. I lifted my wounded brother, so faint and weak, and we soon came to the edge of a large prairie, when as far away as our swimming eyes could see we discovered a company of horsemen. Supposing them to be Indians, frightened beyond expression, and trembling under my heavy burden, I rushed back with him into the woods and hid behind some thick brush. But those brave men, on the alert, dashing from place to place, at last discovered us. Soon we heard the clatter of horses' hoofs and the voices of our rescuers calling us by name, assuring us they were our friends who had come to take care of us. Lifting the almost unconscious little sufferer,

I carried him out to them as best I could. With all the tenderness of women, their eyes suffused with tears, those good men raised us to their saddles and hurried off to camp, where we received every attention and kindness that man could bestow.

I was seven years of age when my parents were murdered. Fifty-nine years have passed since then, and yet my heart grows faint as that awful time passes in review. It is indelibly stamped upon memory's pages and photographed so deeply upon my heart that time with all its changes can never erase it.

REBECCA J. GILLELAND FISHER *was an early Texas settler.*

The Wraith Riding Shotgun

BY LUCIA ST. CLAIR ROBSON

★ When I leave my neighborhood in Arnold, Maryland, the only two places in the world where I'm likely to be recognized in public are Groesbeck, Texas, and Crowell, Texas. I've never been arrested in Groesbeck or Crowell, and as best I can remember, I don't owe anyone money there, but people stop me on the street anyway.

A few have asked for an autograph. Some want their photo taken with me, and one woman started sobbing in sheer agitation. (Another went down on her knees in a crowded bookstore and proclaimed me a goddess, but that was El Paso, and can't be used against me here.) This is not the sort of treatment I'm used to back East, where I could topple beak-first into the gutter and sprout toadstools and no one would break stride.

Even as Texans reckon distance, Groesbeck and Crowell aren't near enough to each other to make an extramural beer run, or send an away-team to the pasture-hockey finals. They do have something in common though. They're both partial to a particular ghost.

I'm partial to that ghost myself. She took me to Texas in 1980 and she keeps me coming back; she, and the fact that the rear view of a rodeo roper in tight Levis is a deeply religious experience. The ghost's name is Cynthia Ann Parker and I have a lot to thank her for. She sent me off on a course I never could have imagined. She changed my life, profoundly and for the better. You can't cannonball deeper into debt to someone than that.

My Texas connection started innocently enough with arrant lust at a Baltimore science fiction convention on Easter weekend, 1979. There, amidst sword fights raging through the hotel lobby and loathsome extraterrestrials crammed into the elevators, I met the science fiction writer, Brian Daley, and his editor. Brian asked me if I had read the new Han Solo novel. I airily replied, no, I didn't read movie spinoffs. His editor's wife, about to bust a gusset, blurted out, "He wrote it." So I took Brian to the hotel bar to mend fences, screwdrivers being the best tool to mend this sort of fence.

That was Saturday night.

Sunday morning, Brian and I watched the pastel-and-polyester Easter breakfast crowd collide with Balticon's google-eyed [sic] aliens, Darth Vader wannabes, and industrial-sized women in dog collars and leopardskin bikinis. In one twelve-hour period, I found love and an editor. Love gave me a reason to wake up grinning like a baked possum in the morning. The editor got me a book contract.

I was looking for love, but not an editor. I already had a respectable job as librarian in Anne Arundel County, Maryland. I mentioned Cynthia Ann Parker to this editor though. At the age of nine Cynthia Ann was taken by Comanches after an attack on her family's fort in east Texas in 1836. She lived with the Comanches twenty-four years, married, and had three children.

Her story, I observed, would make a helluva novel. The editor, who otherwise seemed a sensible specimen, suggested that I write it. I gave him the flounder-eye, as though he'd suggested I run for pope, and said, "I don't know beans about plot development or dialogue or characterization."

He called me at work every Monday anyway, to ask if I'd started writing. To placate him I ordered a few books on Comanches through interlibrary loan, emptied out my recipe box to put note cards in, and squandered $125 of my $15,000 annual salary on a manual portable typewriter. On Halloween night of 1979 I hitched a chair up to the old door laid across two nightstands that still serves as a desk. I cracked my knuckles, tucked my hair behind my ears, poised my bony fingers over the typewriter keys, and made the acquaintance of the wretch who would become my second most faithful companion in life: writer's block.

The first line finally came to me in the shower, and I bolted out, wet and nekkid, to write it down. I solved the problem of plot development by starting with a massacre. My advice to beginning writers: start with a massacre. You don't need sappy dialogue for that.

Maybe it was propitious that I began writing on All Hallows' Eve. My house has been full of ghosts ever since. It's no wonder that writers have a reputation as a whiney, sniveling, substance-abusing lot. We don't just hear voices, we are voices. We historical novelists table-tap in a perpetual séance, trying to get a postcard, a laundry list, a doodle on a bar bill, any sort of communication from those who cashed in their chips a hundred years ago or more.

I'm not the spooky sort; but I could swear, as I tippity-typed away after coming home from work at night, creating carnage in appalling amounts and detail, that someone was standing behind my left shoulder. I knew who she was too, a nine-year-old child witnessing the slaughter of her family in the east Texas wilderness of 1836.

In early 1980 I sent the first six chapters to Brian's science fiction editor. He walked them down the hall to his friend, Pam Strickler, of Ballantine Books. She received the eighty pages on Friday. On Tuesday morning she called me at work to offer me a contract, and to read me my rights—movies rights, foreign rights, serial rights. Cereal rights? Were they going to print it on boxes of Captain Crunch?

All she needed from me, Pam said, was my signature and nine hundred more pages. My boss sneaked out for bubbly, the library staff got royally snockered on the taxpayers' dime, and through a champagne haze the thought festered, "Oh, s***. What have I gotten myself into?"

As a historical novelist with a contract I could now add "Professional Liar" to my résumé. I've since learned that Texas history is the best possible place for a professional liar to hang out, but there was a catch. The only writing course I'd taken was a semester of high school journalism twenty years before. Brian had gone to Los Angeles to spend three months adapting the first *Star Wars* movie for National Public Radio, so I was on my own. I looked through books for advice, and found some.

Somerset Maugham wrote that there are three rules for writing fiction. Unfortunately, no one knows what they are.

Anonymous said that writing fiction is getting your hero up a tree and throwing rocks at him.

Jack Woodford explained plotting: Boy meets girl. Girl gets boy into pickle. Boy gets pickle into girl.

By the time I finished telling the story of Cynthia Ann Parker and her son Quanah, the last Comanche chief to surrender to the U.S. Army, my recipe box of notes would overflow to fill a couple card-files drawers. The bibliography would include ninety-six sources, and I would acquire a fractious pack of imaginary friends.

Historical accounts were helpful, but the map is not the territory. I had to visit Fort Parker. I had to see the hill country where Cynthia Ann's Comanche band, the Honey Eaters, pitched camp. I had to stand in the grass of the Staked Plains and get blown slantwise by the West Texas zephyrs. I had to wade up to my insoles in the Pease River where Sul Ross, a college kid who took a summer job fighting Indians, recaptured Cynthia Ann. I had to bivouac in Palo Duro Canyon where Quanah Parker brooded through his last days with the band of Comanches known as the Wanderers.

I requested my three weeks of annual library leave, packed my sleeping bag and pup tent, hung a GONE TO TEXAS sign on the front door, and decamped. I arrived in Texas in May when the bluebonnets were staging their annual coup. May was when, in 1836, a large coterie of Kiowas and Comanches attacked Fort Parker. They were annoyed, I'd read, because the Parkers had liberated horses from them in retaliation for stock stolen by a bunch of brunets from another tribe. It was a familiar plot line on the frontier.

I flew to San Antonio because it's an enchanting city and because my earliest Texas connection lived there. Darlyne Morales is a fourth generation Texas, born and raised in San Angelo. When I met her in 1968 she told me she included a shoebox full of hometown hardpan in her household inventory so that wherever the Air Force might send her and her husband, their children would be born on Texas soil. That must have generated some lively discussion in the delivery room in Germany when her son was born; and it might explain why the kid had a hankering for humus. Darlyne and her Box O' Dirt gave me the first inkling that Texans were different from us trail-broke critters in the herd.

Darlyne's husband Bill tuned up their spare car, a red Rabbit, until it was humming the key of C, added a CB, and handed me the keys. I threw my tent and sleeping bag into it and took off for Groesbeck where, as any Texan can tell you, Fort Parker has been re-created. It wasn't re-created in my image though.

The countryside matched what I had imagined, but the fort was larger than mine, much larger, and it lacked the small cabin I pictured in the center. The main gate was on the side opposite where I thought it should be, which meant the spring I'd read about was not where I'd assumed.

I asked the ranger in charge if this was the way the fort had looked in 1836. He shifted his chaw to the other cheek and said, no, it would have been smaller. A family couldn't defend a stockade that big. And, he added, we think there was a small cabin in the middle where Elder John and his wife lived. I asked about the gate. He said it would have been on the other side to catch the morning sun.

I stood there in the same morning sun that had shined down on the Parkers and felt the waters of the past rising around me. I'd waded into history's flow, and it was proving to be more mysterious and surprising than I'd expected.

And the spring? I asked. The ranger spit an amber arc, and said the spring had always been right where it was; but he gave me the name of Joseph Cotton, a Groesbeck resident with a lot of information on the Parker story. I went to see him, I asked him about the spring. He shook his head. That spring appeared early in the twentieth century, he said. The one mentioned in the old accounts was another one, and it was where it was supposed to be.

I knew that coincidence accounted for the similarities between the image I'd conjured up, and the fort as it probably was. But even so, that was the first hint that my research trip, and all those to follow, would include far more than current reality. It showed me that truth and fiction, the past and the present are hard to tell apart without an arc lamp and a jeweler's loupe.

I put 3,000 miles and a couple hundred years on the Morales's Rabbit during that first foray into the past, easy to do in Texas. Two decades later odd details come to mind: a thimble-sized hummingbird nest on a mesquite limb at the Alamo movie set in Brackettville; a Don Quixote of a rattlesnake that tilted with my front tire near Enchanted Rock; a fiddle contest in Archer City where the emcee asked me to stand up and eye-dentify myself; tea with four hulking truckers whom the Rabbit and I met via the CB and convoyed with for hours; strangers who gave me the economical, two-fingers-above-the-steering-wheel salute as their pickups rumbled past on the back roads.

I remember watching my first professional wrestling act on TV at two A.M. in San Angelo with Darlyne's grandmother. Darlyne's grandmother more than made up in exuberance what she lacked in size. I'd've put my money on her against any of them in the ring.

I remember joining the grand orbit of dancers two-stepping to the music of Bubba Litrell and his Melody Mustangs. I remember standing on a bluff overlooking the Pease River and imagining the Comanche lodges scattered along it. Imagining soldiers attacking and Cynthia Ann running from them with her youngest child in her arms.

I pitched my tent on the floor of Palo Duro Canyon. I spent a morning on my back watching the buzzards circle between the parentheses of the canyon walls. As I lay there I was careful to twitch before they mistook me for the main corpse, or the cadaver d'jour.

North of Amarillo I followed a ranch road to the site of the buffalo hunters' camp at Adobe Walls where Billy Dixon made his legendary one-mile shot at an army of Indians willing to barber him and his friends by taking some off the top. Two monuments stood there at the base of hills carpeted in flowers and with a magnificent view of the Canadian River threading the plain far below. A coyote passed silently into the tall grass, as indifferent to my presence as any big-city dweller.

That's where I first experienced The Hackle Factor. The hair on the nape of my neck stirred in an old and phantom wind, as though an unseen hand had opened a coffin and released a djin. The air and earth felt charged with the spirits of the people who had died there. I could almost see the force of Comanche, Kiowa, Arapaho, and Cheyenne warriors urging their ponies over the crest of the ridge and racing down the slope, determined to eradicate the heedless entrepreneurs who were destroying their food supply, their families, and their way of life.

On that first jaunt through Texas I acquired a lifelong addiction to time tripping. What I discovered was that solitary travel gives a sense of timelessness, of animated suspension between the nattering of the present and anxieties about the future. On the back roads, sharing the car with their ghosts and a companionable silence, it may be easier for me to understand the lives my characters led than for them to understand mine; although I have found myself trying to explain call forwarding, hyperlinks, rush hour, and RuPaul to the wraith riding shotgun.

The book that came out of that first trip, *Ride the Wind,* is in its seventeenth printing. Thanks to Darlyne's grandmother, I could describe in it how a horse eats thistles, how to peel an armadillo, and bark a squirrel. No, not bark at a squirrel. Even Texans don't bark at squirrels, at least not often. They shoot at the limb just ahead of the animal so the bark explodes up and knocks him out of his tree. Then he can be bulldogged, hog-tied, bludgeoned, skinned, hanged, drawn, butchered, dressed out, and quartered. The resulting forkful of meat can be tossed into the evening stew with no pesky lead to take a bite out of the bridgework.

A writer friend once confessed that early in his career he described two cowboys sitting down to a feast of prairie dog. At a book signing a ranch woman came up to him and pointed out that there's not enough meat on a prairie dog to fill a cavity in a molar. My friend looked at her solemnly and said, "Ah, but, madam, a hundred years ago prairie dogs were much larger." I've given a similar response to skepticism about my description of a rampaging Texas river.

Texans usually eat higher on the hog than squirrel or prairie dog though. While preparing for the barbecue at Fort Parker's Christmas celebration a few years ago, I helped sort and clean seventy pounds of dry beans, also at two in the morning. Do Texans never sleep?

That was my first experience with steer-on-a-stick shish kabob of half a beef carcass. My friends basted it with a mop dipped in a washtub of sauce. That's nothing out of the ordinary for Texans, but we hardly ever use mops as cooking utensils in Arnold. Nor do we carry bottles of our favorite hot sauce with us wherever we go. And the hot sauce we do use cannot double as paint remover.

I recently read, by the way, that while it's not true that Texans will eat armadillos, 'possums, prairie dogs, or rattlesnakes, if times get tough, they know where to find them. I tried that material out on my Groesbeck friends, Celeste and Bob Coffee and Dale McDaniels. At the time we were riding in the Coffee's double-axle, jalapeno-red "fun" truck with a perimeter of flashing running lights. At night the fun truck looks like a casino making house calls.

I got as far as "I hear it's not true that Texans will eat armadillos, 'possums, prairie dogs, or rattlesnakes . . ." when as if on cue they all made the roll-bar ring with, "Yes, they will! Texans will eat anything."

Why I happened to be in the truck that typical Texas weekend involves a tornado, a downpour of red dust, 10,000 cowboys, a shirttail full of Indians, and me on a very pregnant mare in the hundred and sixth annual Fort Worth Stock Show parade. All of that was followed by a multiple smash-and-grab, Civil War reenactors weeping over the loss of their Enfields and Sharps, purloined coggins test that kept us from riding in the rodeo grand entry, a Scottish Comanche vigilante in full regalia on a honking big Yamaha, and waffle-patterned fingerprints in the tornado's deposit of red dust on the fun truck.

That weekend I learned that Booshway, the Coffees' miniature poodle gets his daily grunts by racing in a fluffy white blur around the perimeter of the Groesbeck cemetery, sort of a track-and-potter's field event. For a grand finale, at two A.M., we all crowded onto the sofa in the family room, and watched a video of our friends, the Tahmahkeras, acting in a kung-fu western filmed in Chinese, with English and Comanche subtitles. But that is another story.

Crowell. In 1860 Cynthia Ann Parker was recaptured near Crowell, Texas, so I must have passed through there on that 1980 trip; but it became memorable to me fifteen years later. That was when Crowell's town librarian, Jackie Diggs, called to ask if I would attend their second annual celebration of Cynthia Ann Parker Days. I couldn't refuse a librarian, especially when she made me laugh so hard I had to treat my adenoids for windburn. Jackie has a wit as dry as northwest central Texas dust and as penetrating as chaparral.

I did have one stipulation. I don't do the hood ornament thing. In 1985 I had to wave graciously from the prow of a Buick at a Parker family reunion parade in Quanah, Texas. Hell's hinges can't compare with the hood of a Buick at noontime in August in Quanah, Texas. It's damned difficult to wave graciously when the tail end of your fuselage is on fire.

As I drove to Crowell from the airport at Wichita Falls I began to wonder if I would have a place to sleep when I arrived. Jackie had said she'd saved a room for me at Crowell's only motel. She said that the motel's other thirteen rooms were reserved for Quanah Parker's descendants.

Quanah Parker had five wives and something like thirteen kids. The Parker tribe had had a hundred years to parlay that hand. I could do the math. It would be the Oklahoma land-rush in reverse, with the Indians getting the real estate. It would be the only time the whites wanted in on the Indians' reservation.

What I couldn't find along that stretch of Texas highway, or any other, was a phone booth from which to call and confirm my motel reservation. My theory is that phone booths confuse Texans. They mistake them for Chase and Sanborn cans, "yield" signs, or Wild Turkey bottles, all of which God created on the eighth day for target shooting. And by the way, what Yankee-come-lately in the highway department ever thought Texans would cotton to signs exhorting them to "yield"?

Anyway, I was agitating about that ten-by-twelve-foot parcel of roadside bliss when I remembered that I was in Texas. It didn't matter if I lost the motel room. Someone will always put you up in Texas, whether you want them to or not.

When I got to Crowell I stopped at the library to look for Jackie Diggs. Jackie wasn't there, but a stoolie must have fingered me, because within minutes a Lincoln Continental drove up and a small whirlwind named Eunice shimmered out. Before I knew what hit me, she had chicken-winged me and frogmarched me into the car. Eunice Halbert and her husband Grady hijacked me to their house, hid my clothes in their homey spare room, and fed me beans and ham and corn bread until I was too bloated to resist their kindness.

I happened to be the Halberts' sole sleepover that weekend. I didn't realize then how odd that was. The Texans I know don't put limits on the number of guests. If they have floor space, a yard, or a pickup truck, and what Texan doesn't have one of those, you have a place to bed down.

I've slept under a billiard table in a room paneled in guns, while the family's two pet bisons snored in the corral outside the window. Comanche friends have invited me to share their motel room with them and the room's spare bed with their wolf. I've occupied a pup tent with a barrel racer who shorted out the fun truck's electrical system trying to run her curling iron off the cigarette lighter.

I've curled up with Booshway, the permanently permed cemetery sprinter, on a pullout by the Coffees' back door. I lost count of how many people were staying at the Coffees' that weekend, but their parrot, Charley, greeted everyone as they came in and wandered past my sleeping accommodations with a friendly wave and a "Howdy." Charley shouted "Hello" to callers every time the phone rang too. But I digress.

The Halberts took such good care of me in Crowell, and Jackie made me laugh so much, that I came back the next year for rematch at the third annual Cynthia Ann Parker Days. By then Eunice had written and published her own account of Cynthia Ann's story, a children's book called *Two Feathers* from Red River Press. At the height of the festival we signed our works in tandem on Crowell's main drag, and I became drunk as a fiddler on a brand of eighty-proof celebrity I don't get to sample elsewhere.

That is, I didn't get to sample it until I met Sandi and Monroe Tahmahkera who install air conditioners, raise appaloosas, act, dance, tell jokes, and bless us all in Dublin, Texas, and elsewhere. If Cynthia Ann Parker is my Texas connection, the Tahmahkeras are the Groesbeck-Crowell connection. And as Quanah's great grandson, Monroe Tahmahkera embodies a direct link with Cynthia Ann.

I was driving out of Crowell on Sunday morning and stopped on the courthouse square to say goodbye to Jackie. She introduced me to the Tahmahkeras and their crowd of family and friends. They were all heading out to participate in Monroe's blessing ceremony at the site where Cynthia Ann was recaptured. Did I want to come along? I couldn't think of a better reason to miss a plane flight.

In the years since then I've met many of their vast family, biological and adopted. I've had the privilege of joining them in their celebrations of the past and the present—in Crowell, at Fort Parker, at the Fort Worth Stock Show Parade and the forty-second Annual Comanche Homecoming, and on a two-week, seven-vehicle caravan across three states. I've seen and learned things I never would have experienced in Arnold.

Thanks to Cynthia Ann, I've found family in Texas, too. After *Ride the Wind* came out I received a letter from someone in Austin who wrote, "This can't be coincidence." She included a list of four or five women in her immediate family named Lucia or Lucia Robson. We discovered that my father's grandfather had a family in Texas that he neglected to mention to the one in Georgia.

I'll tell you a secret connection about that book, too. While I was writing it, Brian was working on an alternate-reality fantasy called *Tapestry of Magic.* He wanted his protagonist to enlist the aid of Trickster Coyote. Since Coyote's favorite food is buffalo tongue, Brian used the bison-hunting scene from my manuscript. His guy, Sir Crassmore, met my guy, Nocona, and exchanged gifts. My book was at the point where I could sneak Sir Crassmore's present, a scarf, into *Ride the Wind. Tapestry* is out of print, but I've found copies in used bookstores. Check it out. It's an example of how writers amuse themselves and each other.

Because of *Ride the Wind,* I'm now indexed in Verne Huser's new book, *Rivers of Texas,* put out by Texas A&M Press. Thank you, Verne. I never expected my potboiler to make a scholarly index.

While researching Cynthia Ann's story I came across the subjects of two more books. *Walk in My Soul* chronicles Sam Houston's early life with the Cherokee. Texans have varying opinions on Houston. My favorite description of him is Marquis James's who called him "grand, gloomy, and peculiar." In my book *Fearless,* one of the characters refers to Sam as that "opium-smoking, corset-wearing bag of breeze who only knows how to retreat." I hasten to say that the opinions expressed in my books are not necessarily those of the author. It just proves that fame is like a greased pig, hard chased and difficult to hold onto once caught.

The other book to come out of *Ride the Wind* is *Fearless: A Novel of Sarah Bowman*. It tells the story of the six-foot-tall laundress known in the Mexican War and ever after as the Great Western.

Sarah was so big you had to hug her in installments, and she had enough sand for a lakefront. She earned a reputation as "something of the roughest fighter on the (Texas/Mexico) border." That's like being a den mother in a pack of rattlesnakes.

I'm here to testify that a writer can find more extravagantly uncommon characters in Texas than in all the other states put together. If you're going to take in ghosts anyway, I recommend the Texas variety.

But a lot of those characters are not ghosts. They're still high-stepping through life. I'm looking forward to the next dance with them.

LUCIA ST. CLAIR ROBSON was born in Baltimore, Maryland, and grew up in south Florida. She has been a Peace Corps volunteer in Venezuela, and a teacher in Brooklyn, N.Y. She has also lived in Japan, South Carolina, and southern Arizona. After earning her Master's degree in library science, she worked as a public librarian in Anne Arundel County, Maryland. She is the author of six historical novels, including Ride the Wind, *and* Fearless: A Novel of Sarah Bowman.

Prairie Fire

BY GEORGE WILKINS KENDALL

☆ The side of the bluff was formed of rough, sharp-pointed rocks, many of them of large size, and every little spot of earth had, in former years, given nourishment and support to some scraggy cedar, now left leafless and desolate by fire. Shoots of young cedars, however, were springing up wherever they could find roothold; but they were not destined to attain the rank and standing of their sires.

After reaching the valley, we soon found the sandy bed of what had been a running stream in the rainy season. Immediately on striking it, our tired nags raised their heads, pricked up their ears, and set off at a brisk trot, instinctively knowing that water was in the vicinity. The horse scents water at an incredible distance, and frequently travelers upon the prairies are enabled to find it by simply turning their horses or mules loose.

A tiresome ride of three or four miles now brought us to the river. On reaching its banks, nothing could restrain our nags from dashing headlong down. Equally thirsty ourselves, we had fondly hoped that the waters might prove fresh and sweet; but they were even more brackish than any we had yet tasted. Repulsive as it was, however, we swallowed enough to moisten our parched lips and throats, and ten minutes after were even more thirsty than before. Our horses, more fond of this water than any other, drank until apparently they could swallow no more.

While some of our party were digging into the sand at the edge of the stream, with the hope of finding water more fresh, and others were enjoying the cooling luxury of a bath, a loud report, as of a cannon, was heard in the direction of the camp, and a dark smoke was seen suddenly to arise.

"An Indian attack!" was the startling cry on all sides, and

instantly we commenced huddling on our clothes and bridling our horses. One by one, as fast as we could get ready, we set off for what we supposed to be a scene of conflict. As we neared the camping-ground it became plainly evident that the prairie was on fire in all directions. When within a mile of the steep bluff, which cut off the prairie above from the valley, the bright flames were seen flashing among the dry cedars, and a dense volume of black smoke, rising above all, gave a painful sublimity to the scene.

On approaching nearer we were met by some of our companions, who were hurriedly seeking a passage up the steep. They had heard, from those on the prairie above, that the high grass had caught fire by accident, and that with such velocity had it spread that several of the wagons, and among them that of the commissioners, had been consumed. This wagon contained, in addition to a large number of cartridges, all the trunks and valuables of the mess to which I was attached, making me doubly anxious to gain the scene of destruction and learn the worst. It afterward proved that the explosion of the cartridges in the wagon was what we had mistaken for the report of our six-pounder.

With redoubled exertions we now pushed forward toward the camp, but before we could reach the base of the high and rugged bluff the flames were dashing down its sides with frightful rapidity, leaping and flashing across the gullies and around the hideous cliffs, and roaring in the deep, yawning chasms with the wild and appalling noise of a tornado. As the flames would strike the dry tops of the cedars, reports, resembling those of the musket, would be heard; and in such quick succession did these reports follow each other, that I can compare them to nothing save the irregular discharge of infantry—a strange accompaniment to the wild roar of the devouring element.

The wind was blowing fresh from the west when the prairie was first ignited, carrying the flames, with a speed absolutely astounding, over the very ground on which we had traveled during the day. The wind lulled as the sun went down behind the mountains in the west, and now the fire began to spread slowly in that direction. The difficult passage by which we had descended was cut off by the fire, and night found our party still in the valley, unable to discover any other road to the table-land above. Our situation was a dangerous one, too; for had the wind sprung up and veered into the east, we should have found much difficulty in escaping, with such velocity did the flames extend.

If the scene had been grand previous to the going down of the sun, its magnificence was increased tenfold as night in vain attempted to throw its dark mantle over the earth. The light from acres and acres, I might say miles and miles, of inflammable and blazing cedars, illuminated earth and sky with a radiance even more lustrous and dazzling than that of the noonday sun. Ever and anon, as some one of our comrades would approach the brow of the high bluff above us, he appeared not like an inhabitant of this earth. A lurid and most unnatural glow, reflected upon his countenance from the valley of burning cedars, seemed to render still more haggard and toilsome his burned and blackened features.

I was fortunate enough, about nine o'clock, to meet one of our men, who directed me to a passage up the steep ascent. He had just left the bluff above, and gave me a piteous recital of our situation. He was endeavoring to find water, after several hours of unceasing toil, and I left him with slight hopes that his search would be rewarded. By this time I was alone, not one of the companions who had started with me from the river being in sight or hearing. One by one they had dropped off, each searching for some path by which he might climb to the table-land above.

The first person I met, after reaching the prairie, was Mr. Falconer, standing with the blackened remnant of a blanket in his hand, and watching lest the fire should break out on the western side of the camp; for in that direction the exertions of the men, aided by a strong westerly wind, had prevented the devouring element from spreading. Mr. F. directed me to the spot where our mess was quartered. I found them sitting upon such articles as had been saved from the wagon, their gloomy countenances rendered more desponding by the reflection from the now distant fire. I was too much worn down by fatigue and deep anxiety to make many inquiries as to the extent of our loss; but hungry, and almost choked with thirst, I threw myself upon the blackened ground and sought forgetfulness in sleep. It was hours, however, before sleep visited my eyelids. From the spot on which I was lying, a broad sheet of flame could still be seen, miles and miles in width, the heavens in that direction so brilliantly lit up that they resembled a sea of molten gold. In the west, a wall of impenetrable blackness appeared to be thrown up as the spectator suddenly turned from viewing the conflagration in the opposite direction. The subdued yet deep roar of the element could still be plainly heard as it sped on as with the wings of lightning across the prairies, while in the valley far below, the flames were flashing and leaping among the dry cedars, and shooting and circling about in manner closely resembling a magnificent pyrotechnic display—the general combination forming a scene of grandeur and sublimity which the pen shrinks from describing, and to which the power of words is wholly unequal.

Daylight the next morning disclosed a melancholy scene of desolation and destruction. North, south, and east, as far as the eye could reach, the rough and broken country was blackened by the fire, and the removal of the earth's shaggy covering of cedars and tall grass but laid bare, in painful distinctness, the awful chasms and rents in the steep hillside before us, as well as the valley spreading far and wide below. Afar off, in the distance, a dense black smoke was seen rising, denoting that the course of the devastating element was still onward.

GEORGE WILKINS KENDALL was a reporter from New Orleans on the Texas–Santa Fe Expedition of 1841. He was imprisoned with the other members of the expedition. Later, he was war correspondent in the Mexican War. He continued to write about Texas, and became a sheep rancher. He died in 1867.

INDIAN DEPREDATIONS

BY J. W. WILBARGER

☆ In the spring of 1830, Stephen F. Austin came to his new colony, located on the upper Colorado, with two surveyors and the advance guard of emigrants for the purpose of establishing the surveys of those who had made their selections. Josiah Wilbarger and Reuben Hornsby were among those who had previously been over the ground and picked out locations for their headright leagues. Wilbarger had come to Texas from the State of Missouri as early as 1828 and first settled in Matagorda county, where he remained about one year and then moved up the Colorado. It was in about the month of March, 1830, that he selected for his headright survey a beautiful tract of land situated at the mouth of what is now known as Wilbarger creek, about ten miles above where the San Antonio and Nacodoches road crosses the river where the town of Bastrop now is. After making his selection he immediately moved on his headright league with his family and two or three transient young men and built his occupation house, his nearest neighbor being about seventy-five miles down the river. In the month of April, Austin, with his surveying party, accompanied by Reuben Hornsby, Webber, Duty, and others, who had also previously made their selections, arrived, and commenced work on the Colorado at the crossing of the San Antonio and Nacogdoches road. The river was meandered to the upper corner of the Jesse Tannehill league, when the party stopped work in the month of May. Wilbarger was the first and outside settler in Austin's new colony until July, 1832, when Reuben Hornsby came up from Bastrop (where he had stopped for a year or two) and occupied his league on the east bank of the Colorado river, some nine miles below the site of Austin.

Hornsby's house was always noted for hospitality, and he, like his neighbor Wilbarger, was remarkable for those virtues and that personal courage which made them both marked men among the early settlers. Young men who from time to time came up to the frontier to look at the country made Hornsby's house a stopping place, and were always gladly welcomed, for it was chiefly through such visits that news from the States was obtained. A more beautiful tract of land, even now, can nowhere be found than the league of land granted to Reuben Hornsby. Washed on the west by the Colorado, it stretches over a level valley about three miles wide to the east, and was, at the time of which we write, covered with wild rye, and looking like one vast green wheat field. Such was the valley in its virgin state which tempted Hornsby to build and risk his family outside of the settlements. Until a few years ago not an acre of that league of land had ever been sold, but it was all occupied by the children and grand children of the old pioneer, who lived out his four score years and died without a blemish on his character.

In the month of August, 1833, a man named Christian and his wife were living with Hornsby. Several young unmarried men were also stopping there. This was customary in those days, and the settlers were glad to have them for protection. Two young men, Standifer and Haynie, had just come to the settlement from Missouri to look at the country. Early in August, Josiah Wilbarger came up to Hornsby's, and in company with Christian, Strother, Standifer and Haynie, rode out in a northwest direction to look at the country. When riding up Walnut creek, some five or six miles northwest of where the city of Austin stands, they discovered an Indian. He was hailed, but refused to parley with them, and made off in the direction of the mountains covered with cedar to the west of them. They gave chase and pursued him until he escaped to cover in the mountains near the head of Walnut creek, about where James Rogers afterwards settled.

Returning from the chase, they stopped to noon and refresh

themselves, about one-half a mile up the branch above Pecan spring, and four miles east of where Austin afterward was established, in sight of the road now leading from Austin to Manor. Wilbarger, Christian, and Strother unsaddled and hoppled their horses, but Haynie and Standifer left their horses saddled and staked them to graze. While the men were eating they were suddenly fired on by Indians. The trees near them were not large and offered poor cover. Each man sprang to a tree and promptly returned the fire of the savages, who had stolen up afoot under cover of the brush and timber, having left their horses out of sight. Wilbarger's party had fired a couple of rounds when a ball struck Christian, breaking his thigh bone. Strother had already been mortally wounded. Wilbarger sprang to the side of Christian and set him up against his tree. Christian's gun was loaded but not primed. A ball from an Indian had bursted Christian's powder horn. Wilbarger primed his gun and then jumped again behind his own tree. At this time Wilbarger had an arrow through the calf of his leg and had received a flesh wound in the hip. Scarcely had Wilbarger regained the cover of the small tree, from which he fought, until his other leg was pierced with an arrow. Until this time Haynie and Standifer had helped sustain the fight, but when they saw Strother mortally wounded and Christian disabled, they made for their horses, which were yet saddled, and mounted them. Wilbarger finding himself deserted, hailed the fugitives and asked to be permitted to mount behind one of them if they would not stop and help fight. He ran to overtake them, wounded, as he was, for some little distance, when he was struck from behind by a ball which penetrated about the center of his neck and came out on the left side of his chin. He fell apparently dead, but though unable to move or speak, did not lose consciousness. He knew when the Indians came around him—when they stripped him naked and tore the scalp from his head. He says that though paralyzed and unable to move, he knew what was being done, and that when his scalp was torn from his skull it created no pain from which he could flinch, but sounded like distant thunder. The Indians cut the throats of Strother and Christian, but the character of Wilbarger's wound, no doubt, made them believe his neck was broken, and that he was surely dead. This saved his life.

When Wilbarger recovered consciousness the evening was far advanced. He had lost much blood, and the blood was still slowly ebbing from his wounds. He was alone in the wilderness, desperately wounded, naked, and still bleeding. Consumed by an intolerable thirst, he dragged himself to a pool of water and lay down in it for an hour, when he became so chilled and numb that with difficulty he crawled out to dry land. Being warmed by the sun and exhausted by loss of blood, he fell into a profound sleep. When awakened, the blood had ceased to flow from the wound in his neck, but he was again consumed with thirst and hunger.

After going back to the pool and drinking, he crawled over the grass and devoured such snails as he could find, which appeased his hunger. The green flies had blown his wounds while he slept, and the maggots were at work, which pained and gave him fresh alarm. As night approached he determined to go as far as he could toward Reuben Hornsby's, about six miles distant. He had gone about six hundred yards when he sank to the ground exhausted, under a large post oak tree, and well nigh despairing of life. Those who have ever spent a summer in Austin know that in that climate the nights in summer are always cool, and before daybreak some covering is needed for comfort. Wilbarger, naked, wounded and feeble, suffered after midnight intensely from cold. No sound fell on his ear but the hooting of owls and the bark of the coyote wolf, while above him the bright silent stars seemed to mock his agony. We are now about to relate two incidents so mysterious that they would excite our incredulity were it not for the high character of those who to their dying day vouched for their truth.

As Wilbarger lay under the old oak tree, prone on the ground he distinctly saw, standing near him, the spirit of his sister Margaret Clifton, who had died the day before in Florisant, St. Louis County, Missouri. She said to him "Brother Josiah, you are too weak to go by yourself. Remain here, and friends will come to take care of you before the setting of the sun." When she had said this she moved away in the direction of Hornsby's house. In vain he besought her to remain with him until help would come.

Haynie and Standifer, on reaching Hornsby's, had reported the death of their three companions, stating that they saw Wilbarger fall and about fifty Indians around him, and knew that he was dead. That night Mrs. Hornsby started from her sleep and waked her husband. She told him confidently that Wilbarger was alive; that she had seen him vividly in a dream, naked, scalped, and wounded, but that she knew he lived. Soon she fell asleep and again Wilbarger appeared to her alive, but wounded, naked, and scalped, so vividly that she again woke Mr. Hornsby and told him of her dream, saying, "I know that Wilbarger is not dead." So confident was she that she would not permit the men to sleep longer, but had their coffee and breakfast ready by daybreak and urged the men at the house to start to Wilbarger's relief.

The relief party consisted of Joseph Rogers, Reuben Hornsby, Webber, John Walters, and others. As they approached the tree under which Wilbarger had passed the night, Rogers, who was in advance, saw Wilbarger, who was sitting at the root of a tree. He presented a ghastly sight, for his body was almost red with blood. Rogers, mistaking him for an Indian, said: "Here they are, boys." Then Wilbarger rose up and spoke, saying, "Don't shoot, it is Wilbarger." When the relief party started Mrs. Hornsby gave her husband three sheets, two of them were left over the bodies of Christian and Strother until the next day, when the men returned and buried them, and one was wrapped around Wilbarger, who was placed on Roger's horse. Hornsby being lighter than the rest mounted behind Wilbarger, and with his arms around him, sustained him in the saddle. The next day Wm. Hornsby (who is still living), Joseph

Rogers, Walters, and one or two others returned and buried Christian and Strother.

When Wilbarger was found the only particle of his clothing left by the savages was one sock. He had torn that from his foot, which was much swollen from an arrow wound in his leg, and had placed it on his naked skull from which the scalp had been taken. He was tenderly nursed at Hornby's for some days. His scalp wound was dressed with bear's oil, and when recovered sufficiently to move, he was placed in a sled, made by Billy Hornsby and Leman Barker (the father-in-law of Wilbarger) because he could not endure the motion of a wagon, and was thus conveyed several miles down the river to his own cabin. Josiah Wilbarger recovered and lived for eleven years. The scalp never grew entirely over the bone. A small spot in the middle of the wound remained bare, over which he always wore a covering. The bone became diseased and exfoliated, finally exposing the brain. His death was hastened, as Doctor Anderson, his physician, thought, by accidentally striking his head against the upper portion of a low door frame of his gin house many years after he was scalped. We have stated the facts as received from the lips of Josiah Wilbarger, who was the brother of the author of this book, and confirmed by Wm. Hornsby, who still lives, and others who are now dead.

The vision which so impressed Mrs. Hornsby was spoken of far and wide through the colony fifty years ago; for her earnest manner and perfect confidence that Wilbarger was alive, made, in connection with her vision and its realization, a profound impression on the men present, who spoke of it everywhere. There were no telegraphs in those days, and no means of knowing that Margaret, the sister, had died seven hundred miles away only the day before her brother was wounded. The story of her apparition, related before he knew that she was dead— her going in the direction of Hornsby's, and Mrs. Hornsby's strange vision, recurring after slumber, present a mystery that made then a deep impression and created a feeling of awe which, after the lapse of half a century, it still inspires. No man who knew them ever questioned the veracity of either Wilbarger or the Hornsbys, and Mrs. Hornsby was loved and reverenced by all who knew her.

We leave to those more learned the task of explaining the strange coincidence of the visions of Wilbarger and Mrs. Hornsby. It must remain a marvel and a mystery.

J. W. WILBARGER was an early Texas frontiersman and settler. His Indian Depredations in Texas *is considered a classic.*

BRUSHY CREEK AND PLUM CREEK

BY JOHN HOLLAND JENKINS

☆ The largest, most horrible raid ever made by Indians upon Texas resulted in the famous battle of Plum Creek. A large band of Comanches under the notorious chief, "Buffalo Hump," took possession of Victoria, then came on down Peach Creek, through a sparsely settled country, burning houses and killing until they came to Lynnville. They were supposed to have been guided by Mexicans.

On their way they came upon Mr. Foley and Parson Ponton, who were going across the country to Gonzales. Foley was riding a very fine racehorse, while Mr. Ponton's animal was old and slow. They saw the Indians about a quarter of a mile off and whirled to run. The racehorse soon bore Foley far in advance of Ponton, who was fast losing ground. The first Indian swept past him without even turning his head. Foley on the racehorse was evidently the prize upon which he was bending every energy. The second Indian came on, and in passing, struck him on the head with a spear—he, too, intent upon overtaking Foley. A third drew his bow as he came and shot, the arrow striking Ponton's leather belt with such force as to knock him from his horse. He lay as if dead, and pondered whether or not he should shoot, his double-barreled shotgun being still at his side. He wisely concluded to be still, and the rest of the Indians passed him without a pause, doubtless thinking him dead.

As soon as the last one had gone by, he sprang up and crawled into a thicket and there lay hidden until they came on back with Foley, who had made a brave run but was caught at last. They had chased him to a little creek, where they had hemmed him in and as a last resort, he had dismounted and tried to hide in a water hole. From the signs they had roped and dragged him out, and brought him on to the spot where they had left Ponton, whom they had thought dead. Finding him gone, they made Foley call him, but of course no answer came. The cruel wretches then shot and scalped Foley and, when he was found, the bottoms of his feet had been cut off and he must have been made to walk some distance on the raw stumps! The cruelty of those Comanche warriors knew no bounds. The Reverend Ponton himself gave me an account of this race, and its attendant particulars, and I think I can vouch for its truth.

At Lynnville the Indians burned a few houses, killed a few more citizens, and then went on unmolested. They took two captives, Mrs. Crosby and Mrs. Watts, whose husbands were killed in the fight, and started back on their incoming trail. It is strange, but true, that all this was over before we had heard any of the circumstances. Captain John Tumlinson immediately raised a squad of forty or fifty men, and taking their plain trail came upon them on their way out—a large force of between four and five hundred Indians. Our captain was nothing daunted, however, and ordered our men to fire a charge at them. He was brave, cool, and deliberate, and I have always believed would have whipped them, if a misunderstanding among the men had not forced him to draw off, with the loss of one man. The Indians charged upon the rear of our force, which was composed of Mexicans, who came near stampeding, and thus brought great confusion into our ranks. Tumlinson then followed along at a distance, receiving recruits constantly.

By this time, the news having been well ventilated here around Bastrop, General Burleson had raised all the men he possibly could and started out, anxious to intercept them at Plum Creek. Every now and then we met runners, who were sent to bid Burleson to come on. We rode until midnight, then halted to rest our horses. Very early the next morning we were again on the warpath, still meeting runners at regular intervals beseeching us to hurry.

We fell in with the Guadalupe men in the edge of Big Prairie, near Plum Creek, about two miles from where Lockhart now stands. We were now ordered to dismount, lay aside every weight, examine our arms, and make ready for battle. [General Felix] Huston's men had gotten in ahead of the Indians, and were lying in a little mot of timber, when they heard the Indians coming, they being seemingly ignorant of our close proximity to them, for they were singing, whistling, yelling, and indeed making every conceivable noise. Here, while awaiting the Indians, we of Burleson's force joined them. A double-filed line of march was formed, Burleson's forces from the Colorado marching about one hundred yards to the right of Huston's men from the Guadalupe, and in sight of the Indians.

Four men were sent ahead as spies and the rear guard of the Indians, consisting of four warriors, turned and rode leisurely back to meet them. Slowly and deliberately they came on, making no sign or move for fight. When within twenty steps of our spies, Colonel Switzer raised his gun and killed one, whereupon the others beat a hasty retreat for their main force. Burleson ordered us to "spur up," and we rode very fast. We saw confusion in the Indian ranks, which we could not understand. A squad of men seemed to retreat in the face of a pursuing band of Indians. They were evidently divided against themselves or pursuing some other body of men.

At length, however, we were discovered by the main force of Indians, who immediately formed a line between us and their packmules, stolen horses, and other plunder, and awaited our attack. When in one hundred and fifty yards of this line, we were ordered to dismount; one man of the double file held both horses, while his comrade shot.

It was a strange spectacle never to be forgotten, the wild, fantastic band as they stood in battle array, or swept around us with all strategy of Indian warfare. Twenty or thirty warriors, mounted upon splendid horses, tried to ride around us, sixty or eighty yards distant, firing upon us as they went. It was a superstition among them, that if they could thus run around a force they could certainly vanquish it. Both horses and riders were decorated most profusely, with all of the beauty and horror of their wild taste combined. Red ribbons streamed out from the horses' tails as they swept around us, riding fast, and carrying all manner of stolen goods upon their heads and bodies.

There was a huge warrior, who wore a stovepipe hat, and another who wore a fine pigeon-tailed cloth coat, buttoned up *behind*. They seemed to have a talent for finding and blending the strangest, most unheard-of ornaments. Some wore on their heads immense buck and buffalo horns. One headdress struck me particularly. It consisted of a large white crane with red eyes.

In this run-around two warriors were killed, and also a fine horse. We were now ordered to reload, mount, and charge. They at once retreated, though a few stood until we were in fifteen steps of them before starting. In the meantime, the same warriors played around us at the right, trying to divide our attention and force, while the main body of Indians retreated, firing as they went. Soon, however, they struck a very boggy bayou, into which all of their packmules and horses bogged down. A number of men halted to take charge of these, and such a haul they were making! The mules were literally loaded with all manner of goods, some even carrying hoop-irons to make arrow spikes. They bogged down so close together that a man could have walked along on their bodies *dry*.

Still the Indians retreated while the whites advanced, though the ranks on both sides were constantly growing thinner, for at every thicket a savage left his horse and took to the brush, while every now and then a horse fell under one of our men. About twenty warriors kept up their play upon our right, while an equal number of our men kept them at bay. In this side play, Hutch Reid [Hutchinson Reed] was wounded. He undertook to run up on an Indian and shoot him. As he passed, his gun snapped, and before he could check his horse, an arrow struck him just under the shoulder blade, piercing his lungs and lodging against his breastbone. Then one of the most daring and best mounted of the warriors was killed by Jacob Burleson, who was riding the notorious Duty roan, the racehorse which a while back bore Matthew Duty to his death and which finally fell into Indian hands. This broke up the side play. Burleson, with about twenty-five men, pursued them to within a mile of the San Marcos River, where they separated, so we retraced our steps.

One instance of the hardness and cruelty of some men, even though not savage in form and color, was shown us on this raid. As was often the case, some squaws were marching in Indian ranks, and one of them had been shot, and lay breathing her last—almost dead, as we came by. French Smith, with almost inhuman and unmanly cruelty, sprang upon her, stamped her, and then cut her body through with a lance. He was from the Guadalupe; indeed, I do not think there was a single man from Bastrop who would have stooped to so brutal a deed. Ah! Men almost forgot the meaning of love and mercy and forbearance amid the scenes through which we passed in those early days.

While halting to rest our horses, we heard a child cry, and upon going into the thicket, a Mr. Carter found a fine Indian baby, which had been left in the retreat.

Joe Hornsby and I were riding about two hundred yards in front of Burleson's main army, watching for Indian signs and trails as we went. Suddenly we came in sight of about thirty Indians some distance ahead. At first Joe said they were Tonkawas, who were a friendly tribe living in our midst. Upon seeing their shields, however, we knew they were hostile. I galloped back to notify Burleson, while he kept his eye upon them. When we came up they immediately shied off. We cut in ahead of them and advanced upon them. In thirty steps of them, Burleson ordered us to fire, and the action was simultaneous, though no one was hurt and only two horses killed. At one time here, I felt as if my "time" had come, sure enough. We had fired one round, and I was down loading my gun when I saw an Indian approaching me with gun presented. At this critical moment Joe Burleson shot, killing him instantly. We discovered afterward that the Indian's gun was not loaded, and he was playing a "bluff."

We had a hot race after another warrior on foot, who was unarmed except for bow and arrow, but who would turn and shoot as he ran. General Burleson rushed at him with pistol presented, when an arrow from the Indian would have killed him if he had not stepped back. Then the warrior made another shot at Monroe Hardeman, which missed him, but was driven eight inches into his horse. The hardy warrior made a brave and persistent fight, and even after he was knocked down, drew his last arrow at me, the man nearest to him. I killed him just in time to save myself.

What fancies they had in the way of ornamenting themselves! This savage presented a strange picture as he lay decked in beads, etc., sleeping the "dreamless sleep" of death. He also carried around his neck a tiny whistle and tin trumpet.

The stolen horses, mules, and goods were divided among the soldiers, with the consent of the merchants, who could not satisfactorily identify the articles. Among other things, a Comanche mule fell to my lot, and an odd specimen he was, with red ribbons on ears and tail.

On the return march, we found a Texan dead and scalped. The explanation of his death furnished an explanation of the confusion that was observed in the Indian ranks on the advance. It happened in this way: A squad of men on the Indian trail came upon the savages' advanced guard, and thinking they could easily manage so small a force, dismounted in a live oak grove and awaited them. Seeing the full force, however, they mounted and retreated. One man, the unfortunate one whom we found scalped, was left by his horse as well as his comrades, and thus had met his terrible fate.

We also found the body of Mrs. Crosby, whom they had killed when obliged to retreat, and nearby we found Mrs. Watts, whom they had also left for dead, having shot an arrow into her breast. A thick corset board had received and impeded its force, so that though wounded, she was still alive. She was a remarkably fine looking woman, but was sunburned almost to a blister.

JOHN HOLLAND JENKINS was a Texas settler, frontiersman, and Indian fighter.

The Heart of Texas

BY THOMAS FLEMING

⭐ As a historian, I have visited Texas in my imagination often. In a series of articles on historic sites for *This Week* magazine, I wrote about the heroes of the Alamo. In my history of West Point, I wrote accounts of the battles of Resaca de la Palma and Palo Alto on the banks of the Rio Grande that began the Mexican War.

In my novel, *Promises to Keep,* my main character rode with John J. Pershing and not a few Texans in pursuit of Pancho Villa. I grew to admire the warrior spirit of the Texas male. But not until I visited Austin and met Claudia Alta Taylor Johnson, known to the world as Lady Bird, did I get a glimpse of the other side of Texas, its feminine heart.

I came with Margaret Truman, an old friend of Mrs. Johnson. I was assisting Margaret with research for her 1995 book, *First Ladies.* We had resolved to interview all the living First Ladies and Mrs. Johnson was the first stop on our journey.

Almost immediately I sensed we were in the presence of an extraordinary woman. The melodious Southern voice (acquired from girlhood summers in Alabama), the perfect poise, the careful thought she gave to each of our questions, combined to produce an almost mesmerizing effect.

She told Margaret a delightful story of a memory of visiting the Truman White House. She described herself as the wife of a "mere Congressman" who wended her way toward President Truman and his wife in a long receiving line. When she shook hands with Bess Truman, she was so warm and friendly, Lady Bird exclaimed to Lyndon as they left the White House: "I believe she *knew* me!"

We asked her to tell us some of her favorite Johnson White

House memories. She gave us her recollection of her historic whistlestop tour through the Southern states in 1964. The South was so infuriated by the Civil Rights Act that Congress had just passed, the President did not think it was safe for him to venture in their direction. Instead he sent Lady Bird.

Eyes twinkling, Lady Bird told us how she called governors and congressmen and senators and purred: "Guv-nuh, I'm thinkin' about comin' down to your state . . ."

The initial response of these good old boys was panic. They came up with some of the lamest excuses in history to avoid meeting her. Undeterred, Lady Bird headed in their direction, with a cadre of reporters and advance men and women in tow.

The Lady Bird Special made forty-seven stops in eight states. Everywhere the First Lady delivered the same or a similar message. She did not defend the Civil Rights Act. She simply said she thought it was "right" and eventually most Southerners would agree with her. Instead she told them she was on "a journey of heart"—to tell Southerners that she and her husband loved and respected them. Before the trip was over, the good old boys had come out of hiding and were fighting to get on the train.

"That was the *most* fun," Lady Bird said.

Her other favorite White House memory was her beautification program. Beginning with Washington, D.C., where she and her committee planted 83,000 flowering plants, 50,000 shrubs, 25,000 trees, and 137,000 annuals, she went national and soon had people planting and landscaping and fighting billboard proliferation from Maine to California—with a special push in Texas. Almost single-handedly, she inspired Americans to restore beauty to their cities and towns and countryside.

Mrs. Johnson shared with us many other White House memories, including some that were daunting: Trying to console a bloodcaked Jackie Kennedy on the nightmarish day John F. Kennedy was shot; protestors chanting outside the White House day and night against the Vietnam War; her daughters bursting into tears and objecting violently when they heard LBJ was not going to run for reelection. But there was not a trace of bitterness or regret in her voice.

That night, she invited us to dinner at her Austin home, overlooking the lovely little valley through which the Colorado River winds. As we sipped drinks on the open porch, a Secret Service man came out and whispered in Mrs. Johnson's ear.

"Oh, Margaret," she said. "Jackie's slippin' away. They don't expect her to live the night."

Jackie Kennedy was dying of cancer in New York. The Secret Service man had brought Lady Bird the sad news so she could have a statement ready for the press. But she was moved to tell us what she felt, then and there.

"My heart overflows with love for her, it always has," Lady Bird said. "She went through so much and yet she never lost that beautiful gentle shining quality of pure grace. She was so kind, so thoughtful. I'll never think of her as dead. She'll always be a loving presence in my life until the day I die."

There was not a dry eye on the porch. That was the moment when I saw how large, how generous, how fine, the heart of Texas could be.

Thomas Fleming is a distinguished historian and the author of numerous critically acclaimed and bestselling novels. His masterpiece, The Officers' Wives, *was an international bestseller with over two million copies sold. He lives in New York City.*

INAUGURAL ADDRESS

BY LYNDON BAINES JOHNSON

WEDNESDAY, JANUARY 20, 1965

My fellow countrymen, on this occasion, the oath I have taken before you and before God is not mine alone, but ours together. We are one nation and one people. Our fate as a nation and our future as a people rest not upon one citizen, but upon all citizens.

This is the majesty and the meaning of this moment.

For every generation, there is a destiny. For some, history decides. For this generation, the choice must be our own.

Even now, a rocket moves toward Mars. It reminds us that the world will not be the same for our children, or even for ourselves in a short span of years. The next man to stand here will look out on a scene different from our own, because ours is a time of change—rapid and fantastic change baring the secrets of nature, multiplying the nations, placing in uncertain hands new weapons for mastery and destruction, shaking old values, and uprooting old ways.

Our destiny in the midst of change will rest on the unchanged character of our people, and on their faith.

THEY CAME HERE —the exile and the stranger, brave but frightened—to find a place where a man could be his own man. They made a covenant with this land. Conceived in justice, written in liberty, bound in union, it was meant one day to inspire the hopes of all mankind; and it binds us still. If we keep its terms, we shall flourish.

FIRST, JUSTICE WAS the promise that all who made the journey would share in the fruits of the land.

In a land of great wealth, families must not live in hopeless poverty. In a land rich in harvest, children just must not go hungry. In a land of healing miracles, neighbors must not suffer and die unattended. In a great land of learning and scholars, young people must be taught to read and write.

For the more than thirty years that I have served this nation, I have believed that this injustice to our people, this waste of our resources, was our real enemy. For thirty years or more, with the resources I have had, I have vigilantly fought against it. I have learned, and I know, that it will not surrender easily.

But change has given us new weapons. Before this generation of Americans is finished, this enemy will not only retreat—it will be conquered.

Justice requires us to remember that when any citizen denies his fellow, saying, "His color is not mine," or, "His beliefs are strange and different," in that moment he betrays America, though his forbears created this nation.

LIBERTY WAS THE second article of our covenant. It was self-government. It was our Bill of Rights. But it was more. America would be a place where each man could be proud to be himself: stretching his talents, rejoicing in his work, important in the life of his neighbors and his nation.

This has become more difficult in a world where change and growth seem to tower beyond the control and even the judgment of men. We must work to provide the knowledge and the surroundings which can enlarge the possibilities of every citizen.

The American covenant called on us to help show the way for the liberation of man. And that is today our goal. Thus, if as a nation there is much outside our control, as a people no stranger is outside our hope.

Change has brought new meaning to that old mission. We can never again stand aside, prideful in isolation. Terrific dangers and troubles that we once called "foreign" now constantly live among us. If American lives must end, and American treasure be spilled, in countries we barely know, that is the price that change has demanded of conviction and of our enduring covenant.

Think of our world as it looks from the rocket that is heading toward Mars. It is like a child's globe, hanging in space, the continents stuck to its side like colored maps. We are all fellow passengers on a dot of earth. And each of us, in the span of time, has really only a moment among our companions.

How incredible it is that in this fragile existence, we should hate and destroy one another. There are possibilities enough for all who will abandon mastery over others to pursue mastery over nature. There is world enough for all to seek their happiness in their own way.

Our nation's course is abundantly clear. We aspire to nothing that belongs to others. We seek no dominion over our fellow man, but man's dominion over tyranny and misery.

But more is required. Men want to be a part of a common enterprise—a cause greater than themselves. Each of us must find a way to advance the purpose of the nation, thus finding new purpose for ourselves. Without this, we shall become a nation of strangers.

THE THIRD ARTICLE was union. To those who were small and few against the wilderness, the success of liberty demanded the strength of union. Two centuries of change have made this true again.

No longer need capitalist and worker, farmer and clerk, city and countryside, struggle to divide our bounty. By working shoulder to shoulder, together we can increase the bounty of all. We have discovered that every child who learns, every man who finds work, every sick body that is made whole—like a candle added to an altar—brightens the hope of all the faithful.

So let us reject any among us who seek to reopen old wounds and to rekindle old hatreds. They stand in the way of a seeking nation.

Let us now join reason to faith and action to experience, to transform our unity of interest into a unity of purpose. For the hour and the day and the time are here to achieve progress without strife, to achieve change without hatred—not without difference of opinion, but without the deep and abiding divisions which scar the union for generations.

UNDER THIS COVENANT of justice, liberty, and union we have become a nation—prosperous, great, and mighty. And we have kept our freedom. But we have no promise from God that our greatness will endure. We have been allowed by Him to seek greatness with the sweat of our hands and the strength of our spirit.

I do not believe that the Great Society is the ordered, changeless, and sterile battalion of the ants. It is the excitement of becoming—always becoming, trying, probing, falling, resting, and trying again—but always trying and always gaining.

In each generation, with toil and tears, we have had to earn our heritage again.

If we fail now, we shall have forgotten in abundance what we learned in hardship: that democracy rests on faith, that freedom asks more than it gives, and that the judgment of God is harshest on those who are most favored.

If we succeed, it will not be because of what we have, but it will be because of what we are; not because of what we own, but, rather because of what we believe.

For we are a nation of believers. Underneath the clamor of building and the rush of our day's pursuits, we are believers in justice and liberty and union, and in our own Union. We believe that every man must someday be free. And we believe in ourselves.

Our enemies have always made the same mistake. In my lifetime—in depression and in war—they have awaited our defeat. Each time, from the secret places of the American heart, came forth the faith they could not see or that they could not even imagine. It brought us victory. And it will again.

For this is what America is all about. It is the uncrossed

desert and the unclimbed ridge. It is the star that is not reached and the harvest sleeping in the unplowed ground. Is our world gone? We say "Farewell." Is a new world coming? We welcome it—and we will bend it to the hopes of man.

To these trusted public servants and to my family and those close friends of mine who have followed me down a long, winding road, and to all the people of this Union and the world, I will repeat today what I said on that sorrowful day in November 1963: "I will lead and I will do the best I can."

But you must look within your own hearts to the old promises and to the old dream. They will lead you best of all.

For myself, I ask only, in the words of an ancient leader: "Give me now wisdom and knowledge, that I may go out and come in before this people: for who can judge this thy people, that is so great?"

Born near Stonewall, Texas, in 1908, LYNDON BAINES JOHN-SON served as a United States congressman, senator, and vice-president. On November 22, 1963, after John F. Kennedy was assasinated, Johnson was sworn in as the thirty-sixth president of the United States of America and served until 1968 when he retired to his ranch in Texas. He died January 22, 1973.

The Spirit of Texas

BY DENTON A. COOLEY, M.D.

★ As a native Texan, I have always taken pride in my origin. My grandfather moved to Houston in 1884 and lived the rest of his life here as did my father who practiced dentistry in Houston for some fifty years. As a Texan, myself, I have enjoyed a very special pride wherever my travels took me.

I recall vividly my early years in Europe in the military service just after the war. It always pleased me when I was introduced not just as an American, but as a Texan. That identification has seemed to inspire achievement and contribution.

The spirit of Texas seems to pervade our everyday existence. Our desire is to be superlative, not only the largest, but also the best in the United States. I know that Alaska may now compare in size, but will never compare in other respects. I am proud to be a Texan.

DENTON A. COOLEY, M.D. has been a pioneer in the field of medicine, and professional colleagues worldwide have recognized his remarkable accomplishments. In 1968 he performed the first successful U.S. heart transplant and in 1969 performed the first artificial heart transplant. Today he is the surgeon-in-chief and president of the Texas Heart Institute in Houston, Texas.

Denton A. Cooley, M.D.

The Time of Her Life

by BRYAN WOOLLEY

☆ She was born in 1892 in a Texas community that has disappeared, except for the cemetery where her mother and father and little brother are buried. When the great storm destroyed Galveston in 1900, she lived at Brazoria, not far inland, and remembers being a refugee in the old courthouse while the water went down. Some of her friends who went to school on the island were swept away. While she was still a girl, her father—a schoolteacher and a storekeeper—was bedridden with a terminal disease and died young. When she was seventeen, she and her older sister, Voleta, became schoolteachers, to help support their mother and five surviving younger brothers and sisters. She lived in boarding houses in communities with such names as Sunshine and Honey Grove and rode a pony to her one-room schools, where some of her pupils were older and twice as big as she was. She kept discipline and taught many country youngsters all they would ever know of book learning. She married Audie Lee Gibson, a farmer, and bore a daughter, Beatrice, and taught in a small town called Carlton. Her husband accepted a job as deputy sheriff and was shot to death by robbers in 1932, a few nights before Christmas. When her daughter's marriage ended in 1945, she trekked beyond the Pecos in a 1939 Chevrolet with Beatrice and five grandchildren to help create a new life in Fort Davis, a small, isolated mountain town. She taught for twenty years there. Among her pupils were all five of her grandchildren. "An education is the most important thing you can have," she told us, "because nobody can take it away from you," and the grandchildren would get eight college degrees among them.

She remembers veterans of the Lost Cause parading in their

gray uniforms, Teddy Roosevelt and the Spanish-American War, the first automobile that came through and scared all the horses, the Wright brothers' first flight, the Mexican Revolution, World War I, the Great Depression, World War II, the A-bomb, the Korean Police Action, the Cuban Missile Crisis, the death of President Kennedy, Neil Armstrong walking on the moon, Vietnam, Watergate, and the births of thirteen great-grandchildren. Through it all, she has been sustained by her faith in God, in the country, in her unshakeable belief that there's some good in all of us. "The Lord helps those who help themselves," she has said to the generations. "All things work for good for those who love the Lord." "It's always darkest just before the dawn." "If at first you don't succeed, try, try again." "There's more than one way to skin a cat." "Be sure you're right, then go ahead." Her mottos and slogans are engraved as deeply in my mind as the Beatitudes and the Bill of Rights. Whether they're lived up to or not, they're still true for me and for hundreds of others whose lives she has touched and helped shape. When I was very small, I, her first grandchild, gave her a name—Mommy. For forty-five years the name has remained right for her. Everyone in the family calls her that. "Children have been my life," she says, "and nobody's ever made a better investment."

Clora Laura DeVolin Gibson is ninety now. Months before her birthday, my mother, her daughter, started making plans and calling the members of the scattered clan.

"Everybody's got to come," she said. "Anybody missing will ruin it."

She rented nearly all of the historic Limpia Hotel on the Fort Davis town square and ordered birthday cakes, cookies, gallons of "Baptist punch," flowers. She published notices in the *Alpine Avalanche and the Big Bend Sentinel,* inviting all Mommy's friends to come celebrate. She hired a photographer. "Who knows when we'll all get together again?" she said. Some of the great-grandchildren are in college now, and soon will go their own ways.

All day Friday and Saturday morning, relatives, in-laws, step-relatives, and in-laws-to-be arrived—Isabel and me from Dallas; Ted and Pat from Saint Louis; Chris from New York; Linda, Jim, David, Scott, Terry, and Laura from Marfa; Dick, Sandra, Audie, Michael, Janice, and Allyson from Cisco; Mike, Linda Kay, Alden, and Lori from Lubbock; Sherry, Lee, Mark, Susan, and Tara from Midland. Aunt Helen, Mommy's baby sister, and only other surviving DeVolin of their generation, arrived from Las Cruces, and cousin Joanne and husband Jim from El Paso. Cousin Emmett and wife Dorothy and daughter Linda came from Marfa. Cars seemed to be breeding and multiplying in the town square and up the street from the courthouse in front of the rambling old adobe house where a generation of us had grown up. "We can always tell when the Woolleys are in town," a merchant said. "The population of Fort Davis doubles." In the side yard the male cousins of the youngest generation played a nonstop touch football game. Inside, the youngest females, aglow with adolescent vanity, showered and curled and blow-dried and primped and perfumed. The old house groaned under their energy. Down at the Limpia, Mommy's grandchildren, now in middle age or getting there, traded old jokes and memories over coffee and wine—the first vintage from Fort Davis's own vineyard, a small and appropriate new industry for the old town, which has never seen the smoke of a factory or even a railroad train.

It was toward the middle of the afternoon, before things got really hectic, that I took my bourbon out to the second-floor porch of the Limpia and sat on a bench in the sun and looked down on the town square. I had never seen Fort Davis from that perspective, perched like God above the ground and buildings where I had spent my boyhood. To my left was the stone Union Mercantile, established in 1879 and in business ever since, its steel-barred windows still misleading tourists into thinking it's the jail. How many nails and boards had I bought from Tyrone Kelly there over the years? How many ropes and pocketknives? No telling. The Union was where we bought nearly everything that wasn't to eat or drink in those days. Across the square was El Cerro Books and the office of the newly arrived doctor, the first physician Fort Davis has had in years. Their building had been the Harry Jarratt Motorport in my youth, and later, Mrs. Tarvin's beauty shop. Next to it, in a red-stone, two-story building, the twin of the hotel, were the Fort Davis State Bank, where I had worked for a year once, hating every minute, and the post office, where I had waited desperately for love letters from high school sweethearts in Alpine and Marfa. And to my right was the Jeff Davis County Courthouse, where my mother had been county and district clerk for more than thirty years, and its town clock that now, as thirty years ago, tolls each hour five minutes early, and its lawn and trees and sidewalks, where I learned to roller-skate and played capture-the-flag on soft summer nights. Below me, on the first floor of the Limpia, the drugstore had been in the old days and Bill Fryar gave me my first job, sweeping up, jerking sodas, washing windows, to pay off an Ansco box camera that I had to have but could not afford. When I was in high school I once fell through the floor where I now stood. The Limpia had caught fire, and the Fort Davis Volunteer Fire Department had tried to save it. The floor collapsed under me and I fell to the sidewalk below, not hurt at all and feeling very much the hero. And around the rim of the town stood the mountains—Sleeping Lion, Blue, Dolores—the rugged, changeless hills where I had wandered with my friends and alone, shooting jackrabbits, camping, just standing and looking at the vast world in which I felt so small and unique. The names and faces of dozens of good people passed through my memory—old relics of the pioneer days who were still alive and lively then, the mothers and fathers of my friends, and my old buddies and girlfriends—nearly all of them gone, either dead or moved to God-knows-where. One of them, Barry Scobee, who had loved that town with a rare passion, had told me once: "After Fort Davis, heaven is all that's left." And I knew that, given the choice, he would rather stay in Fort Davis. Sitting there in the sun with my

Clora Laura "Mommy" DeVolin Gibson
on her ninetieth birthday.
PHOTO COURTESY OF CHRIS MARZULLI.

bourbon, I also knew that I'm a privileged person, having grown up in that place and having known its people.

The party wasn't to begin until 3:00 on Saturday afternoon, but the florist arrived at 12:30 to pin the color-coded flowers on us—red for Mother and the grandchildren, blue for the great-grandsons, pink for the great-granddaughters, white for the in-laws, and an orchid for Mommy. And the photographer, setting up his camera and lights in the Limpia lobby, already was looking worried. "It's like photographing the crowd at a Dallas Cowboys game," he said. For half an hour he arranged and adjusted us, trying to fit the whole family onto one small negative, Mommy sitting in an armchair in the midst of us like the queen bee in her hive. And then the smaller groups— Mother and Mommy; Mother and Mommy and the five of us who arrived so long ago in the '39 Chevy, then each of us and our own progeny and spouses. It took hours, and by the time we were through, the grunts were arriving.

It was the duty of us grandsons to stand at the hotel door and greet them, while the women presided over the guest book and the punch bowl and coffeepot. I was glad I still recognized so many—J.D. and Dale Crawford, old family friends and parents of my best high school buddy; Alice Swartz, the only math teacher to ever teach me anything; Lucy Foster Miller, whose lawn and garden I used to water when she was out of town; Ralph Russell, who taught me how to type and thus gave me a livelihood; Tyrone Kelly, still proprietor of the Union, and his wife Audrey, pianist for the Baptist church and the whole community; Bit Miller, who could sing "Sweet Little Jesus Boy" and bring a tear to every eye in the house; Annie Lou Clark, music teacher who, nearing ninety herself, had a student recital scheduled for the next day; Fritz Kahl, the best pilot in the Davis Mountains, and his wife Georgie Lee. Some of them I'd seen before on my infrequent trips home. Others I hadn't laid eyes on since I went off to seek my fortune in 1955. But having known them once, I know them always, and our conversations were as if they had been interrupted only a few minutes ago, not twenty-seven years before.

"When I die," I told Fritz, "I'm to be cremated, and you're to take my ashes up and scatter them over the Davis Mountains."

"You'd be surprised how often I do that," he said. And to my wife, a New Yorker, he said, "This place must look small to you, but the kids who went to school in Fort Davis were lucky. My daughters had only three teachers in elementary school—Lillian Mims, Clora Gibson, and Hazel Rau. They handled two grades apiece. They were kind, friendly women, but when they closed their classroom doors, believe, me they *held school*. When the kids got out of there, they had *learned* what they were supposed to learn."

There were people I didn't know, too—newcomers, retired

people, most of them, who had fled the dangerous, expensive cities or the rigors of Northern winters to find a place to live comfortably on their pensions. Some have lived there ten years or longer, but if you didn't grow up in Fort Davis, you can be a newcomer for twenty or thirty years. It depends on your finding your place in the community, in the churches, the Fort Davis Historical Society, the schools, and on how often you show up at potluck suppers and the ice cream parties on the courthouse lawn.

I don't know what Mommy's duty at the party was supposed to be. Probably to sit in a comfortable chair near the punch bowl and accept the congratulations. But soon she was standing at the hotel door with her grandsons, greeting the guests. She stood there for two hours, not getting tired at all, for what was happening to her was love. And I wondered what it felt like to live almost a century and be loved by so many for so long. "Why don't you sit down a minute, Mommy?" we would say. Our own legs were screaming for relief. "Oh no," she would say. "I'm having the time of my life."

BRYAN WOOLLEY has been writing about Texas and Texans for more than thirty years. He is a senior writer for the Dallas Morning News *and the author of several books about Texas including his most recent,* Mythic Texas. *He wrote "The Time of Her Life" in January 1983, not long after the party celebrating his grandmother's ninetieth birthday. She died in 1984 and is buried in Fort Davis.*

"What Kind of People?"

BY SENATOR PHIL GRAMM

All over the world, people want to know what kind of people Texans are, and I explain that Texans are America's ideal Americans. Texas became an independent nation and then a sovereign state not because the most brilliant and talented people came to live here. Texas was built by common people. Sam Houston and Stephen F. Austin were the kinds of leaders who trusted the future of our country to the hard work and achievement of ordinary people like you and me. And it is in Texas that ordinary people can still find the freedom and opportunity to do extraordinary things.

Respectfully,

PHIL GRAMM
UNITED STATES SENATOR

Senator PHIL GRAMM of College Station is fifty-seven years old. He holds a Ph.D. in economics, the subject he taught at Texas A&M University for twelve years. He has published numerous articles and books on subjects ranging from monetary theory and policy to private property to the economics of mineral extraction, and currently serves as chairman of the Senate Banking Committee. He is married to Dr. Wendy Lee Gramm, former chairman of the United States Commodity Futures Trading Commission under Presidents Reagan and Bush. They have two sons, Marshall and Jeff.

Phil Gramm, United States Senator.
PHOTO COURTESY OF SENATOR PHIL GRAMM.

The Kioways

By J. W. Abert

☆ September 12.—Last night we were startled at midnight by the alarm of Indians. They had been heard early in the evening, as they followed in our path, and an occasional dark form was seen flitting across the hill and disappearing in the canyon below. The mules, which are the best sentinels, were very restless, snorting, and some broke the tugs by which they were attached to the pickets, showing by their actions that a concealed enemy was prowling around. Just as the moon was setting, Hatcher, awakened by the unusual stir, got up, and, taking his rifle, sat himself beside the door of our tent. Upon first hearing the alarm we all sprang to our feet, rifle in hand, but as no hostile demonstration succeeded, we again returned to rest, having first examined the fastenings of our mules, and taken every precaution to guard against surprise.

At daylight we were stirring, and, on examining the neighborhood, found the tracks of Indians, and soon discovered a band of natives riding toward our camp. We invited them in, and gave them breakfast, of which they partook with great confidence. They proved to be a band of Kioways, and several of the "Up-sah ro-kees," or Crows, who lived on the head water of the Missouri. They said that their village was on a branch of the creek upon which we were encamped. They, discovering our trail, which indicated the presence of strangers, had followed on until warned to proceed more cautiously by the alarm given in the early part of the evening. We had been mistaken by them for their enemies, the Texans, and they had remained near out camp during the night in order to satisfy themselves. One of them had crawled, in the shadow of the ravine, to within ten feet of our tent, where he lay quietly, entirely screened from observation by a rocky wall which ran perpendicularly down into the ravine. From this point he saw Hatcher, and closely observed every motion; his rising in bed on his elbow, rolling up his sleeves, scratching his arm, and taking his rifle and seating himself at the door of the tent. Determined to improve so fine an opportunity of revenging himself on one whom he considered as an enemy, he fitted his arrow to the bowstring and drew it to the head; but, he added, "here my heart whispered to me that he might be an American, and I did not shoot." This was, indeed, a dread moment—the lives of our whole party hung upon the Indian's bowstring. We were just entering their country; they were around us in numbers, and had blood been shed they would have hung about us until every individual was cut off; but the hand of Almighty Providence prevented this sad termination. The Great Spirit whispered in the ear of the savage, "He may be an American." To confirm his statement to us, as well as to prove to his brother warriors the boldness of his daring approach, he had piled a heap of stones on the ledge of the rock, after yielding to the fortunate suggestion of his heart. We were also approached on the opposite side of our camp by several, who had crept upon their bellies and watched the men sleeping under the wagons, and said that they could have stabbed them to the heart and retreated without being discovered.

We gave our new friends some tobacco, and expressed our regrets at having nothing else to offer them. Hatcher made them some "cigaritos;" they smoked them with seeming satisfaction, and then mounted their horses and accompanied us on our road, which led us nigh their camp; they laughed heartily at a party of Comanches they had previously met, who had been frightened at our approach and fled, leaving their mules and furniture scattered over the prairie; and, meeting these Kioways, advised them to fly, as they reported us to be as numerous as the blades of grass on the prairie. These, however, were determined to satisfy themselves, and, striking on our trail, had followed until last evening. The Kioways are a people excelling the Comanches in every respect, and, though far inferior to them in number, not counting more than 200 lodges in all, yet exercise almost absolute control over them. On inquiring the origin of their nation, and the cause of their having such influence, they replied, that many years ago, so long as to be lost to the memory of their oldest tradition, their fathers had left a land far to the north, and coming hither, and finding the Comanches, had smoked the pipe of peace, and had remained in close friendship ever since. They speak an entirely different language, being much more deep and guttural, striking upon the ear like the sound of falling water. Their manners and customs are also quite different, yet they are firmly bound together by some unseen bond, and appear to feel a mutual desire to benefit each other. The Kioways sustain a character for bravery, energy, and honesty, while the Comanches are directly opposite, being cowardly, indolent, and treacherous. The Kioways are particularly noted for their honesty; and, while we remained with them, nothing was stolen—an occurrence sufficiently uncommon to merit special notice. Arrived at their village, we found it in a well wooded valley embosomed by high hills. Their horses had eaten the grass very short, therefore ours found but indifferent pasturage. We encamped a quarter of a mile lower down, and had scarcely pitched our tents before the squaws and children came flocking round anxious to trade—some bringing ropes made of plaited thongs, some moccasins, and others skins. We had nothing but tobacco to offer them in exchange, and with this single article we effected a few purchases; for, had we refused to trade altogether, they would have imputed it to an unfriendly motive. We wished to conciliate them as much as possible, hoping to derive some benefit from them during our passage through the Indian settlements below, which they represented to be very numerous. We were much struck by the noble bearing and fine athletic figures of these people, which we partly attributed to their being continually on horseback, which not only gives them palpable evidence of their superiority over the animals they bestride, but makes them conscious of their elevation over all the lower orders of creation, which is communicated to their whole character. These Indians ride beautifully, and manage their horses with astonishing skill. Knowing their fondness for large American horses, I endeavored to exchange mine, which, although it had been led all the way from Bent's fort, was very stiff, but the chief said he had "two hearts" about it. We noticed the singularity of their mode of mounting; wrapping a blanket several times around their body and legs, they throw themselves lengthwise upon the horse, and then rise up in the seat. The blanket, binding the limbs, assists greatly in clinging to the animal.

These people, contrary to the general opinion, appeared to be gay, cheerful, and fond of frolic; they laughed, chatted, and joked, much to the astonishment of some of us, who possessed preconceived notions which were, doubtless, obtained from the popular writers of the day. Some of the men had formed a shooting match between the boys, and they spent an hour or two in shooting at a button at the distance of 15 or 20 paces. We were all surprised at the remarkable skill which they displayed. Among the people who came to visit us in the camp, were some whose features and hair betokened Spanish blood; they had been taken prisoners, and, being well treated, were perfectly content with their new situation; they said that they were in fact better situated than in their own country, for they had plenty to eat, and were more kindly treated than in the place whence they had been taken. In dress, the Kioways resemble the other roving tribes of the great desert, being habited in buckskin. Their moccasins are furnished with a fringed appendage, 8 or 10 inches in length, which is attached to the heel, which could not be conveniently worn by other than mounted Indians, and is said to be peculiar to their tribe. They all have the blanket or buffalo robe, and their long hair is braided so as to form a queue, sometimes lengthened by means of horse hair until it reaches the ground; and this queue is often ornamented with convex silver plates, which they procure from the

Spaniards. The dress of the women differs but little from that of the northern tribes—the same leathern cape, tunic, leggins, and beaded moccasins.

We were particularly struck with the profusion of trappings with which the men ornamented themselves and their horses, and which they had procured either by robbery or barter from the Spaniards, with whom they had considerable intercourse.

After finishing our trade, we endeavored to persuade some of the Indians to travel with us, for we apprehended difficulties in coming into collision with some roving band, that might attack us by night under the idea that we were Texans. There was one young man whose frank and generous demeanor elicited the sympathies and procured the friendship of all of us, and he, too, seemed at once to have his whole heart enlisted in our behalf. We endeavored to persuade him to accompany us as far as Bent's houses, where we would perhaps meet a large assemblage of Indians awaiting the arrival of Bent's wagons. We told him at once that we had nothing to give him, and therefore could not press him to incommode himself. He appeared undecided, and returned to the village to consult the chiefs.

We were struck with the affection which an old squaw manifested for Hatcher. She wept over him for joy when they met, and insisted on his receiving a bale of tongues, and some "pinole" which she had manufactured from the musquit. She always calls him son, having adopted him ever since his first trading with her nation.

J. W. ABERT led a United States exploratory expedition across the Texas Panhandle in 1845.

Old Texas Days

BY NOAH SMITHWICK

☆ There were herds of fine, fat deer, and antelope enough to set one wild who had never killed anything bigger than a raccoon, but, to my astonishment and disgust, I could not kill one, though I was accounted a crack marksman; but I found it was one thing to shoot at a mark, the exact distance of which I knew, and another to hit game at an uncertain distance.

The colonists, consisting of a dozen families, were living—if such existence could be called living—huddled together for security against the Karankawas, who, though not openly hostile, were not friendly. The rude log cabins, windowless and floorless, have been so often described as the abode of the pioneer as to require no repetition here; suffice it to say that save as a partial protection against rain and sun they were absolutely devoid of comfort. Dewitt had at first established his headquarters at Gonzales, and the colonists had located their land in that vicinity, but the Indians stole their horses and otherwise annoyed them so much, notwithstanding the soldiers, that they abandoned the colony and moved down on the Lavaca, where they were just simply staying. The station being in the limits of the reserve, they made no pretense of improving it, not even to the extent of planting corn, one of the first things usually attended to, for the Texan Indians, unlike their eastern brethren, scorned to till the soil, and the few Mexicans scattered through the country did so only to the extent of supplying their own wants; so when the colonists used up the breadstuff they brought with them they had to do without until they raised it. This, however, was no very difficult matter near the coast, where there were vast canebrakes all along the rivers. The soil was rich and loose from the successive crops of cane that had decayed on it. In the fall, when the cane died down, it was burned off clean. The ground was then ready for planting, which was done in a very primitive manner, a sharpened stick being all the implement necessary. With this they made holes in the moist loam and dropped in grains of corn. When the young cane began to grow they went over it with a stick, simply knocking it down; the crop was then laid by. Game was plenty the year round, so there was no need of starving. Men talked hopefully of the future; children reveled in the novelty of the present; but the women—ah, there was where the situation bore heaviest. As one old lady remarked. Texas was "a heaven for men and dogs, but a hell for women and oxen." They— the women—talked sadly of the old homes and friends left behind, so very far behind it seemed then, of the hardships and bitter privations they were undergoing and the dangers that surrounded them. They had not even the solace of constant employment. The spinning wheel and loom had been left behind. There was, as yet, no use for them—there was nothing to spin. There was no house to keep in order; the meager fare was so simple as to require little time for its preparation. There was no poultry, no dairy, no garden, no books, nor papers as nowadays—and, if there had been, many of them could not read—no schools, no churches—nothing to break the dull monotony of their lives, save an occasional wrangle among the children and dogs. The men at least had the excitement of killing game and cutting bee trees.

NOAH SMITHWICK first came to Texas as a colonist and a gunsmith. He was a volunteer from Gonzales in the Texas Revolutionary Army. Later, he settled on the Colorado River above Austin where he became an Indian agent for the Republic of Texas. He also owned mills and engaged in other enterprises. He left Texas for California in 1861 because he opposed secession. He was the author of a classic book on early Texas, **Evolution of a State.**

FOREVER TEXAS

BY SENATOR KAY BAILEY HUTCHISON

☆ When asked what Texas means to me, I think first of the courageous, resilient people. I think of the early pioneers carving out their corner of earth and building Texas into the great state it is today.

I think of my adventurous great-great-grandfather, Charles S. Taylor. He was born far from Texas, in London, England, in 1808. His parents died when he was a child. After being educated in law by his uncle, he sailed off to the New World and landed in Nacogdoches, Texas, when it was a territory of Mexico.

Taylor soon became prominent in the territory and was appointed *alcalde* (mayor) by the government of Mexico. But, he and his fellow Texans wanted freedom and joined other leaders in the territory in signing the Texas Declaration of Independence. While he was at that convention, his wife Anna Maria fled with their children seeking safety in Louisiana. Tragically, all four of their children died en route.

Undaunted, the Taylors remained strong supporters of the Republic of Texas and eventually its statehood. They and their brave compatriots forged the only state that came into our nation as a nation.

Thomas Rusk was Charles's friend and fellow delegate to the convention that voted to declare independence. He was appointed Secretary of War, and when General Sam Houston was wounded at San Jacinto, he finished the battle, later describing it:

> *The sun was sinking in the horizon as the battle commenced; but at the close of the conflict, the sun of liberty*

and independence rose in Texas, never, it is hoped, to be obscured by the clouds of despotism . . . it was freemen fighting against the minions of tyranny and the results proved the inequality of such a contest.

Thomas Rusk joined Sam Houston as Texas's first two senators. I am a successor in the Rusk line. Since the heroic era of Rusk, Houston, and Taylor, Texas has flourished from cattle to oil to high tech. Our entrepreneurs thrill the world. But despite the vast physical wealth, the state's most powerful resource is the spirit of the people.

Senator KAY BAILEY HUTCHISON is the first woman to represent her state in the United States Senate. Senator Hutchison grew up in La Marque, Texas, and graduated from the University of Texas and UT Law School. She was twice elected to the Texas House of Representatives. Senator Hutchison lives in Dallas with her husband, Ray, a former colleague from the Texas House. The senator's heritage in Texas is historic.

I have ridden a horse in the Houston Rodeo parade every year that I have held office since I was a State Representative for Houston in 1973.

PHOTO COURTESY OF SENATOR KAY BAILEY HUTCHISON.

The YO Ranch and the Texas Legacy

BY CHARLIE SCHREINER III

⭐ Charles Armand Schreiner was my grandfather. He arrived with his family by boat in Indianola, Texas, in 1852, at the port on the Gulf when he was fourteen years old. By this time several thousand predominately German immigrants had already landed in Texas. The family made their way by foot to San Antonio and then North to Camp Verde, an Army outpost that was destined to be the headquarters for Jefferson Davis's great camel experiment in just a few years.

By today's way of thinking, Grandfather was just a boy but back then he had already taken on the responsibility of a man. Most boys grew up fast back then—mostly because they had to. For a while he did some rangering in '54, '55, and '59 with Captain John Samson's rangers. Then he married Magdalena Enderle and settled in Kerrville. Kerrville was named for James Kerr who was a friend of Sam Houston and was at the battle at San Jacinto. I don't think James Kerr ever set foot in Kerrville, but Sam Houston wanted to honor his friend by naming a county and the town after him.

In the late fifties my grandfather got married and went into the mercantile business in Camp Verde with his brother-in-law, Casper Real. In 1861 grandfather's first child was born. It was that same year when he joined up with General Walker's "greyhounds" to fight for the Confederacy in the Civil War. At the end of the war, he came back to Texas and went into the cattle business. In 1869 he started a general store in Kerrville with a partner who kept a store in Comfort, Texas. They had a simple agreement between them—grandfather would man the store in Kerrville and in ten years he would buy out his partner. He did.

When General Phil Sheridan led a campaign against the Indians, he advised my grandfather to move his cattle out of "Indian country," but Grandfather was a man of vision. Texas was his home and he stayed to realize his dreams in Texas.

There came a time in Texas when a homestead law was passed. If a man chose to live on a piece of land for three years and make at least three hundred dollars in improvements, that land would legally become his. Since this was "Indian country" there were plenty of places available, so Grandfather began to employ ranch hands to live out on a place, to work cattle, and do a few improvements. He picked up property from Kerrville to Harper and Redshole to Mountain Home. At that time this was all open range but grandfather was able to control the herds around the watering holes. Not long after that, he put the windmills over wells and had water available elsewhere.

Sometime in about 1883, '84, or '85, Grandfather brought Hereford cattle down from Oklahoma to improve his herds of Longhorn, but that proved detrimental to both the Longhorns and the Herefords.

After the last big cattle drives in the '80s, Grandfather stayed busy with many other interests, but after the Inheritance Tax was introduced, he decided to give his assets to members of his family. Uncle Gus got the Southfork Ranch; Uncle Louis the Schreiner Bank; Uncle A.C. took over the Schreiner Department Store; the James River Ranch at Mason went to Aunt Francis; Aunt Lena, Aunt Mimi, and Uncle Charles, Jr. got the Live Oak Ranch; and my father took over the operations of the Sawyer Ranch known as the YO and named for Y. O. Coleman.

Y. O. Coleman came from Kentucky to Corpus Christi and then Goliad in about 1850 and was in a partnership with a man named Fulton who had interest in land near Goliad, the site of the Sutton/Taylor feud. Together [Coleman and Fulton] formed a company called the Coleman/Fulton Pasture Company. Taylor wanted to keep his children away from any harm arising out of the feud, so he moved his half of the cattle business and the family to Mason and started a ranching operation there. The cattle had been branded YO (for Coleman) back in Goliad. When Taylor sold the ranch and all the holdings to grandfather back in 1880, Grandfather bought all the cattle and the rights to the brand and renamed the ranch the YO. It was easier than rebranding all the herd.

My father died when I was a young boy. My mother raised me at the ranch and then later I went to school at the San Antonio Academy in San Antonio. I also attended Schreiner Institute in Kerrville, Texas Military Institute in San Antonio, and the University of Texas in Austin.

Today when considering the future of the Texas rancher and their landholdings there are many adversary forces that make it difficult to be entirely optimistic about the ranching business today.

There was a time when a man could make a living for his family on cattle, but now when land sells for what it does and cattle sell for what they do, it just doesn't make any sense for a man to stay a rancher these days. So many forces, you might say, work against the man.

We've been luckier than some. We've had the resources and the opportunities to diversify the operation of the YO Ranch. Today we operate as an exotic game preserve, as a guest ranch, and an adventure camp for children. Tourism brings in a steady flow of people year-round to the ranch.

But I do worry about the future. What with taxes and federal control on just about every aspect of a man's business, it's sad to think that what generations of a family sacrificed to build a legacy for the future can be severely jeopardized by sprouting special interest groups.

CHARLIE SCHREINER III was among the twenty-six founding members of the Texas Longhorn Breeders Association of America. In Don Worcester's book, The Texas Longhorn: Relic of the Past, Asset for the Future, *Schreiner is quoted, "The breed got a start in Texas and that's where the association is going to stay." In 1964 he was elected the first president of the association and served three terms. Charlie Schreiner III continues to live in Mountain Home, Texas, at the famous YO Ranch.*

RECOLLECTIONS OF STEPHEN F. AUSTIN

BY MOSES AUSTIN BRYAN

☆ Having been often requested to write out my personal recollections of Stephen Fuller Austin, I do so to perpetuate some facts that might never be known unless I record them; for I am the only person living who was closely associated with him in private life at home, in Mexico, in the army, and during his last days, while Secretary of State. I have, then, a knowledge of much of the inner life of this benefactor of Texas and the human race.

In this communication, I can state those delicate facts of persons and things which I have not heretofore stated, because I have not desired to provoke controversy or wound the feelings of others, by stating them for the public. But now, that I feel I shall soon pass away, it is but an act of justice to my uncle that I leave them behind me, for information to his family and for the use of the honest and truth-loving historian.

In January, 1831, I came to San Felipe de Austin, where Uncle Austin lived in a log cabin with two rooms, one his bed chamber and the other his office. An old French negro woman, named Mary, was his cook, and an intelligent mulatto man, by name Simon, was his body servant; these he owned up to his death and they were very much attached to their master. He left them by will to my mother, and they served her during her life and died in the service of my half-brother, Stephen Perry. These servants attended to Austin's domestic wants and comforts, which were few and simple; he took his meals with the family of his secretary, Samuel M. Williams, who lived near him. It has been said by Thrall, in his *History*, that his home was with his sister after she came to Texas; this is a mistake. When he was on the coast near his sister, he spent as much time with her as his duties would permit, but his home was always in San Felipe after that town was laid out in 1824. He kept "a bachelor's home" as he called it, at first taking his meals with Mrs. Picket, and afterward with Samuel M. Williams when he married and kept house. His home was the log cabin I have spoken of, and here he did his business and received all who called on him—it was a thoroughfare.

Austin was slender, sinewy, of graceful figure and easy, elastic movements, with small hands and feet, dark hair inclined to curl when damp, with large, hazel eyes, fair skin when not sunburned, about five-feet-eight or-nine inches in height. His face was grave and thoughtful when not in the social circle—then it was animated and lit up by the gentle soul within; his voice was manly and soft, his colloquial powers fluent, persuasive, and attractive, without his being conscious of it himself; his magnetic power over others gave him the great influence he possessed over the leading men of Texas when with them, and his lofty, practical intellect, his thorough forgetfulness of self and devotion to Texas, bound to him the great mass of the people, especially the agriculturists, who formed four-fifths of the population.

His office was also the land office of the colony; consequently he had no privacy of home. I have often wondered at his equanimity amid all his self-sacrifices, discomforts, and annoyances, of which no one of this day can have the least idea. He had acquired the most perfect self-control of anyone I ever knew; naturally (he said) he was quick and irritable, but no one would suppose so from intercourse with him, for with others he had such ways as to make every one like and be easy with him. I have often seen him pace backward and forward, with hands behind him, in deep thought; lost to everything about him. When I would remind him that persons wanted to see him, he would in the most pleasant manner say, "Austin, you did right to interrupt me; always call me back when I have duties to discharge to others, for I have so many things to think of and attend to that my mind becomes absorbed, and I need to be reminded of their presence." I have seen him enjoy himself in the dance and in the society of ladies of San Felipe. He was then cheerful and courtly in his attentions and movements; cultivated and refined himself, he appreciated and enjoyed the society of such ladies as Mrs. William H. Jack, Mrs. Ira R. Lewis, Mrs. Nancy McKinney, Mrs. Townsend, and others. He was a graceful dancer and he said such society and amusements were a great recreation to him. The ladies were all of them his friends. Mrs. Bell, Mrs. Jack, Mrs. Lewis, Mrs. Wharton, Mrs. Long, Mrs. Calvit, long after his death, have talked to me of him and spoke of his habits, charming manners, neatness in dress and person, his temperance in all things, his chaste language (I never heard him utter an oath) so free from slang; of his manly modesty and dignified ways, rarely speaking of himself and inclined to pass over the faults of others and to make the most of their virtues. He told me of an incident happening to him on his first trip to Texas, which he said had great influence in forming his disposition in intercourse with others. He said he had with him for the benefit of his party an old hunter, with whom he went out frequently to hunt when the party encamped. The hunter would from time to time caution him to be careful, when he would make a noise treading on leaves or rotten wood. Finally he said to him, "Mr. Austin, you will never make a hunter." "Why?" "Because you need *patience.*" Reflecting on this, he said to himself, "Here am I on the outset of a great enterprise, and I am told by a faithful person that I can't succeed in a small matter for the want of *patience;* if I am wanting in the ability to do this, how much more will I be wanting in the ability to succeed in my great undertakings? From this day I will devote myself to obtain every requisite necessary for my success. I will *possess patience* and every other quality I need." "My friends at times tell me I have too much patience and forbearance, but I think not, for without these, I never should have succeeded in my colonization of Texas."

MOSES AUSTIN BRYAN was a nephew of Stephen F. Austin, and his aide during the Texas Revolution.

The Cowboy's Paradise

BY PATRICK DEAREN

☆ He rode "hell-bent-for-leather" along a Southwest river likened to hell and entered the myth of the West.

He was a cowboy of the Pecos.

With skills tailored to the river's unique demands and with character honed by a no-man's land in which "pecos" also meant *murder* and "pecos swap," *theft,* he was a breed of cowhand unlike any other. F. S. Millard, a Pecos cowboy of the 1880s, recalled one cowhand reckoning that "the Pecos boys were the most expert cowboys in the world" and another one adding, "Yes, with the ex left off."

They were maybe the "best damned cowboys" who ever sat a horse, men who rode wild broncs by day and even wilder ones over a plate of beans by night. But no Pecos hand ever had need to brag of his skill in working cattle; either he rode out into a midnight storm muttering, "If I couldn't hold this damned herd alone, may I go to hell," or he rolled up his bedroll and went home to mama.

It was a confidence that many would carry into the sunsets of their lives.

"If we could turn back fifty years now [from the 1950s]," reflected septuagenarian Julius D. Henderson, a Pecos hand of the late 1890s, "we could show those drugstore cowboys how it was done."

They lived like coyotes, said the old-timers, out of a chuck wagon or a cow camp and never "made a kick," unless someone cut them out a string of "dogs" to ride—that is, sorry old beaten-out horses. And "quittin' time" wasn't determined by a pocket watch or the rise or fall of the sun; they worked, as one

old-time hand put it, from "you can till you can't." A young
cowhand with a Texas cattle outfit at Pope's Crossing in 1867
wrote, "All anybody asks of a man in the Pecos is a good day's
work and to keep his privacy."

The Pecos seemed uniquely suited to nurturing the lifestyle
of a cowboy; a fact not lost on newspapers of the nineteenth
century. The *San Angelo* [*Times*] *Standard* in the fall of 1886,
even went so far as to proclaim the valley of the Pecos "the
cowboy's paradise." Nevertheless, no cowhand ever smiled
when he pulled rein at the river's banks.

"The Pecos—the graveyard of the cowman's hopes . . . I
hated it!" lamented Charles Goodnight, who first drove cattle
along its bank in 1866.

It was a river cursed with a vengeance by all, and few cowhands would have disputed the buffalo hunters claim that,
"When a bad man dies, he goes either to hell or the Pecos."

Its headwaters, 11,300 feet high in the Sangre de Cristo
range in northern New Mexico, would have looked more like
Heaven to a Texas cowboy, however. Cradled by pristine peaks
rising 13,000 feet, the singing stream cascades down through
columbine-spangled meadows and alpine-green forests before
emptying into the lowlands and setting a course to the southeast. Striking Texas as the lone river in an arid empire three
hundred miles wide, it slithers on through forbidding desert
flats, carves a mighty rockwalled canyon, and intersects the Rio
Grande and Mexican border near Langtry, Texas 926 river
miles from the Sangre de Cristos.

Along much of its Texas stretch today, the Pecos is only a
polluted trickle, squeezing through a jungle of salt cedars that
choke banks sloughed and neglected. The motorist crossing it
by bridge today is more likely to greet it with a yawn than with
visceral emotion. But were he to read the history buried deep
in its banks, he would find the sweat and blood of cowhands
who knew this ghost as the most formidable and treacherous
river in the West.

"Just two things that cowboys were afraid of—the Pecos River and rattlesnakes," wrote James Hinkle, a Pecos cowboy of the 1880s.

Generally four to fifteen feet deep and forty to sixty feet wide in the flats, it flowed without a murmur but swift as a war-horse between treeless banks as perpendicular as the walls of an edifice. "An animal may wander along the banks half a day," said one traveler, "without finding a point where he may drink." In fact, in the hundreds of miles between the New Mex-ico line and the Rio Grande, a cowboy could cross the Pecos only at a handful of sites.

Seldom less than half-bank full, the Pecos was so turbid with red sediment that, said one cowboy, "A bucket of its water would yield an inch of sand," a condition that led to the for-mation of quicksand below the unscalable walls. So tenacious was this mire, went one yarn, that whenever a Forty-Niner crossed a wagon and bogged an ox, efforts to pull it our suc-ceeded only in putting another bend in the river.

Judging by the "unmatchable sinuosity" of this waterway, cursed by one cowpuncher as the "crookedest river in the world," more oxen must have succumbed to the Pecos sands than ever reached the California gold fields. Consider the experience of cowhand F. S. Millard: "We used to go in a-swimming. We would jump in the river [depositing their gar-ments at that point], go about half a mile downstream, and come out at our clothes."

Cattle drover Pete Narbo found the river's horseshoe bends less obliging. Sighting a stray steer across the river and shooting it for beef, he swam his horse to the far bank only to find the carcass still across-river; he and the steer had been on the same side.

SNAKING UNDER A relentless sun through a barren land with "the curse of thirst upon it," as U.S. Army Captain W. H. C. Whiting observed in 1849, the Pecos was, first and foremost, a study in nature's sovereignty. "I lost my brand-new hat . . .

when trying to cross the river just last week when brim-full and the wind blowing every which way," a cowhand wrote home in 1867. "You folks just can't believe how the wind blows out here. It has so much room to get started in."

Nevertheless, cattlemen seeking open range for their herds saw promise in the Pecos and "luxuriant growth of nutritious grasses" beyond its flood plain. "The hills and plains east and west of it," noted a correspondent of the *San Antonio Daily Express* in 1877, "furnish a stock range almost unlimited in extent and of the best quality for cattle, horses, sheep, and goats.

But even as cattle found sustenance, the scrub mesquite, cat-claw, lechuguilla, and cacti proved inhospitable to any cow-hand not astride a horse. "Every thing that grows," lamented, *The* (Clarksville, Texas) *Standard* in July 1861, "has a thorn on the end of the leaves, or spears of grass so sharp they will stick you."

This then was the river and land known as the Pecos, which loomed a vast wilderness known only to Indians afoot from 9000 B.C. until the coming of the Spaniards in the sixteenth century.

WERE IT NOT for the horse, there could never have been a cow-boy. "A cowboy without a horse," observed Billy Rankin, a Pecos cowhand of the 1920s, "is just like a one-legged man at a butt-kicking."

When future New Mexico governor Don Juan de Oñate imported seven thousand horses to the Southwest in 1598, native Indians quickly absorbed the animal into their cultures. By the latter 1600s, the Apaches and Comanches were horse peoples, and by the middle of the eighteenth century, the Comanches had seized the Southern Plains, established rancherias on the Arkansas and Red rivers, and marked the Pecos as the south-western boundary of Comancheria. For the next hundred twenty-five years, while Mescalero Apaches raided from western strongholds in the Guadalupe and Sacramento mountains, Comanches pushed down by fall to cross the Pecos at Horsehead Crossing and plunder deep into Mexico.

No cowboy of the Pecos ever envied the free haircuts meted out by these warriors, whom he hated and feared even while sometimes respecting their courage. "I have often heard it said that Indians were sneaking cowards and would not fight," said cattle drover G. F. Banowsky, survivor of two Indian battles on the Pecos in the 1870s. "In my dealings with them, I found it the other way about. I never knew them to decline a battle in the open with the white man, when they had anything like as good guns; nor do I believe that anybody else ever did [know them to decline]."

Even as Spain's rule over the Pecos ended in 1821, and on through fifteen years under the flag of Mexico and a near decade of Republic of Texas dominion that ended when Texas joined the United States, the Pecos largely was shunned by white men, who settled no closer than hundreds of miles to the east. Then came a gold strike near Sutter's Mill, California, stirring the imaginations of men and women throughout the nation. Soon, the Pecos witnessed the approach of not only emigrants, but also their herds of work oxen, beeves, and breeding stock. A caravan setting out from Fredericksburg, Texas, in early 1849, for example, had "numerous herds of cattle," reported a Houston newspaper of the day. And riding in the dust raised by the hooves were "herdsmen"—the first cowboys of the Pecos—pointing the way into myth and history for all the cowhands who would follow.

PATRICK DEAREN is a well-known and respected author of several books on cowboy history and legend, including A Cowboy of the Pecos, Crossing Rio Pecos, Castle Gap and the Pecos Frontier, Portraits of the Pecos Frontier, The Last of the Old-Time Cowboys, *and* When Cowboys Die, *a Spur Award finalist.*

LIVING IN THE LAST FRONTIER

BY CRAIG CARTER

⭐ Texas: It brings so many thoughts and emotions that it's hard to get them all into words, but honor, independence, strong character, and deep cultural roots come immediately to mind.

I've had the good fortune of growing up and living in a very remote part of Texas: where the Rio Grande makes the Big Bend in Brewster County, one of the largest and least populated counties in the United States. At a very early age I came to understand the true meaning of the word "neighbor."

Most folks who come to visit for the first time in this harsh, rough, arid, scary, wide-open, spectacular, and beautiful part of Texas have one of two reactions. They either love it or hate it. I can't get enough of it.

If a person had a couple of years to just travel around and really get to know the State, they would experience people, traditions, climates, and terrain uncomparable to any other one place in the world.

I could write for days and still not get it all down on the page what Texas means to me. But after elaborating, I'll sum it all up in one word . . . HOME!

Regards from the Last Frontier

Cowboy, songwriter, singer, actor, CRAIG CARTER is a versatile performer from the Big Bend country of West Texas. Recent film credits include Dancer, Texas, Pop 81 *released by Tri-Star,* Hi Lo Country *produced by Martin Scorsese and starring Woody Harrelson, Sam Elliott, and Billy Cudrup. He has toured Europe an amazing twenty-seven times, and has just completed a music video titled* Living in the Last Frontier. *He divides his time between acting, writing, singing, and al-ways training horses.*

Craig Carter.

A Texas Cowboy

BY CHARLES A. SIRINGO

☆ We commenced work about the first of September on "Big Sandy" in Lavaca county, a place noted for wild "brush" cattle. Very few people lived in that section, hence so many wild unbranded cattle.

As the cattle remained hidden out in the "brush" during the daytime, only venturing out on the small prairies at night, we had to do most of our work early in the morning, commencing an hour or two before daylight. As you might wish to know exactly how we did, will try and explain: About two hours before daylight the cook would holloa "chuck," and then Mr. Wiley would go around and yell, "Breakfast, boys; d—n you get up!" two or three times in our ears.

Breakfast being over we would saddle up our ponies, which had been staked out the night before, and strike out for a certain prairie maybe three or four miles off—that is all but two or three men, just enough to bring the herd, previously gathered, on as soon as it became light enough to see.

Arriving at the edge of the prairie we would dismount and wait for daylight.

At the first peep of day the cattle, which would be out in the prairie, quite a distance from the timber, would all turn their heads and commence grazing at a lively rate toward the nearest point of timber. Then we would ride around through the brush, so as not to be seen, until we got to the point of timber that they were steering for.

When it became light enough to see good, we would ride out, rope in hand, to meet them and apt as not one of the old-timers, may be a fifteen- or twenty-year-old steer, which were continuously on the lookout, would spy us before we got twenty yards from the timber. Then the fun would begin—the whole bunch, maybe a thousand head, would stampede and come right toward us. They never were known to run in the opposite direction from the nearest point of timber. But with cattle raised on the prairies, it's the reverse, they will always leave the timber.

After coming in contact, every man would rope and tie down one of the finest animals in the bunch. Once in awhile some fellow would get more beef than he could manage; under those circumstances he would have to worry along until some other fellow got through with his job and came to his rescue.

If there was another prairie close by we would go to it and tie down a few more, but we would have to get there before sunup or they would all be in the brush. It was their habit to graze out into the little prairies at nightfall and go back to the brush by sunrise next morning.

Finally the herd which we had gathered before and which was already "broke in," would arrive from camp, where we had been night-herding them and then we would drive it around to each one of the tied-down animals, letting him up so he couldn't help from running right into the herd, where he would generally stay contented. Once in awhile though, we would strike an old steer that couldn't be made to stay in the herd. Just as soon as he was untied and let up he would go right through the herd and strike for the brush, fighting his way. Under those circumstances we would have to sew up their eyes with a needle and thread. That would bring them to their milk, as they couldn't see the timber.

I got into several scrapes on this trip, by being a new hand at the business. One time I was going at full speed and threw my rope onto a steer just as he got to the edge of the timber; I couldn't stop my horse in time, therefore the steer went on one side of a tree and my horse on the other and the consequence was, my rope being tied hard and fast to the saddle horn, we all landed up against the tree in a heap.

At another time, on the same day, I roped a large animal

and got my horse jerked over backward on top of me and in the horse getting up he got me all wound up in the rope, so that I couldn't free myself until relieved by "Jack" a negro man who was near at hand. I was certainly in a ticklish predicament that time; the pony was wild and there I hung fast to his side with my head down while the steer, which was still fastened to the rope, was making every effort to gore us.

Just before Christmas, Moore selected our outfit to do the shipping at Palacious Point, where a Morgan steamship landed twice a week to take on cattle for the New Orleans market.

We used to ship about five hundred head at each shipping. After getting rid of one bunch we would strike right back, to meet one of the gathering outfits, after another herd. There were three different outfits to do the gathering for us.

We kept that up all winter and had a tough time of it, too, as it happened to be an unusually cold and wet winter.

CHARLES A. SIRINGO *was a Texas cowboy, a Pinkerton detective, and an author who wrote about his experience, his first book,* A Texas Cowboy, *is considered a classic.*

"...One Riot, One Ranger"

BY MIKE COX

⭐ I grew up hearing wonderful stories from my grandfather, L. A. Wilke, about the old-time Texas Rangers he knew as a newspaperman back in the teens, twenties, and early thirties.

Sitting back in his chair while twiddling his thumbs on his ample belly, with a chuckle he'd tell me about some Ranger reaching out from the witness stand to slap an impertinent defense attorney or pistol-whipping some ill-mannered miscreant. As assassinations and riots seemed to grip the nation in the sixties, Granddad longed for what he considered the good ol' days when a Ranger could kill someone just because he needed killing with complete confidence that he had the full pardoning power of the Governor behind him. Many would say that wouldn't be a bad idea today, but those days are long gone, as is my granddad.

Regrettably, Granddad never got to know that one day I would have what may be the best job in Texas. As spokesman for the Texas Department of Public Safety, which includes the Texas Rangers, I get to do a lot of the talking for these lawmen and -women. Most of the Rangers I know would as soon get in a gunfight as face a TV camera, and that's good, because it gives me job security.

Before I went to work for the DPS, I spent nearly twenty years as a newspaper reporter, following in Granddad's footsteps. One of the Rangers I dealt with quite a bit was A. Y. Allee, Jr. He was the son of a famous Ranger captain.

When some labor trouble broke out in the oil patch during the late 1960s, I went to Eldorado where the Rangers were investigating a case of oil field vandalism. When I got there, I found two Rangers—Allee and Arthur Hill.

"Well, so much for 'One Ranger, One Riot,' " I popped off. "No, just one of us is here for the riot," Allee said, chewing on a cigar. "Arthur's here to stop the vandalism. I'm here to handle you."

Seventeen years after that smart aleck remark, I went to work for the DPS. Now it's my job to handle reporters with an attitude. I get a lot of telephone calls from reporters who want to know more about the history of the Rangers. Usually, they have just seen *Walker, Texas Ranger* on TV.

If someone is interested in doing what TV types call a "package" on the Rangers, I often suggest that we meet at the Texas Ranger Museum and Hall of Fame in Waco. I walk them through the museum, do an interview on the history of the Rangers, and then, if one is available, introduce the reporter to a real live Texas Ranger.

During one such interview in Waco, a golden-voiced TV anchor who was personally handling a *Walker*-inspired Ranger story, asked me to tell him the history of the Rangers in twenty-five words or less. I thought about it for a moment, inwardly fuming at the superficiality of the electronic media, and replied, "The Texas Rangers have evolved from a mounted paramilitary organization primarily concerned with Indian fighting into a civilian law-enforcement agency." That took twenty-one words, giving him a little change back.

The news reader pondered my condensed history for a moment and then asked, a hint of suspicion in his voice, "What's 'paramilitary' mean?"

Oh well, he wasn't from Texas.

One Ranger who made the transition from horse to automobile was Frank Hamer, a giant Texan credited with killing dozens of men in the line of duty. While that number surely was exaggerated, it's well documented that during a career that began in 1906 and continued through the 1930s, he did a lot of killing for the State of Texas in the name of law and order. My granddad said Hamer had the coldest eyes of any man he ever knew. And Granddad lived to be eighty-seven years old.

Though Hamer became a legend in his own time, the public had just about forgotten about the captain by 1967. That's the year the movie *Bonnie and Clyde* became a hit film. In the movie, Hamer is kidnapped by a sexy couple of Depression-era bank robbing killers portrayed by Warren Beatty and Faye Dunaway. Eventually freed by the couple, Hamer tracks them down and kills them in an ambush in Louisiana.

That Hamer played a key role in the killing of the couple was certainly accurate, but the captain never met Clyde Barrow and Bonnie Parker before he and three other officers gunned them down on May 23, 1934. Warner Bros. ended up paying an undisclosed amount of money to Hamer's family in settlement of a lawsuit filed by them over Hamer's unflattering portrayal in the movie.

This Wanted poster was circulated during
the search for Bonnie and Clyde.
PHOTO COURTESY OF MIKE COX.

Granddad, so far as I know, never saw the movie. But he had known Hamer before his reputation was solidified by the killing of Bonnie and Clyde.

I don't know for sure when Granddad first met Hamer. I imagine it was in the summer of 1922 when Hamer and other Rangers came to Corpus Christi to settle a bloody local political dispute involving the Ku Klux Klan. Granddad was editor of the Corpus Christi *Caller* at the time. During his tenure as editor, the KKK tossed a brick through the window of Granddad's house.

Five years later, Granddad was in Fort Worth, working as city editor of the Fort Worth *Press,* a long since extinct Scripps-Howard sheet. He had no shortage of news stories to cover. The West Texas oil boom was in full sway, as was Prohibition. With each major oil discovery, new towns sprang up like gushers. Despite federal law, bootleg whiskey flowed as freely as black crude.

One of the wildest of these alcohol-lubricated boomtowns was Borger, a brand new, wide open city of nearly 30,000 in Texas's Panhandle. When local authorities proved unable or unwilling to enforce the law, Governor Dan Moody declared a state of martial law and sent in National Guard troops and Texas Rangers.

When the train that would carry the Rangers to Borger left Fort Worth, Granddad was on it. The Ranger contingent was led by Captain Hamer.

Hamer had an almost animal-like instinct when it came to telling whether a man was packing a pistol. Granddad would learn that firsthand.

During the 1920s, Fort Worth was Texas's Chicago. When a whiskey raid that Granddad had gone along on deteriorated into a gunfight between the cops and bootleggers, Granddad found a telephone and called in a story as the lead continued to fly. Back in the *Press* newsroom, the rewrite man taking his dictation heard each shot in what we refer to today as "real time." Possibly on the heels of this incident, Granddad persuaded the Fort Worth police chief to commission him to carry a pistol.

Granddad started toting a gun, but not much of one: If he felt he was going somewhere where he might get in a tight place, he stuck a .25 caliber semiautomatic in his vest pocket. When he boarded the train for Borger with the Rangers, he had the little pistol.

When the train pulled out of the station in Fort Worth, Granddad was soon asleep, lulled into slumber by the rhythmic clacking of the rails.

As Granddad snored away, Hamer fished into Granddad's vest pocket and pulled out the pistol. Granddad woke up with the giant Ranger standing next to his seat, tossing the small pistol up and down in his big hand.

"Wilke," he said, "you better not ever shoot me with this thing and let me find out about it! When I go to hub a little hell, I want a .45."

Satisfied, Granddad was no threat to anyone with the .25, Hamer gave it back to him.

Once they got to Borger, one of the first things the Rangers did was order all the prostitutes out of town, some 1,100 of them. The ladies of the evening departed so fast that they left hundreds of fancy dresses on hangers at the local dry cleaning establishments. The Rangers collected all the dresses and donated them to Borger's few churches.

Years later, long after Borger had settled down to a quiet county seat town, I was there for a pheasant hunt. My host's grandfather had been a lawman during the boom and the Ranger takeover.

"Borger would've been a lot bigger today if Rangers hadn't run all the wimmen off," the old man liked to say.

Though Hamer was generally idolized by the press, he never had too much to say to reporters. This was back before the term news media had entered our jargon: Back then, the Rangers were more likely to refer to journalists as "damn reporters."

Though Hamer was the ranking Ranger captain, he was not

the only captain in Borger. Tom Hickman, captain of Fort Worth-based Company B, was a good friend of Granddad's. As the Rangers proceeded with their cleanup, Hickman cordially kept my grandfather apprized of Ranger activities and impending developments. These leaks were beginning to irritate Hamer.

At one point during the period of martial law, Hamer saw Granddad talking to a fellow Scripps-Howard reporter who was in Borger representing the Houston *Press*. The big Ranger walked over to the two average-sized men, towering over them like an oil derrick. He draped his long arms around each man's shoulder and remarked, "Now I know how Jesus Christ felt crucified between two thieves."

Three years after what came to be known as the Battle of Borger, Granddad and Hamer crossed paths again, this time in Sherman, a county seat town north of Dallas. Hamer and several other Rangers had been dispatched there to protect a black man accused of raping a white woman.

On May 9, 1930, a lynch mob charged the Grayson County courthouse in its frenzied effort to get to the prisoner. The Rangers managed to fend off the mob until someone set fire to the building. Smoke and flames forced Hamer and the other Rangers out of the building. They had left the prisoner locked in the county vault and he died, either from lack of air, intense heat, or the dynamite the mob later used to blow open the safe.

As word of the riot reached the outside world, reporters from Fort Worth and Dallas rushed to Sherman. Among them was Granddad. The Rangers, meanwhile, had retreated to the county jail to await the arrival of National Guardsmen. Granddad went to the jail and stayed with the Rangers. Periodically, someone fired a .22 round into the jail, the bullet rattling around against the bars.

After a while, the Rangers and Granddad got hungry. Granddad agreed to leave the jail and walk to a nearby drugstore for sandwiches and coffee. On his way back to the lockup, carrying a galvanized bucket full of steaming coffee and a sack of sandwiches, Granddad was accosted by one of the townsfolk and told he could not proceed. Stealing a page from Ranger crowd control technique, Granddad hit the man in the head with his metal flashlight, knocking him to the ground. The crowd parted and the Rangers had their sandwiches and coffee.

In 1932, when Miriam A. "Ma" Ferguson was elected governor, Hamer resigned his Ranger commission. When Hamer went on the trail of Bonnie and Clyde in 1934, Granddad was up in Ohio, working for the Scripps-Howard flagship, the Cleveland *Press*. Granddad eventually returned to Texas, but soon went into chamber of commerce work and had no further occasion to write about Hamer.

The old Ranger died of natural causes in the summer of 1955. He went to his grave with fourteen pieces of buckshot in his body, souvenirs from one of his many gun battles. I was six years old when he died. Though I never met him, I can say that Hamer and I shared the same barber.

In the mid-1990s, the senior barber at Austin's Sportsman's Barber Shop was Jimmy Frost. Nearly ninety years old, he was still cutting hair. As a young man, he had worked at a shop on Congress Avenue in downtown Austin. One of his customers was the noted Ranger captain, Frank Hamer.

Mr. Frost told me that Hamer never allowed him to completely cover his face when he was shaving him and never turned his back to the shop window. The Ranger captain either got a haircut or a shave, Mr. Frost said. Never both. A shave cost extra, and Hamer, being a state employee, had to make a choice.

By the time I became a customer at Mr. Frost's shop, he was getting a little shaky and only cut hair part-time. But just to be able to say that the man who once cut Frank Hamer's hair also gave me a haircut, one day I sat down in his chair and told him to take a little off the top and the sides. But when Mr. Frost grabbed his straight razor and asked if I'd like a shave, I politely declined. Hamer had earned his living being a tough guy—not me.

Like the ever-changing seasons, things have come full circle. My daughter Hallie is beginning to understand that Daddy writes and tells stories about the Rangers. Some day I'll tell her about getting a haircut from Frank Hamer's barber or she'll read it in this book.

As early as four, she already knew that there's something special about the Texas Rangers.

For a time, Hallie went through what I call her "kitty stage." One of her favorite things was meowing. On a visit to Amarillo, where my father lives, Hallie thrust her little feet into a pair of my boots and shuffled into the living room, where my father reposed in his easy chair.

When she meowed, my father said, "Hallie, I don't think kitties wear cowboy boots."

I did not see this, but according to my father, she squared her shoulders, looked him straight in the eye, and said, "Texas Ranger kitties do!"

MIKE COX is chief of media relations for the Texas Department of Public Safety, Texas's state law enforcement agency. He came to the DPS in 1985 after a twenty-year career as an award-winning newspaper reporter. Cox is the author of many books and numerous magazine articles, essays, and book reviews. In 1993 he was elected to receive membership in the Texas Institute of Letters. His book Texas Ranger Tales, *a collection of stories dealing with the history of the Texas Rangers, was the 1997 recipient of the Austin Writers League Violet Crown Award.*

Bandit Queen Belle Starr

BY DANNY SHIRLEY

★ My grandfather, Tom Shirley, used to gather us boys (my cousins and I) around him and tell us stories about Belle Starr. She was killed before he was born, of course, but his father, Oliver Shirley, was a young boy when Belle was active, and he had firsthand experiences. My granddad ("Dad") would tell us stories of how his father remembered Belle, Cole Younger, Frank and Jesse James, and other members of their gang coming to the Shirley Ranch and hiding from the lawmen, or recovering from gunshot wounds. Dad always glamorized these stories for us young'uns, so I don't know how much was actual fact and how much had become legend over the years. But, his father, Oliver, was Preston Shirley's son, and Preston was Belle's brother, so there's little doubt he had real exposure to Belle and her famous outlaw friends.

The Shirley family in 1913. Front row, left to right: Lessa, Ressa, Grandma Sarah, Grandpa Oliver. Back row, left to right: George, Walter, Elsie, Tom, Ethel. A pioneer family.

The thing I remember most about these old family stories was the fact that they involved real people and not some fictional characters or Hollywood stars. These people included Shirleys, and while they committed criminal acts and lived, for the most part, outside the law, I always thought of them as heroes. To me, sitting on the ground under the old redbud tree, and listening to Dad tell tales of Belle Starr, Cole Younger, Jesse James, and their good friend Blue Duck riding into some little Texas or Oklahoma town, robbing the bank and escaping in hail of gunfire was the ultimate adventure. Belle was a Shirley, and I was a Shirley, and that made us partners and kindred spirits. I never thought of her as anything but a wonderful young girl who had been driven to harass the Yankee carpetbaggers by the horror and loss of the Civil War. I loved her, and always secretly wished that I had been born in a time when I could have ridden with her.

TRAIN ROBBERS

BY JAMES B. GILLETT

☆ I well remember the hot July evening when Corporal Wilson arrived in our camp with his orders. The company had just had supper, and the horses had been fed and tied up for the night. We knew the sudden appearance of the corporal meant something of unusual importance. Soon Sergeant Nevill came hurrying to us with orders to detail a party for an immediate scout. Lieutenant Reynolds's orders had been brief, but to the point: "Bass is at Round Rock. We must be there as early as possible tomorrow. Make a detail of eight men and select those that have the horses best able to make a fast run. And you, with them, report to me here at my tent ready to ride in thirty minutes."

First Sergeant C. L. Nevill, Second Sergeant Henry McGee, Second Corporal J. B. Gillett, Privates Abe Anglin, Dave Ligon, Bill Derrick, and John R. and W. L. Banister were selected for the detail. Lieutenant Reynolds ordered two of our best little packmules hitched to a light spring hack, for he had been sick and was not in condition to make the journey horseback. In thirty minutes from the time Corporal Wilson reached camp we were mounted, armed, and ready to go. Lieutenant Reynolds took his seat in the hack, threw some blankets in, and Corporal Wilson, who had not had a minute's sleep for over thirty-six hours, lay down to get a little rest as we moved along. We left our camp on the San Saba River just at sunset and traveled in a fast trot and sometimes in a lope the entire night.

Our old friend and comrade, Jack Martin, then in the mercantile business at the little town of Senterfitt, heard us pass by in the night, and next morning said to some of his customers that hell was to pay somewhere as the Rangers had passed his store during the night on a dead run.

The first rays of the rising sun shone on us at the crossing of North Gabriel, fifteen miles south of Lampasas. We had ridden sixty-five miles that short summer night—we had forty-five miles yet to go before reaching Round Rock. We halted on the Gabriel for a breakfast of bread, broiled bacon, and black coffee. The horses had a bundle of oats each. Lieutenant Reynolds held his watch on us and it took us just thirty minutes to breakfast and be off again. We were now facing a hot July sun and our horses were beginning to show the effects of the hard ride of the night before and slowed down perceptibly. We did not halt again until we reached the vicinity of old Round Rock between one and two o'clock in the afternoon of Friday, July nineteenth. The lieutenant camped us on the banks of Brushy Creek and drove into new Round Rock to report his arrival to General Jones.

Bass had decided to rob the bank on Saturday, the twentieth. After his gang had eaten dinner in camp Friday evening they saddled their ponies and started over to town to take a last look at the bank and select a route to follow in leaving the place after the robbery. As they left camp, Jim Murphy, knowing that the bandits might be set upon at any time, suggested that he stop at May's store in old Round Rock and get a bushel of corn, as they were out of feed for their horses. Bass, Barnes, and Jackson rode on into town, hitched their horses in an alley just back of the bank, passed that building, and made a mental note of its situation. They then went up the main street of the town and entered Copprel's store to buy some tobacco. As the three bandits passed into the store, Deputy Sheriff Moore, who was standing on the sidewalk with Deputy Sheriff Grimes, said he thought: one of the newcomers had a pistol.

"I will go in and see," replied Grimes.

"I believe you have a pistol," remarked Grimes, approaching Bass and trying to search him.

"Yes, of course I have a pistol," said Bass. At the words the robbers pulled their guns and killed Grimes as he backed away to the door. He fell dead on the sidewalk. They then turned on Moore and shot him through the lungs as he attempted to draw his weapon.

At the crack of the first pistol Dick Ware, who was seated in a barber shop only a few steps away waiting his turn for a shave, rushed into the street and encountered the three bandits just as they were leaving the store. Seeing Ware rapidly advancing on them, Bass and his men fired on him at close range, one of their bullets striking a hitching post within six inches of his head and knocking splinters into his face. This assault never halted Ware for an instant. He was as brave as courage itself and never hesitated to take the most desperate chance when the occasion demanded it. For a few minutes he fought the robbers single-handed. General Jones, returning from the telegraph office, ran into the fight. He was armed with only a small Colt's double-action pistol, but threw himself into the fray. Connor and Harold had now come up and joined in the fusillade. The general, seeing the robbers on foot and almost within his grasp, drew in close and urged his men to strain every nerve to capture or exterminate them. By this time every man in the town who could secure a gun had joined in the fight.

The bandits had now reached their horses, and realizing their situation was critical they fought with the energy of despair. If ever a train robber could be called a hero, Frank Jackson proved himself one. Barnes was shot down and killed at his feet and Bass was mortally wounded and unable to defend himself or even mount his horse, while the bullets continued to pour in like hail from every quarter. With heroic courage, Jackson held the Rangers back with his pistol in his right hand while with his left he unhitched Bass's horse and assisted him into the saddle. Then, mounting his own horse, Jackson and his chief galloped out of the very jaws of hell itself. In their flight they passed through old Round Rock, and Jim Murphy, standing in the door of May's store, saw them go by on the dead run. The betrayer noticed that Jackson was holding Bass, pale and bleeding, in the saddle.

Lieutenant Reynolds, entering Round Rock, came within five minutes of meeting Bass and Jackson in the road. Before he reached town he met posses of citizens and Rangers in pursuit of the robbers. When the fugitives reached the cemetery they halted long enough for Jackson to secure a Winchester they had hidden in the grass there; then they left the road and were lost for a time. The battle was now over and the play spoiled by two overzealous deputies bringing on a premature fight, after they had been warned to be careful. Naturally, Moore and Grimes should have known that the three strangers were the Sam Bass gang.

Lieutenant Reynolds started Sergeant Nevill and his rangers early next morning in search of the flying bandits. After traveling some distance in the direction the robbers had last been seen we came upon a man lying under a large oak tree. Seeing we were armed, as we advanced upon him he called out to us not to shoot, saying he was Sam Bass, the man we were hunting.

After entering the woods the evening before, Bass had become so sick and faint from loss of blood that he could go no farther. Jackson had dismounted and wanted to stay with his chief, declaring he was a match for all their pursuers.

"No, Frank," replied Bass. "I am done for."

The wounded leader told his companion to tie his horse near at hand so he could get away if he should feel better during the night. Jackson was finally prevailed upon to leave Bass and make his own escape.

When daylight came Saturday morning Bass got up and walked to a nearby house. As he approached the place a lady, seeing him approaching covered with blood, left the house and started to run off, as she was alone with a small servant girl. Bass saw she was frightened and called to her to stop, saying he was perishing for a drink of water and would return to a tree not far away and lie down if she would only send him a drink. She sent him a quart cup of water, but the poor fellow was too far gone to drink it. We found him under this tree an hour later. He had a wound through the center of his left hand, the bullet having pierced the middle finger.

Bass's death wound was given him by Dick Ware, who used a .45 caliber Colt's long-barreled six-shooter. The ball from Ware's pistol struck Bass's belt, cutting two cartridges in pieces and entering his back just above the right hipbone. The bullet mushroomed badly, and made a fearful wound that tore the victim's right kidney all to pieces. From the moment he was shot until his death three days later Bass suffered untold agonies. As he lay on the ground Friday night where Jackson had left him the wounded man tore his undershirt into more than a hundred pieces and wiped the blood from his body.

Bass was taken to Round Rock and given the best of medical attention, but died the following day. While he was yet able to talk, General Jones appealed to him to reveal to the authorities the names of the confederates he had had that they might be apprehended.

"Sam, you have done much evil in this world and have only a few hours to live. Now, while you have a chance to do the state some good, please tell me who your associates were in those violations of the laws of your country."

Sam replied that he could not betray his friends, and that he might as well die with what he knew in him.

He was buried in the cemetery at old Round Rock, where a small monument was erected over his grave by a sister. Its simple inscription, defaced in recent years by relic-seekers, read:

SAMUEL BASS
Born July 21st, 1851
Died July 21st, 1878

A brave man reposes in death here.
Why was he not true?

JAMES B. GILLETT was a Texas Ranger from 1875 to 1881.

"Not Afraid to Go to Hell by Himself" A Short History of the Texas Rangers

by DALE L. WALKER

☆ The adage that to be a Texas Ranger you had to shoot like a Kentuckian, ride like a Mexican, track like an Indian, and fight like the devil, belongs to the mid-1830s when impresario Stephen F. Austin, whom Sam Houston called "the father of Texas," was developing his colony, San Felipe de Austin, in the then-northernmost Mexican province of Coahuila y Tejas. The settlement of about 4,000 Americans lay on high ground overlooking a bend of the Brazos River fifteen miles from the Gulf of Mexico and 175 miles from San Antonio de Bexar, and was being scourged by Indian raids: Karankawa war parties in the first years, later by the most feared of Texas tribes, the Comanches. To combat these marauders, settlers formed "ranging companies" of militiamen, mostly southern farmers, tradesmen, and adventurers, and these outriders functioned as the only law, and only army, Texas had in its formative years.

In 1835, Antonio Lopez de Santa Anna proclaimed himself dictator of Mexico and overthrew the Constitution of 1824, the liberal document which had opened Coahuila y Tejas to colonization. On November 3 that year, less than four months before the battle at the Alamo, a "consultation" was held in San Felipe de Austin and there fifty-eight prominent Texans set forth the foundation for the revolution against Mexico and, among lesser business, formally organized the Texas Rangers.

The original force of twenty-five was soon increased to three fifty-six-man companies, each member ordered to be ready "with a good horse, saddle, bridle and blanket and a hundred rounds of powder and ball." The riders were paid $1.25 a day and had as their assignment to protect Texans from Indians on the frontier between the Brazos and Trinity Rivers. Later the boundaries were moved westward to the Guadalupe River and to the duty of protecting settlers in the fledgling republic from the hostile Indians were added assignments to fight in the war with Mexico, and to guard Texas from raids by Mexican border bandits and from the miscellaneous depredations by American outlaws.

Among the early rangers who made significant marks in Texas history were:

- Ben McCulloch (1811–1862), a Tennessee frontiersman and friend of Davy Crockett's who fought as an artillerist with Sam Houston at San Jacinto, against Comanches at Plum Creek, Texas, in 1840, and with Zachary Taylor in the Mexican War at the head of a company of Rangers. (McCulloch became sheriff of Sacramento County, California, and U.S. marshal in Texas, and died at the Battle of Pea Ridge, Arkansas, in the Civil War.)

- William Alexander Anderson "Big Foot" Wallace (1817– 1899), a huge Virginian (6'2", 240 pounds and wearing a size twelve boot), became a buffalo hunter, a veteran of the Mier Expedition and the Mexican War, and served as a stagecoach driver. Texas folklorist J. Frank Dobie said Wallace "was as honest as daylight but liked to stretch the blanket and embroider his stories." He didn't need to. One of Wallace's exploits as a Texas Ranger occurred in the early 1840s when he tracked down a horse thief named Antonio Corrao and "executed" the man on the spot. Later, in a San Antonio cantina, Big Foot was accosted by a drunk who said he was a friend of Corrao's. Wallace turned, drew his Bowie knife from his belt, and said, "I killed Corrao and I want to kill all his friends, too." The Corrao partisan, so the story goes, fled town.

- John Coffee "Jack" Hays (1817–1883) was born at Little Cedar Lick, in the same part of Tennessee where his uncle, Andrew Jackson, had built his home, "The Hermitage." In his youth, Hays became acquainted with Sam Houston and in 1836 left Tennessee to join up with Houston, becoming at age nineteen an unpaid member of the Army of the Republic of Texas. By 1840 he was a captain of Rangers and, as was said of him, "He had mauled Indians from the Nueces to the Llano and never with more than fifty men." The Lipan Apache chief Flacco, who scouted for Hays, once said, "Me and Red Wing [another scout] not afraid to go to hell together. Captain Jack not afraid to go to hell by himself."

IN THE DECADE of the 1840s there is scarcely an Indian fight, border problem, or Mexican battle in which Jack Hays was not conspicuously involved.

In August 1840, a band of Comanches and some Kiowas swooped down east of San Antonio near Gonzales, looting, and killing in the sparsely settled communities and isolated farms. The raiders surrounded the town of Victoria, killed fifteen people, and stole nearly 2,000 horses, driving the vast herd ahead of them as they poured south along Plum Creek (near present-day Lockhart, Texas) to Lavaca Bay and toward the Gulf. They raided the town of Linnville, killed five people there, and after loading their loot on stolen mules, drove these, their *caballado* now swollen to 3,000 animals, and their prisoners, northward again.

Meantime, a force was gathering at Plum Creek to intercept and fight the Comanches: farmers, townspeople, soldiers led by veteran Indian fighter Captain Matthew "Old Paint" Caldwell, and Rangers such as Captain John J. Tumlinson, Ben McCulloch, and Jack Hays.

At daybreak on August 12, after Tonkawa scouts reported to the Texans that the Comanches and their great horse herd and loot-carrying mule train were but three miles away, the Texans rode out to meet them. The Comanches formed for battle, the warriors prancing about adorned with bright pieces of calico, tall stovepipe hats, and black swallow-tailed coats looted from Victoria and Linnville, others scurrying to drive

the horses ahead of them, and to hide their booty. One Comanche chief finally rode toward the Texans in a show of courage and was instantly shot down. The Texans then charged,
scattered the great *caballado* to the four winds and in a hard
fight that stretched over fifteen miles along Plum Creek, killed
at least eighty of the Comanche band while suffering but a
single casualty.

The Texans rescued three of the four captives taken at Linnville (at least one female captive was killed by the Comanches),
and recaptured many horses and most of the loot—mostly silverware, cloth goods, and whiskey.

JACK HAYS ALSO took a significant part in the events leading
up to the disastrous Mier Expedition of 1842–1843, a signal
event in early Texas—and Texas Ranger—history that was to
have ramifications later during the war with Mexico.

In September 1842, a Mexican army of at least a thousand
troops commanded by a French mercenary general and crony
of Santa Anna's named Adrian Woll, invaded Texas, and captured San Antonio. Woll's mission was a "demonstration" to
show the Texans that Mexico did not recognize their "republic" and would countenance no annexation of the territory by
the United States. Woll made his point and quickly abandoned
the town, but on September 17 his retreating force was met by
a small contingent of militiamen under Matthew Caldwell, who
sent out an appeal for more volunteers with a message ending,
"Huzza! Huzzah for Texas!"

Among those who answered the call was twenty-five-year-
old Captain Jack Hays at the head of a Ranger company that
included Ben McCulloch and Big Foot Wallace. Hays, in con-
tributing to the effort to force the Frenchman and his army
back to the Rio Grande, led one cavalry charge into Woll's
artillery, the result being that every Mexican gunner was killed
at his post by Ranger pistols and newly issued shotguns.

Woll is said to have offered $500 in gold for Jack Hays's
head.

Meantime, Sam Houston, president of the Republic of Texas, dispatched orders for the gathering of a volunteer army to the Rio Grande to harass Woll's retreating force and, in fact, to make an answering "demonstration" by invading northern Mexico. This "army," consisting of Jack Hays and his company of Rangers plus an undisciplined rabble scrapped together from the settlements, 750 men in all, was led by Brigadier General Alexander Somervell, and Houston's orders contained this admonition: "You may rely upon the gallant Hays and his companions . . . Godspeed you."

Somervell and his rough border troopers rode south from San Antonio on November 8, 1842, and captured Laredo on December 8. Here the abysmal quality of the force showed its face: the volunteers terrified the citizenry, carried off and raped a number of women, and plundered the town. Somervell attempted to exact some punishment for these acts, returned to the town *alcalde* as much of the loot as he could find and arrested a number of his volunteers. As a result of these acts of apology, about 200 of the men simply left Somervell's army and rode back home.

The general then led his depleted and near-mutinous force downriver, crossed the Rio Grande, and captured the Mexican town of Guerrero. But now his dogs of war had lost bark and bite, had become so rife with dissension that Somervell abandoned the expedition and retreated north with about 250 men, among them Hays and McCulloch. Of the 300 who decided, or were perhaps ordered by Somervell, to continue Houston's now-faltering invasion, four were notable Ranger captains: Big Foot Wallace; Ewen Cameron, described as "a powerful Scotsman"; William N. Eastland, who had fought with Houston at San Jacinto; and Samuel H. Walker, a thirty-two-year-old Maryland stalwart who had fought with Andrew Jackson in the Seminole War in Florida.

The 300 freebooters from Somervell's army elected one William S. Fisher their commander and marched down the Mexican side of the river to the adobe hamlet of Mier, near Camargo.

There the Texans were surrounded by a far superior Mexican force and, with Fisher wounded, fell apart into squabbling factions. After being assured they would be treated as prisoners of war and kept on the border during negotiations for their return, the Texans took a vote and surrendered.

The promises were lies. In late December the prisoners were marched south to Monterey and in early February 1843, set out again, to a place called Hacienda Salado near Saltillo. On the march through the desert the Rangers laid plans for escape and at daybreak on February 11, Cameron and Walker disarmed a guard and with Eastland's and Wallace's assistance, captured the Mexican ammunition stores, took several other prisoners with them and set out north toward the Rio Grande.

In the trackless desert above Saltillo, the escapees (the exact number unknown) became lost on the waterless flatlands, struggling vaguely northward. They abandoned their arms, survived a few days eating grasshoppers and snakes, dug into the sand for precious moisture to relieve their swollen tongues, and finally were found by Mexican soldiery, placed in irons, and returned to Salado.

In Mexico City, the furious Santa Anna ordered that all the captured Americans be shot. Only after outcries by American and British ministers did the Mexican president relent and modify his order. Now, he decreed, every tenth man would be executed.

At Salado, the decimation order was put into effect: There were 176 Texas survivors of the Mier raid and so a pitcher containing 159 white beans and seventeen black ones was carried to the prisoners. Those who drew the black beans were to be shot.

Big Foot Wallace, who noticed the black beans seemed to have been poured on top of the white ones, managed to get his huge paw deep into the pitcher and drew a white bean.

In fact, all four of the Rangers drew white beans, but Ewen Cameron, who had led the escape, had earned the special hatred of his captor, the Salado *comandante* General Antonio

Canales, and after receiving a sanction from Santa Anna, Canales ordered Cameron to be executed with the other seventeen. The survivors were marched to Mexico City and imprisoned. Ranger historian Walter Prescott Webb says they were "horribly mistreated," but all were finally liberated before the U.S.–Mexican War erupted in the spring of 1846.

Wallace and Sam Walker would return to Mexico that year, riding with a victorious army—and would find retribution for the experiences at Salado.

CAPTAIN JACK HAYS, although seldom credited for it, revolutionized mounted warfare in 1843 by the simple expediency of recognizing the worth of a new weapon.

In 1836, the year of Texas independence, Samuel Colt, that Hartford, Connecticut, avatar of Yankee ingenuity, began producing a new percussion revolver in his struggling Paterson, New Jersey factory. The weapon was a .36 caliber pistol with a folding trigger, blued steel frame, five-shot cylinders (with spare cylinders to be carried in belt pouches) and a rifled barrel for a range and accuracy far exceeding that of the muzzleloaders then in use. The U.S. War Department was showing little interest in the weapon (it was somewhat fragile and prone to misfiring) but Colt sold a quantity of them to the Republic of Texas and among those who obtained the pistols were Jack Hays and his company of Rangers.

The first documented use of the new colts by the Rangers took place in the spring of 1844 when Hays and fifteen men, including Mier veteran Sam Walker, left their Medina River camp near San Antonio to scout against "hostiles"—Comanches—in the Pedernales River country around present-day Johnson City. A Comanche band led by Yellow Wolf was watching them and his band soon engaged the Texans, preceding the charge with a shower of arrows. Hays and his men, backed into a stand of timber along the river, managed to rout the Indians from the woods, then turned to face Yellow Wolf and about seventy-five warriors coming toward them, lances lowered. Hayes ordered his men to stay their fire until the Indians were within pistol range, then the Paterson Colts (each Ranger had a brace of them) were fired in a crashing volley as Hays shouted "Powder-burn them!"— in other words, shoot at closest quarters. A hundred rounds banged into the Indian vanguard in a matter of seconds and the Comanches broke and ran as the Rangers snapped their spare cylinders into their gun frames. The Texans mounted up and pursued; Yellow Wolf and his remaining band rallied momentarily; Walker and another ranger were wounded; another Ranger named Peter Fohr was killed; and the Texans withdrew again, this time to the river. As the Comanches prepared their frontal charge, Hays ordered Ranger Richard A. Gillespie, wounded from a lance thrust, to take his muzzleloader and draw a bead on Yellow Wolf. Gillespie shot the chief from his horse and the startled Comanches fled, dragging their leader's body with them.

Hays later reported twenty-three Comanches dead, another thirty wounded. He added, "Had it not been for the five-shooting pistols, I doubt what the consequences would have been."

Later, Hays sent Sam Walker to New Jersey to help Colt modify the weapon. The result was the famed six-shot, durable and easy-loading Walker Colt, soon to be adopted for use by U.S. cavalry in Mexico.

ON DECEMBER 29, 1845, Texas was admitted to statehood. The Mexican government had previously served notice that annexation would be regarded as an act of war but that shrewd, humorless expansionist, President James Knox Polk, stole a march or two on Mexico. He declared war on May 13, 1846, after the opening two battles, at Palo Alto and Reseca de la Palma had been fought by General Zachary Taylor north of the Rio Grande.

Jack Hays, now a colonel of volunteers, organized and commanded six companies of Rangers for service in the Mexican War, and they fought with Generals Taylor and Winfield Scott, operating as cavalry and reconnaissance troops and often treating the war as their private time of reprisal for the Mier executions.

The Rangers in Mexico were known for their steadfastness, their stealth, and their brutality. Ranger Captain Ben McCulloch, for example, led forty men through Mexican lines to find a route from Matamoros west to Monterey. Then he and his little force traveled 250 miles in ten days, raided several villages and *rancheros* without once being discovered by the Mexican army.

Jack Hays, described by his peers as "a gentleman of purest character," was ultimately responsible for the reputation for brutality the Ranger regiment earned in Mexico. Samuel Chamberlain, a Bostonian and dragoon private in Taylor's army, described in his post-war memoirs the "uncouth costumes and bearded faces" of Hays's men and of their "lean and brawny forms, fierce wild eyes, and swaggering manners." Chamberlain said the Rangers were "fit representatives of the outlaws which make up the population of the Lone Star State."

To the Mexican citizenry the Rangers were *Los Tejanos Diablos* and *Los Tejanos Sanguinarios*, looting, raping, and killing innocents as they ostensibly sought out Mexican soldiers and Santa Anna adherents. The names became especially poignant after the capture of Mexico City on September, 1847, when, after a Ranger was killed on a city street, Hays's enraged men rampaged through the capital, killing eighty citizens in realization.

Now, Ranger Sam Walker, described as a "rather short, slender, spare, slouchy man with reddish hair, small reddish beard, mild blue eyes, and a quiet, kindly manner," who had fought valiantly throughout the war as a regular army captain of mounted rifles, died as the curtain on the war fell. He was at the besieged city of Pueblo in the fall of 1847 and on October 9, in a battle against Santa Anna's army in the village of Humantla, was shot through the head and chest. When his men saw his brutalized corpse they burst into tears.

After the war, Jack Hays quit the Rangers and led an expedition to California via the Gila River route, and in January 1849, reached San Francisco. He was elected sheriff there, sent for his wife, and joined in partnership with the Surveyor General of California John Clar, in founding the city of Oakland. Hays died there in April 1883.

Following the Mexican War, the Rangers returned to patrolling duties, concentrating on ending the persistent Comanche threats in the east, south, and northern reaches of the vast new state of Texas.

AMONG THE GREATEST Rangers in the post-war era was Captain John Salmon "Rip" Ford (1815–1897), a South Carolinian who came to Texas just after the San Jacinto battle of 1836. He was a man of varied talents—a tough frontiersman, newspaper editor, politician, and sometime physician—who commanded scouts for Hays in the Mexican War and whose nickname (from the tombstone epitaph) derived from the death notices he sent to the families of Rangers killed in battle. Among Ford's greatest Ranger exploits occurred in May 1858 when he led a force of 215 men—rangers and militiamen plus Shawnee, Tonkawa, and Anadarko Indian "friendlies"— against Comanche raiders. Ford and his men tracked the Indians to the Canadian River in Indian Territory and attacked a village of about 300 Comanches led by a chief known as Iron Shirt (or Iron Jacket—the name describing the ancient Spanish chain-mail breastplate he wore into battle). In an eight-hour battle Ford's force killed Iron Shirt and seventy-six Comanches, took eighteen prisoners and 300 horses while losing only two men killed and two wounded.

FORD AND THE Rangers were also deeply involved in the so-called "Cortina Wars" of 1859–1860, bringing to an end the border raids by the renowned cattle rustler, Juan Nepomuceno "Cheno" Cortina, who had fought in northern Mexico battles against Zachary Taylor in the late war and who gained notoriety as a sort of Robin Hood of Mexico for his talent of extracting Mexican citizens from Texas jails.

In September 1859 Cortina and his band rode across the border from Matamoros, captured the Texas town of Brownsville, and were pursued by Rangers under Captain W. C. Tobin who captured and hanged a Cortina lieutenant. After Brownsville was retaken, a force of Texas troops, including 120 Rangers, routed Cortina and his 350-man guerilla army at Rio Grande City, killing sixty of his men. Cortina, slippery as the fabled Robin Hood, escaped but was defeated again the next year, eight miles upriver from Brownsville, by Rip Ford and 100 of his rangers.

Cortina again evaded capture, subsequently became governor of Tamaulipas and died in Mexico City in 1894.

DURING THE CIVIL War, most of the Rangers fought for the Confederacy and during the Reconstruction era, continued their pursuit of Indian raiders, Mexican bandits, miscellaneous outlaws, rustlers, and train and stagecoach robbers.

In the post–Civil War period, Leander H. McNelly made his mark in Ranger history late in his brief life. He was a Virginian who came to Texas with his family in 1860 at the age of sixteen. He had fought at Valverde in the New Mexico campaign of the Civil War, and later at Galveston, and became a feared Confederate guerilla leader along the lower Mississippi, known for his soft voice and shy nature. In the summer of 1874, after the Rangers were reorganized, McNelly joined up and was quickly thrust into resolving a rustling operation in Matamoros headed by a former Cortina lieutenant named Guadalupe Espinoza. The Rangers trapped thirteen of Espinoza's men on the American side of the Rio Grande and killed them. McNelly shot Espinoza's horse and when the rustler ran into the swampy brush along the river, the Ranger dismounted, pulled his rifle from its boot, and calmly walked into the thicket. The other

Texans soon heard six pistol shots, then the crack of a .44 caliber Winchester. McNelly walked out, sheathed the carbine, and calmly mounted up.

On July 13, 1875, in the Brownsville plaza, the corpses of Espinoza and thirteen of his rustlers were place on display, laid out neatly like a row of adobe bricks in the summer sun. McNelly was tubercular, an effect of his rigorous Civil War service, and in 1877 he died on his farm in Washington County, Texas at the age of thirty-three.

THE 1870s ALSO produced celebrated exploits against the worst killer in Western history, John Wesley Hardin, and one of the best-known outlaws, Sam Bass.

In Comanche, Texas, in May 1874, Hardin shot and killed a deputy sheriff named Charley Webb when Webb tried to arrest him in a local saloon. With a $4,000 reward offered for his capture and the rangers on his trail, Hardin fled to Louisiana, was arrested there four months after the murder but escaped his captors. For three years he was not seen—in Texas, at least—but in August 1877, acting on various fragments of information, Ranger Lieutenant John B. Armstrong, who had trained under Leander McNelly, tracked the killer to Pensacola, Florida. Acting alone, the Ranger found Hardin sitting in a passenger car at the Pensacola railroad station with four of his cronies. Armstrong boarded the train, drew his long-barreled Colt .45, entered Hardin's car, and commanded the killer and his cohorts to surrender. Hardin is said to have recognized the weapon Armstrong held as the one favored by Rangers, exclaimed "Texas, by God!" and reached for his own sidearm. Everything happened in a few desperate seconds: Hardin's gun got hung up in his suspenders and one of the Hardin gang members fired quickly and blew Armstrong's hat off. The Ranger shot this man through the heart and wrestled for Hardin's weapon, ending up kicking the killer into an empty seat, smacking him on the head with the .45 and putting him in irons. Hardin was unconscious two hours and when he awoke was the Ranger's prisoner on a train heading across Alabama toward Texas. There he received a sentence of twenty-five years in Huntsville prison for the murder of Charley Webb. Armstrong collected the $4,000 reward—Rangers were bounty hunters of a sort in that era—and used it to build a ranch in southeast Texas.

The Ranger who smoked out Sam Bass was Major John B. Jones, originally of South Carolina, a college graduate, Civil War veteran, and fighter against Comanches, Kiowas, and Apaches. Known as the "Littlest Ranger," Jones was actually a respectable five-foot-eight, weighed 135 wiry pounds, had black hair, and moustache, and was considered a fine horseman as he rode at break-neck speed on his bay stallion Golden Eye.

Jones already had earned a certain celebrity in the Rangers for his dramatic 1877 clean up of outlaw operations in Kimble County, Texas, along the Llano River, around the towns of Bear Creek, and Fredericksburg. He carried a list of forty-five known outlaws, and he and his Rangers, in a maneuver that newspapers called "the Kimble County Surround," succeeded in capturing forty-one of them in ten days without shedding a drop of Ranger or outlaw blood.

Jones had a spy in Sam Bass's gang who informed the Ranger leader that there would be a bank or train robbery in the town of Round Rock, a few miles north of Austin, on a certain day in July 1877. Jones and three other Rangers came to the town a few days before the planned holdup and took local law officers into their confidence in setting their trap. On July 20, two deputies stationed in a dry goods store next to the bank were shot trying to arrest Bass while outside three gang members ran for their horses. One of them was shot dead, and Ranger George Harrell wounded Bass, who still managed to get on his horse and flee. The next morning, John Jones and the Rangers trailed Bass and found him propped under a mesquite tree north of town. "Don't bother shooting, boys," the outlaw said. "I am the man you are looking for." Bass lived two more days, dying on his twenty-seventh birthday. As Walter Prescott Webb wrote, "Every attention was given him by Major Jones."

DURING THE MEXICAN Revolution that began in 1910, the Rangers' reputation suffered much as it had during the Mexican War of 1846–47. The Texans, supposed to be protecting the Texas border, were accused of shooting innocent Mexican citizens, illegally crossing into Mexican territory, performing as bounty hunters, and being generally uncontrollable.

In 1919, the Rangers were again reorganized, the force cut to seventy-six men, then were merged with the Highway Patrol becoming in their centennial year of 1935 a branch of the Texas Department of Public Safety.

They remain so today, the oldest law enforcement agency in America.

THE STORY IS still told, with endless variations: an outlaw gang was terrorizing a Texas town and the mayor sent for the Rangers to restore order. Soon a single horseman rode in and tethered his horse in front of City Hall. The panicked mayor asked, "Where are your men? We need at least a company of Rangers!" "Why?" the lone Ranger responded, "You've only got one gang, right?"

The tale, while no doubt apocryphal, illustrates—as does the Ranger statue at Love Field Airport in Dallas, upon which is inscribed the legend "One Riot, One Ranger"—a salient fact: for 160 and more years, the Texas Rangers have been, in the words of the premiere Texas historian T. R. Fehrenbach, "one of the most colorful, efficient, and deadly bands of irregular partisans on the side of law and order the world has seen."

DALE L. WALKER an award-winning historical writer, is the author of seventeen books, the most recent of which is Pacific Destiny. *He lives in El Paso, Texas.*

Frontiers Old and New

BY DOUGLAS V. MEED

⭐ As a young boy I grew up listening to tales of high adventure on the Texas frontier and the borderlands with Mexico. My father, a soldier, came to the Mexican border in 1916 to protect against the raids of the various brigands that roamed the Rio Grande Valley during those revolutionary times.

As I sat wide-eyed at my Dad's feet he recounted stories of those exciting but bloody years when Pancho Villa, General "Black Jack" Pershing, *bandidos*, and Texas Rangers clashed in the hot and passionate lands of South Texas and the Mexican state of Chihuahua. But mostly he told me of the adventures of my great-grandfather, Emil Frederick Wurzbach, who he met at the family home in San Antonio while courting the young lady who became my mother. Waiting in the drawing room until my mother made her appearance, the old frontiersman regaled my dad with tales of his adventures on the wild Texas frontier.

Emil, called Dutch by his compadres, was eight years old when he arrived with his family at Galveston Harbor in 1846. They were among those idealistic bands of German immigrants who grew restive at the limited opportunities offered in the old country that supported the pomposities of the titled aristocrats reigning over the patchwork of German states.

They were mostly well-educated people who yearned not only for economic opportunity and political freedom but dreamed of a Texas, vast, uncrowded, and unspoiled; land unencumbered by the crowded, regimented, and growing urbanized societies of Europe. As the poet Emma Lazarus wrote, "They yearned to breathe free."

Settling mostly around San Antonio, New Braunfels, and the

Hill Country, they made an unprecedented peace treaty with the Comanches and by hard, very hard work, many achieved their dream. But young Emil was not content with the life of the prospering merchant or productive farmer. He was one of the frontier youths who suffered from incurably itchy feet—what his forebearers termed *"die wanderlust."* And like some itinerant knight, he roamed the frontier seeking new adventures, driven by an insatiable desire to see what was over the next hill.

Emil "(Dutch)" Frederick Wurzbach.
PHOTO COURTESY OF DOUGLAS V. MEED.

He was not a leader in the conventional sense. He commanded no troops, acquired no vast lands, nor did he gain great wealth. He battled Apaches and Comanches as a sixteen-year-old Texas Ranger; hauled wagons over the desert, prospected for gold, drove herds of wild Longhorns, and fought the hell out of the Yankee legions.

He knew "Big Foot" Wallace, broke horses for Robert Neighbors, trailed with Albert Sidney Johnson. He charged the Yankee lines at Newtonia alongside a wild bunch of Cherokee Indians and Missouri guerrillas, and he helped to shatter a Union invasion at Mansfield, Louisiana, under a general who was a French prince.

Like many of his compadres, he was present but unnoticed in the annals of the day. He didn't give a damn for rank, titles, wealth, or outward signs of prestige. On the frontier, men were judged by their honesty, loyalty, industriousness, and courage. You worked hard for your family, you helped your neighbor, and you told the truth. Nothing else much mattered.

After the War Between the States ended, Dutch settled down, married Matilda Stowe, and operated a small ranch where he both increased his herds and fathered thirteen children. He died peacefully in his sleep when he was ninety-two years old.

One could not hope to match Dutch's adventures, but his frontier philosophy, tested in hardship and danger, was a way of life that one could, however imperfectly, try to emulate.

But, one wondered on reaching adulthood, could those pioneer virtues survive in twentieth century Texas, where automobiles replaced the horse, the urban megalopolis crowded into rural communities, people worked in large organizations, consumerism was rife, and television babble replaced the easy conversation of neighbors?

As a young reporter on a Houston newspaper during the post–World War II boomdays in Texas, I learned that the old values were alive and well, at least in some people, for I met Johnny Klevenhagen.

Johnny was the paradigm of the unchanging Texas Ranger. He was tall, lean, leathery with blue-gray eyes that could sparkle with humor and sometimes mist with sympathy. He bridged the gap between the old and the new ways of the Rangers, holding fast to the best traditions of dedication, honesty, and courage while eagerly grasping new and scientific methods of detection.

Klevenhagen solved complex murders, shot it out with bandits, snuffed a race riot, shut down Galveston vice, and arrested an alleged mafia hitman. He tracked killers on horseback in the Brazos River bottoms and confronted callous murderers in the concrete canyons of Dallas, Houston, and San Antonio.

During his career Texas underwent one of its most dramatic changes. During the depression-wracked 1930s the state was rural with agriculture, ranching, and the growing petroleum industry—mainstays of the economy. By the end of the 1950s however, the state had undergone a massive transformation. World War II and rapid industrialization had turned Texas into a land of big cities with exploding populations. Petrochemical complexes, steel mills, shipyards, and aircraft plants changed the face of the land.

It was a far cry from the Texas of 1912 when Johnny was born on a hardscrabble ranch in Comal County where people were outnumbered by both cattle and rattlesnakes. In that harsh environment he learned to do chores, ride and rope only a few years after he learned to walk. Responsibility and initiative came with the hard work while excuses and complaining were simply not in the makeup of Texas ranch lads.

Johnny first met Texas Rangers when some of his family's cattle were rustled and the Rangers were called in to investigate. They were big men with high boots, big sombreros, wearing a distinctive badge fashioned from a Mexican silver peso. Their "Thumbbuster" Colt six-shooters were slung on belt holsters or stuck in their trousers to lay across their bellies. They walked with the swagger of men who feared little and knew much. From his first glimpse of these swashbucklers, Johnny determined his life would belong to the Texas Rangers.

But that ambition had to wait. Johnny was too young and his dad needed his help on the ranch so he dropped out of school during the eighth grade and went to work full-time. In 1930 he joined the San Antonio police as an underage motorcycle cop. After a decade of hard study and a reputation as an excellent investigator, he rose to the rank of chief investigator for the Bexar County District Attorney. In 1940 he was selected as a Texas Ranger where he soon became a legend to lawmen and a curse to the underworld. Following spectacular successes he was promoted to captain of the Ranger company whose jurisdiction included the turbulent Houston and Gulf Coast areas.

For all of the lethal gunfights, Johnny's proudest claim was, "I never fired the first shot. I never shot a man unless he first fired at me."

His reluctance to kill was put to the test one afternoon when he cornered an escaped felon on a street corner in downtown Houston. As the Ranger approached, the criminal drew his gun and started shooting. At that moment a city bus pulled up beside the gunman disgorging a stream of men, women, and small children.

"I couldn't shoot back," Johnny said later, although bullets were buzzing past his head, "and I damned sure couldn't run, so I waited until the bus driver roared off and his passengers ran down the street, giving me a clear shot." He fired once with his .45 and the bullet hit the sleeve of the gunman's coat, jarring the pistol out of his hand. After Johnny jailed the man his laconic report to Ranger headquarters stated, "Shot him loose from his pistol and put him under arrest."

Johnny was tough but he was also fair and kind and never lied. His widow, Viola, said, "Over the Christmas holidays we used to get dozens of cards postmarked from the state prisons. They [prisoners] never showed any bitterness, but always thanked Johnny for being fair and square with them."

If Johnny had a fault, it was too much dedication to duty. On a tough case he would work eighteen hours straight, grab a sandwich, drink a cup of coffee, smoke too many cigarettes, and stumble into bed for a few hours and then repeat he process.

He dedicated his life to the protection of the people of Texas and his zeal proved fatal. Overwork finally caught up with him and after his second heart attack he died in 1958. He was only forty-six years old.

There were many accolades from the governor, the legislature, civic leaders, and lawmen, testifying that Johnny Klevenhagen was one of the great captains of the Texas Rangers. Perhaps the most telling compliment was paid by fellow Ranger Jerome Preiss who told newsmen, "What really inspired me about Johnny was that no matter how tired he was, how long he had worked, he always had time to pat some kid on the head who wanted to talk with him. That made him a great man in my eyes."

Yes, the old frontier virtues lived on in the twentieth century in many men like Johnny Klevenhagen; but what of the twenty-first century? Can those same standards survive in the go-go society of a Texas where high plains adventure has given way to high tech?

I believe they can, albeit in different ways. In the rash of new ventures, a handshake and a smile between Texans can still breed more confidence among young entrepreneurs than a bevy of lawyers.

University laboratories are bulging with eager young men and women searching for new truths with the same steadfastness with which their forebears cultivated new lands.

If there are no longer barn raisings, volunteers flock to offer unpaid services to hospitals, libraries, and disheartened children.

Time and again, National Guardsmen and women are called to remote lands on humanitarian missions. They leave family and careers without complaint and serve with courage and enthusiasm.

In your neighbors, and proudly in your children, you still see the fierce individualism of the pioneer. They face a challenging future with the same courage and optimism with which those early immigrants marched confidently into a strange and savage frontier.

Texans still maintain a strong, if sometimes crusty, independence of thought even if their lack of conformity sometimes seems abrasive.

They prefer to place on their own shoulders responsibilities for family and community rather than rely on the dictates of more distant authorities.

There are tough problems ahead. Life in Texas will never be a continual tea party. It never was. But guided by their heritage of those old time virtues of hard work, neighborliness, honesty, and courage, these newer Texans will prevail.

Dutch and Johnny would be proud.

DOUGLAS V. MEED, a highly respected journalist and editor with several major Texas newspapers, has served as a foreign service officer with the U.S. Information Agency. He is the author of several books, including Texas Ranger Johnny Klevenhagen. *He lives in Round Rock, Texas.*

Be Good to the Indians

BY PA-HA-YOU-CO

⭐ BROTHERS: Never give up your efforts to make peace with your Red brothers. Whenever any of them come to see you, smoke the pipe of peace with them and give them good talk before they leave. If you do that, everybody will know you are appointed by the great chief, and they will come to you to make peace. And you must give them presents when they come. That will not hurt you, but if they should cut your meat off, that would hurt you.

The reason I came here was to bring the white prisoner and deliver him up to you. I know his people are anxious about him. I do not keep my words hid nor tell lies, but what I say is true. I am anxious and so are all my tribe to make peace, and what I say now I will stick to as long as I live.

My people are now gone to the Spanish country [Mexico] for foolishness, and when they get their fill of foolishness they will come back here.

When Colonel Eldridge told me that Texas wished to make peace with me, I was glad. I listened to his talk good. And I have told Buffalo Hump that he must not forget what he heard at the last council, but hold fast to it and never give it up.

When I was a young man we were accustomed to go among the white people and trade. I am anxious that that time should return. We wish to be at peace with all, and raise our children at peace. My war chief, The-Bear-With-a-Short-Tail, is brave, but he prefers peace to war. He has come to see that peace is good. He is next war chief to Buffalo Hump. Now we love our White brethren the same as our Red brothers.

When my brother came back from the council we were all glad to hear his words, for they were good. All the other tribes of Indians know me, and know that I wish for peace with all. You that are listening to me may think that I am telling lies, but the Great Spirit who looks upon me now knows that I speak truth.

Whenever any of my men or chiefs come in to see you, you must give them presents; so that when they return home the people may see that the whites are friendly. The Spaniards when they send for us to make peace, steal our horses; but we believe that what the white people tell us is true.

The buffaloes are close by here, and we are obliged to come down with our families among them. All tribes and nations have some bad men who will steal, but none but my good men shall come, and we will do our best to keep all from stealing.

In the spring some of my men will be down about San Antonio, and they may wish to go into the settlements. If they do, they will come with a white flag, so that the whites may know they are friendly and not hurt them. We shall range from the Colorado to the Guadalupe, and we wish to be friendly. I mention this so that they may know that we will be there hunting, and not to steal.

The Wichitas are like dogs. They will steal. You may feed a dog well at night, and he will steal all your meat before morning. This is the way with the Wichitas.

This is all I have to say. If you listen to my talk, I shall be glad, and everything will be good.

Beyond this speech, little is known of Comanche Chief PA-HA-You-Co.

The Death of Flaco

BY SAM HOUSTON

EXECUTIVE DEPARTMENT,
WASHINGTON, MARCH 28, 1843.

To the Lipans.

MY BROTHERS: My heart is sad. A dark cloud rests upon your
nation. Grief has sounded in your camp. The voice of Flaco is
silent. His words are not heard in council. The chief is no more.
His life has fled to the Great Spirit. His eyes are closed. His
heart no longer leaps at the sight of the buffalo! The voices of
your camp are no longer heard to cry, "Flaco has returned from
the chase!" Your chiefs look down on the earth and groan in
trouble. Your warriors weep. The loud voice of grief is heard
from your women and children. The song of birds is silent. The
ear of your people heard no pleasant sound. Sorrow whispers
in the winds. The noise of the tempest passes—it is not heard.
Your hearts are heavy.

The name of Flaco brought joy to all hearts. Joy was on
every face! Your people were happy. Flaco is no longer seen in
the fight; his voice is no longer heard in battle; the enemy no
longer makes a path for his glory; his valor is no longer a guard
for your people; the right arm of your nation is broken. Flaco
was a friend to his white brothers. They will not forget him.
They will remember the Red warrior. His father will not be
forgotten. We will be kind to the Lipans. Grass shall not grow
in the path between us. Let your wise men give the council of
peace. Let your young men walk in the white path. The gray-

headed men of your nation will teach wisdom. I will hold my red brothers by the hand.

Thy brother,
SAM HOUSTON.

Before coming to Texas, SAM HOUSTON was a soldier, lawyer, member of the United States House of Represenatives, and the governor of Tennessee. In Texas, he served as commander in chief of the Republic of Texas Army, and defeated Santa Anna at San Jacinto. He was twice president of the Republic of Texas (1836–38 and 1841–44), a United States senator from Texas (1846–59), and the governor of Texas (1859–61). He was removed from office for refusing to take the oath of alligiance to the Confederacy.

LOST AND FOUND IN A BORDER TOWN

BY RANDY LEE EICKHOFF

> . . . AFTER THE KINGFISHER'S WING
> HAS ANSWERED LIGHT TO LIGHT, AND IS SILENT,
> THE LIGHT IS STILL
> AT THE STILL POINT OF THE TURNING WORLD.
> —T. S. Eliot,
> *"Burnt Norton"*

⭐ Ghosts ramble the old streets of El Paso despite the asphalt covering the bricks and limestone quarried from the Franklin Mountains that loom above the city like barren breasts. She is a battered old whore, ugly by day but when one climbs up the mountains or stops on the road going through Smuggler's Gap at night, the glittering lights, yellow and white to the Rio Grande, then blue on the Mexican side of the river, sparkle like diamonds on the plain to the Sierra Blanco and Hueco Mountains in the east. Then, she is beautiful and it is only when one descends to the city streets that one finds the ugliness.

At least, that is a metaphor for the city that vainly tries to slip away from its Old West image of gunfighters and prostitutes, smugglers, corrupt politicians, rustlers, and horse thieves. Pancho Villa lived here and used to walk down the cobbled street to the Elite Confectionary, an ice cream parlor where each day where he had an ice cream cone promptly at two P.M. Vanilla. He was addicted to vanilla as much as a cook, in the sprawling houses of the rich on Rim Road that look arrogantly out over the rest of the city, will sneak sips of sherry while preparing meals for the Old Moneyed and, more recently, nouveau riche. General "Black Jack" Pershing lived here as well and chased Villa throughout northern Mexico after the self-styled general led a raid into Columbus, New Mexico, igniting national indignation with his boldness. Albert Jennings Fountain lived here while he helped bilk the Tigua Indians out of their lands with others of his "ring."

This is the city where citizens would gather with picnic lunches along the banks of the river and sip cocktails from the balconies of hotels while they watched the Villistas battle for possession of Juarez across the river during the Mexican Revolution.

This is what the city leaders would like to forget, but it is difficult to forget as there are ghosts that keep cropping up every day, constantly reminding them of the past. A plaque is bolted into the cement wall of Lerners Dress Shop, marking the site as the old Acme Saloon where John Wesley Hardin, who killed some thirty-odd men before he was twenty-four and the law caught up with him and locked him in prison for fifteen years, was killed himself by Constable John Selman who wisely shot him in the back of the head while Hardin shook dice for drinks at the bar. There is another plaque marking where Selman himself was shot not long after by George Scarborough for what reason is anyone's guess.

Hardin and Selman are buried in Concordia Cemetery, which lies in the heart of the city now, a burnt scar of weeds and desert where old tombstones crumble and scorpions live. Hardin's grave is marked quite well just outside the gate to the Chinese section but no one knows where Selman is buried.

The hypocrisy of the city is seen as well when the city council rose up in indignation when a developer proposed naming a street in a new housing section after Beulah M'Rose, Hardin's lover, when the developer suggested that it run right alongside another street named John Wesley Hardin Street. The humorous allegory was ignored in righteous wrath as they considered Beulah M'Rose a "fallen woman" who deserted her husband to live with Hardin in the last few months of his life. Yet, it was Beulah who paid for his funeral when no one else wanted to have anything to do with the gunman/lawyer. Strangely, the town saw nothing wrong in naming a street after the Old West's most accomplished murderer. They also overlooked the fact that other streets were named after several questionable characters of the Old West such as Billy the Kid Street and Western Avenue named after an accomplished prostitute, Sarah Borginnis, better known as "the Great Western."

Today, graffiti covers the walls of most downtown buildings, overpasses, street signs, almost every conceivable surface, the result of a constant war among street gangs for "ownership" of territory. A car once owned by the mayor was stolen and discovered three days later being driven by the chief of police in Juarez. It is a place that could easily be called "the City of Lost Souls" as prostitution was not made illegal until the Roaring Twenties when ladies congregating at the elite country club in town finally managed to convince the mayor to outlaw the Cyprian practitioners. Property taxes jumped nearly a thousand percent immediately. Later, it was discovered that inhabitants of the "Tenderloin District" had been fined monthly for practicing that ancient art and the fines, collected since 1882, had been paying for the running of the city government. Husbands were annoyed, not only for additional cost in taxes they had to pay, but for the loss of the Gentleman's Club and other richly adorned houses of ill repute.

This is the place where two madams, Big Alice and Etta Clark, got into a fight over the services of Bessie Colvin, a busty lady who accused Big Alice of cheating her out of her money for services rendered. In a huff, Colvin went across to the street to Clark's establishment, causing Big Alice embarrassment and, most importantly, great monetary loss for Colvin was quite a popular entertainer by that time. Big Alice stormed over to Clark's parlor and knocked Clark to the floor with a hard right hook. Clark bounced up, snatched a pistol from a drawer, and shot Big Alice in the pubic arch. Big Alice staggered outside and collapsed on Utah Street. The incident was reported by one wag as an unfortunate incident in which Big Alice had been shot in the "public arch." Clark was acquitted.

On April 14, 1881, the city marshal, Dallas Stoudenmire, was eating in the Globe Restaurant when he heard gunfire in the street outside. Rushing out, he saw John Hale shoot Gus Krempkau, an El Paso constable. Stoudenmire drew his long-barreled pistol and fired at Hale. The bullet missed Hale and killed an innocent bystander. George Campbell, another by-stander seeing Stoudenmire, shouted, "This ain't my fight!" He threw his hands above his head and waved them frantically. Stoudenmire calmly plugged him, then cocked his pistol and, taking better aim this time, shot the stunned Hale in the middle of his forehead. Four men went to their Maker in a shootout that is referred to as the "Four Dead in Five Seconds Gun Bat-tle." Three days later, while Stoudenmire was walking the streets, an embittered former deputy marshal, Bill Johnson, tried to kill him with a double-barreled shotgun. He missed. Stoudenmire didn't, pumping nine bullets into him after draw-ing both ivory-handled pistols from his leather-lined back pock-ets.

But there is more to El Paso than its rough Old West image. The University of Texas–El Paso is here, once described by noted historian C. L. "Doc" Sonnichsen as the "Harvard of the Border" and currently the home of one of the world's foremost Victorian scholars, Robert Bledsoe, and world-recognized Faulknerian scholar, Gail Mortimer. The poet Leslie Ullman and novelist Ben Saenz head the creative writing program that has produced several of today's popular writers. Noted histo-rian Leon Metz lives just a couple of blocks from me. In fact, a directory of writers, published on legal-sized paper, runs about a half-inch thick and includes Robert Skimin and Cor-mac McCarthy. Cinco Puentes Press, run by poet Bobby Byrd, has become nationally known for its daring publications in fic-tion and poetry. One of the local high schools, J. M. Hanks High School, one of the state's largest, has produced an award-

winning literary magazine, *The Exeter,* for well over ten years
and the national fiction writing champion Gabriel Herrera.

The El Paso Public Library is the oldest in Texas, and the
city's symphony orchestra is renowned for its standard of excellence.

When I first came here, I eagerly rented a car and drove
down to the Rio Grande to see the famous river that slices
between El Paso and Juarez. My head was filled with visions
of John Wayne splashing across the river in pursuit of or
flight from Indians. It was here as well that novelist, journalist, and raconteur Ambrose "Bitter" Bierce crossed to disappear into the Mexican Revolution. I was disappointed to see
the size of the mighty river reduced to a trickle by Corps of
Engineer dams upriver in New Mexico, yet there were several
women washing clothes in the river and children splashing in
its shallows from one of the haphazard *colonias* that surround the city of Juarez.

I had flown down here to see the city after being recruited
as a possible teacher. I vaguely recalled a song by that name
sung by Marty Robbins years before and wondered if Rosa's
Cantina ever existed (it did and does, although it is little known
today by those who live there). A strange sense of "coming
home" swept over me as I called a friend who lived there and
joined him for supper in one of the numerous Mexican cafes
that line its streets.

"You don't want to come here unless you can handle the culture," he warned over enchiladas, tacos, and pico de gallo. "The
weather is nice, but you'll have to leave your Midwestern pen-
chants behind. You'll have to totally reorganize your life and
thinking." He laughed. "And don't think that this is only His-
panic. The German Air Force trains here and we have a large
Jewish and Greek community as well. This is where the cross-
roads of culture come together. You have to be ready for that."

And one must, for El Paso, Texas, is a state of mind as well
as a state of being. It is a place where the lost souls gather,
coming from all over the United States, up from inner Mexico,

all searching for a place where they can call home, a place where they can belong, a place where the sun shines ninety-five percent of the time. But at the moment, I wasn't ready for that. I was still floundering, searching for a place to belong. I had never lived more than ten years in my entire life in the same place and those ten years had more than one move to them. Vietnam had left me an outcast among my peers who had joined the antiwar movement (I remember being spat upon in Oakland when I made the mistake of appearing in my uniform after flying back from Vietnam in '66) and saw me as representing everything they considered wrong with their world.

Quietly, I slipped away from them and others, shutting myself more and more into my own world, losing myself in books and solitude.

I flew back home right into the middle of one of the largest blizzards in history. El Paso was beginning to take on a whole different perspective, but it took a lot of soul-searching before I agreed to make the shift and a whole lot of arguing to convince my wife that the move would be good for us.

Now, we recognize El Paso for what it is and there is a strange comfort in that, knowing that many of those who have congregated here where water is at a premium and in danger of running out as the bolson becomes more and more depleted and where pollution is heavy in the winter months when the poor burn old tires in stoves made out of old oil drums to heat their shacks in Juarez across the river. We all have something in common. We are all lost souls who come together when the need is there and apart when the need is there as well.

But I discovered I could work well here. I write, I translate, I can think. Behind the house in far north El Paso is The Shack, a building so christened by the poet Michael Carey who joins us yearly in January for "therapy" from the frost and snows of Iowa, regaling us with his Irish humor and warm person.

"Ruairi, that building is the same size as George Bernard Shaw's potting shed," he mused. "He made it into his office and called it his writing shed."

"I'm not as important as Shaw," I said. "So, I guess it's going to have to be my writing shack."

"The Shack it is, then," he pronounced solemnly, blessing it. *"In nomine, et Patre, et Fili, et Spiritus sanctus."*

In the cool morning, I take coffee out to The Shack and pause for a moment to view the mountain called Saint Anthony's Nose, the quiet desert beyond my rock wall from which the quail come in the early morning to drink the dew from my grass. I watch jackrabbits play among the saltgrass and mesquite. I look to the north to the Organ Mountains and breathe deeply of the cool air, take a sip of coffee, then open the door to The Shack and enter, closing the door softly behind me. I look out the window again at the desert, then settle myself contentedly at my desk.

I write. My spirit calm and content for the moment.

As it can only be in Texas.

RANDY LEE EICKHOFF has written four novels in addition to having been awarded grants by the National Endowment for the Humanities for his scholarship. He is the author of A Hand to Execute, The Gombeen Man, The Raid, *and was a Spur Award finalist for* The Fourth Horseman, *a novel based on the life of Doc Holiday—gambler, gunfighter, and sardonic gentleman.*

HELL AND TEXAS

BY PAUL ANDREW HUTTON

⭐ Strange, how hell and Texas have come to be paired in famous quotes. Perhaps it is that fortunate combination of fabulously eccentric inhabitants and exceedingly warm climate, so common to both regions, that has resulted in this historical happenstance. Hard to tell—but the fact remains that the verbal pairing can be credited to two eminently quotable American characters.

No less a distinguished personage than Colonel David Crockett, something of an authority on both subjects, is first credited with the pairing. Crockett's West Tennessee constituency, displaying a decided lack of appreciation for half-horse, half-alligator living legends, declined to return the colonel to Congress in 1835. He took it hard, resolving to strike out for a new land where his remarkable talents might be better appreciated. So it was that the colonel and several of his cronies from the Tennessee political wars embarked on a grand farewell tour of the saloons of Memphis on the night of November 1, 1835.

It was the grandest bender in the recorded history of the Bluff City. They staggered from Jeffries' tavern in the old Union Hotel to Hart's Saloon on Market Street, picking up new compatriots all along the way, until finally reaching McCool's Saloon. Davy's friends carried him on their shoulders and, after dumping him on the bar counter, demanded a speech.

"My friends," said the colonel, "I suppose you are all aware that I was recently a candidate for Congress in an adjoining district. I told the voters that if they would elect me I would serve them to the best of my ability; but if they did not, they might go to hell, and I would go to Texas. I am on my way now!"

There was much applause and shouting, as everyone agreed it was a grand speech. That is, all save saloon proprietor Neil McCool. He had just covered his bar counter with a new oil-cloth that he would not have allowed a coonskin cap to be laid upon, much less a two-hundred-pound man in muddy boots to tramp across while speechifying. McCool flew into a rage, began to swear something awful, and proceeded to throw everything he could lay a hand on at the offending party. Retreating in disarray to the street, Crockett and company composed themselves and headed for Cooper's Saloon on Main in search of better whiskey and a more appreciative proprietor.

The drinking went on all night, with Crockett giving several more speeches. They were good ones, too, for the colonel indeed had the gift, but the only one they all remembered was "Hell and Texas." They saw him off the next morning. As he was rowed across the Mississippi on an oar-driven ferry-flat that marked the first leg of a westward trek leading to the Alamo, those left behind could not help but remark that, between "Hell and Texas," the colonel had most certainly gotten the worse end of the bargain.

Thirty years later, another prominent American made an even more direct connection between hell and Texas. Major General Philip Henry Sheridan was ordered to Texas in 1865 to reconstruct the place and make it as suitable as possible for readmission to the Union. "Little Phil," although only thirty-five, was at the peak of his powers, having emerged from the Civil War as the youngest member of the Union's trinity of great captains. Quick-tempered, irascible, pragmatic, and not burdened with the slightest bit of patience, he was quickly frustrated by the exceedingly difficult task of reconstructing the Texans.

In particular, Sheridan hoped to disabuse white Texans of their habit of regularly slaying their political opponents. These bold gentlemen most particularly favored killing folks whose skin was of a darker hue (between June 1856 and June 1868, 379 blacks were murdered by whites, while only 10 whites were slain by blacks). Sheridan responded by concentrating his soldiers in settled areas and by hauling suspected murderers before military tribunals. Texans howled over the unjustness of these military courts, and indignantly complained that pioneer Texans were being slaughtered on the frontier while Sheridan's troopers camped amongst decent, law-abiding East Texans. Sheridan, in no mood to oblige the Texans, grumbled that, "If a white man is killed by the Indians on an extensive Indian frontier, the greatest excitement will take place, but over the killing of many freedmen in the settlements, nothing is done."

In August 1866 the general was on an inspection tour along the Rio Grande when word reached him of a ghastly massacre of black Republicans in New Orleans. He rushed to the Crescent City, hiring relays and coaches from San Antonio to Galveston. Since it had not rained in weeks the ill-tempered general was pretty well covered with dust, both inside and out, by the time he reached Galveston. He was at the registration desk of the Washington Hotel, slapping a great cloud of dust off his uniform, when a local reporter rushed up and asked how the general liked the Lone Star State. Sheridan gave the newspaperman a withering stare and responded, "If I owned hell and Texas, I would rent Texas out and live in hell."

The reporter dashed off with his prize quote while Sheridan headed for the bar to lubricate the acre or so of Texas soil that lined his throat. All Texas was soon in an uproar over the remark. A little border newspaper, however, stuck up for the general, editorializing that it was only fitting and proper for him to want to live in his place of origin.

President Andrew Johnson, responding to Texan protests, eventually removed Sheridan from command in Texas and banished him to the Great Plains to fight Indians. There the feisty Irish soldier endeared himself to posterity all the more with an infamous quote when, in response to humanitarian protests that his soldiers were slaughtering good, peaceable Indians, he remarked that "the only good Indian is a dead Indian."

Sheridan, who went on to become general-in-chief of the U.S. Army, returned to Texas in 1880 in the company of his friend, ex-President U. S. Grant. At a March 24 banquet at the Tremont Hotel the general, considerably stouter and mellower than in 1866, again directed his remarks to hell and Texas. "Now I want to assure you," declared the hero of the Shenandoah, "that by that expression I only meant to convey how much I was disgusted with that newspaper man. It did not represent my opinion of Texas . . . Every time I visit Texas I think a little more of it than ever before."

This was hardly a warm endorsement of the virtues of the Lone Star state, but Texans, also grown a bit mellower with the passing years, accepted the remarks in good spirit. Responded humorist Alex Sweet, in his *Galveston Daily News* column for March 26, "I have never understood that there was any feeling of bitterness toward General Sheridan on account of his having made that remark. The only reason people thought hard of him, at all, was on account of his failing to kill the reporter."

PAUL ANDREW HUTTON, Executive Director of the Western History Association, is the author of Phil Sheridan and His Army *(1985),* Soldiers West *(1987),* The Custer Reader *(1992), and* Frontier and Region *(1997). His biography of David Crockett is forthcoming from the University of Oklahoma Press. He was raised in San Angelo, Texas.*

A Letter from David Crockett

"This is the first I have had an opportunity to write you with convenience. I am now blessed with excellent health and am in high spirits, although I have had many difficulties to encounter. I have got through safe and have been received by everyone with open cerimony of friendship. I am hailed with hearty welcome to this country. A dinner and a party of ladys have honored me with an invitation to partisapate both at Nacing docher and at this place. The cannon was fired here on my arrival and I must say as to what I have seen of Texas it is the garden spot of the world. The best land and the best prospects for health I ever saw, and I do believe it is a fortune to any man to come here. There is a world of country here to settle.

"It's not required here to pay down for your League of land. Every man is entitled to his head right of 400–428 acres. They may make the money to pay for it on the land. I expect in all probability to settle on the Border or Chactaw Bro of Red River that I have no doubt is the richest country in the world. Good land and plenty of timber and the best springs and will mill streams, good range, clear water and every appearance of good health and game aplenty. It is the pass where the buffalo passes from north to south and back twice a year, and bees and honey plenty. I have a great hope of getting the agency to settle that country and I would be glad to see every friend I have settled thare. It would be a fortune to them all. I have taken the oath of government and have enrolled my name as a volunteer and will set out for the Rio Grand in a few days with the volunteers from the United States. But all volunteers is entitled to vote for a member of the convention or to be voted for, and I have but little doubt of being elected a member to form a constitution for this province. I am rejoiced at my fate. I had rather be in my present situation than to be elected to a seat in Congress for life. I am in hopes of making a fortune yet for myself and family, bad as my prospect has been.

I have not written to William but have requested John to direct him what to do. I hope you will show him this letter and also Brother John as it is not convenient at this time for me to write to them. I hope you will all do the best you can and I will do the same. Do not be uneasy about me. I am among friends. I will close with great respects. Your affectionate father. Farwell."

Born in Tennessee in 1786, DAVID CROCKETT *became a soldier, frontiersman, humorist, and a United States Represenative from Tennessee. He came to Texas in 1836, and was killed at the Alamo.*

An Expatriate's Lament: A Texas Pilgrim in Arkansas

BY W. C. JAMESON

⭐ It is almost painful to have to relate a wearied and hackneyed old cliché such as the one that follows, but the absolute and unbendable truth is it has special meaning for a large number of us expatriate Texans. The saying, at least one version of it, goes like this: You never appreciate a place until you have left it. It was a statement I paid little attention to until I was forced to depart my beloved West Texas homeland for the Ozark environs of Darkest Arkansas, and learned to cope with the loss of horizons.

From time to time and for a variety of reasons, many of us are placed in a position of migrating to new places, new towns, new states, new lands. It may be because our employers sent us there or it may be that we desired a change of climate. Sometimes family considerations force or cause us to relocate.

In my case it was a career opportunity. There was spare chance for me to pursue what I had prepared myself to do in the West Texas of my youth, but coincident with receiving a college degree, one such an opportunity opened up in the verdant foothills of the Arkansas Ozarks.

The idea of moving to the Ozarks offered an immediate appeal for me—I had images of craggy, forested ridges, and deep cool valleys through which ran trickled streams of clear water. In my mind I saw speckled trout swimming in those streams just below the surface, trout that I imagined eagerly awaited my hook. By contrast, my West Texas homeland is often characterized by its lack of water. We West Texans think about water a lot but seldom see much of it, so the prospect of encountering some of it on a regular basis in the Ozarks was darned fascinating.

In my mind I imagined visiting remote Ozark communities and towns peopled by bewhiskered old men in overalls seated on wooden benches whittling animal figures out of small pieces of oak. I also assumed all the young women living in the Ozarks looked like Daisy Mae. I couldn't wait to get there.

I recall as I was packing my bags and loading the car for the move to Arkansas, I was harboring some partially developed regrets about leaving home and the attendant cultures that had shaped me and made me, to a large degree, what I am now, whatever that is, and what I was to become. So great was my eagerness to embark on the adventure of a new career that I thought little or not at all that I would deeply miss any of this arid land, the adjacent mountains, the climate, and the West Texas folk.

Regrets, however, began overwhelming me almost from the moment I began unpacking and moving into my new home. Among the first things I noticed were that there were no whiskered old men in overalls seated on wooden benches and no Daisy Maes frolicking through the woods. Things were considerably more different in my new home than I expected, than I would have believed. But the most dramatic differences, those that caused considerable adjustment and getting used to, had to do with the absence of, for want of a better term, some important Texas things—things I never thought much about until then.

One of the most profound differences was in the color of the landscape. I never thought much about environmental colors before; it was just something I took for granted. You see, in West Texas, the dominant color for most of the year is beige. The sandy deserts were beige. The dry watercourses were beige. Even the vegetation was beige for much of the year when the already scarce moisture was scarcer. Everyone has heard of culture shock, but I am convinced there is such a thing as color shock.

In the Ozarks everything was green: vast carpets of green

pasture and meadow; hillsides verdant with various shades of green trees, bushes, and briars a shade of green that was almost sharp to the eyes. Even the craggy uplands where the Ozark soils were thin and not much moisture was trapped were green with juniper and pine. The only beige I could find was the occasional weathered outcropping of limestone along a slope too steep to support a covering of vegetation.

Green is not an unpleasant color and is perceived by many to be restful. In this case, however, for a Texan raised on beige to be bombarded by so much green in such a short time amounted to a verdure overdose that actually caused headaches for about three weeks until my system adjusted to the color shock.

Another think I missed was space. One would think that space—room to roam, room to stretch, elbow room—and lots of it, would be available in the Ozarks.

Not so.

In West Texas, one more or less takes space for granted, and space is as much or more a part of the natural landscape as is color.

I can recall as a youth in the 1960s driving a vehicle down secondary and tertiary West Texas roads for hours without seeing a single soul, a single dwelling, not even telephone poles. Nothing but space—grand, glorious, soul-stirring space. This was nirvana for me, for from time to time I revel in the deliciousness of solitude that only lots of space can provide. There exists to this day many places in West Texas where one can still do this.

Believe it or not, there is not much space in the Ozarks, and even less remoteness. In fact, in the Ozark Mountains one is seldom more than a couple of miles from a road or a dwelling. This is just not satisfactory for a West Texan whose life was significantly impacted by so much open space and remoteness. On backpacking expeditions through the Ozarks, I've often been inundated with sounds not of nature but of vehicular traf-

fic, barking dogs, and even conversations between neighbors
that carried across the distances of the narrow valleys. Not
satisfactory at all.

Related to space, but perhaps more important to the soul
and psyche, are horizons. Lord, I missed the horizons of West
Texas. One never thinks of horizons—their availability and
their influence—I suspect, until one is forced to do without
them. It took me a few weeks to realize the impact the horizons
of West Texas had on my life. The aforementioned change in
environmental color was instant, and ultimately coped with.
But the horizon deprivation came about three weeks later.

As I was adjusting to new surroundings in the Ozarks, I had
this feeling that something was not quite right, something
slightly out of kilter, something I couldn't quite put my finger
on at first. Then I realized that this feeling was a growing sense
of claustrophobia—not the claustrophobia associated with
crowded and closed-in spaces like elevators, but the claustrophobia associated with an environment possessing limited horizons.

The claustrophobia I experienced in the Ozarks was caused
by the high ridges, the low and narrow valleys, and the tall
trees. What these elements did was to shorten the horizons, and
in some cases virtually eliminate them. In West Texas, on a
clear day one can see for fifty, sixty, or more miles. I can once
recall looking south from a high peak in the Guadalupe Mountains in the days before advanced air pollution and picking out
landmarks I knew were over one hundred miles away. In the
Ozark Mountains, delightful as they are, it is not uncommon
to have one's horizons constricted such that they are only forty
yards away, or less.

An expansive horizon is a beautiful and powerful thing, and
I can't help but believe it shapes one's life for eternity. I believe
horizons represent many things: an invitation to roam, a sense
of place, a sense of perspective with the landscape, the sun, and
the stars. With these kinds of horizons you always knew where

W. C. Jameson.
PHOTO COURTESY OF EMILY JAMESON.

An Awareness

BY FESS PARKER

I believe that an awareness of the spirit of previous Texans first came to me when I was very young through an illustrated book of Texas history. I had gone to the library and found the book—a book in the form of cartoons. I believe it still exists today, but I recall that it began with the six flags over Texas and the history of those people—about the Indians, the early settlers, and the heroes of the Alamo and San Jacinto. I was a young boy just learning to read, but I remember reading that particular book over and over.

I think back now about the character of the people, the neighbors of my mother and father, who lived out in West Texas in San Angelo, and the stories about the not-too-distant years of my childhood when the Indians and Texan settlers were still at constant war. I think one of the things that impressed me from those stories was the self-sufficiency exhibited by those earlier Texans.

Fess Parker in early or mid-1930s.
PHOTO COURTESY OF FESS PARKER.

As a boy, every summer from 1930 to 1940, I had an opportunity to live with my grandparents on the farm and on the ranch. My grandfather on my father's side had a farm in Comanche County, Texas. He grew cotton, peanuts, and watermelon. He also raised cattle, hogs, and goats. My grandmother on my mother's side had a cattle ranch in Erath County. She raised Hereford cattle. My grandparents exhibited that same self-sufficiency as Texans who came before them. I believe there is a spirit that is imbued in all Texans and it is a *wonderful* thing. I won't try to describe it except to say that it has been a powerful influence in my life and remains so to this day.

FESS PARKER is a man for all seasons, an American icon, but he is perhaps best known as an actor. His portrayal of frontiersmen Davy Crockett and Daniel Boone impacted millions of young viewers and created an international phenomenon in the '50s and '60s. Parker began professional acting in 1951 as a stage performer in Mister Roberts. *In 1954, Walt Disney signed him to play the title role in* Davy Crockett, King of the Wild Frontier. *His young fans, now today's decision-makers, are still in awe of their childhood hero. Those who have met Fess Parker are not disappointed. This overriding impression is one of gentleness, kindness, and wisdom. He is unpretentious. His walk is amble, his voice resonant yet soft, and his countenance is one of sincere concern and responsibility. Today he is a successful businessman, and, in many ways, as much an American hero as Davy Crockett.*

Real Texans

BY DALE EVANS ROGERS

☆ I was born in Uvalde at the home of my maternal grandparents. As a child, I spent many Christmases and summer vacations here. Texas has always meant very much to my heart. As a child I used to plan to return to San Antonio—and I still cherish my visits in Texas.

Real Texans are great down-to-earth people—warm and caring, and I cherish the years in my life that I have lived in Texas, and the years I worked in Dallas on radio WFAA on the "Early Bird" program.

I loved the privilege of visiting the Alamo in San Antonio. I feel it a privilege to have my roots in Texas.

God Bless You,
Dale Evans Rogers

Singer and actress DALE EVANS ROGERS appeared in many films and television shows throughout her career. Married to the late Roy Rogers, King of the Cowboys, she continues to make her home in California and is active with family, friends, and community.

Dale Evans.

"It Ain't Much to Look At..."

BY MAC DAVIS

✪ I can probably sum up my feelings about growing up in West Texas in one sentence: It ain't much to look at, but if I were to have a flat tire and no spare, West Texas is where I'd want to be.

In my song, "Texas in my Rearview Mirror," I wrote "... when I die, you can bury me in Lubbock, Texas, in my jeans." It's in my will.

MAC DAVIS continues to write music and today hosts a regular radio show on KZLA, a Los Angeles station that plays classic country music. He coaches little league for his two young sons and replies that "life is good."

Patriots

BY CAPTAIN BURL TERRILL, USMC RET.

☆ The year was 1941 when I was born in a small West Texas town called San Angelo. I have lived here for the past fifty-nine years and now live within twenty-five miles of the hospital where I was born. I did spend four years at Texas A&M in College Station and four years in the United States Marine Corps.

There is something special about Texas, and for me West Texas, that is hard to define on paper. I have been in most states of the U.S. and I have not yet found a place that I would rather live. I have been in several foreign countries including Switzerland, Germany, Spain, Italy, New Zealand, and Australia, and have never once been asked if I was from the United States. It was more like a statement: "I'll bet you're from Texas." It could have been the hat, the boots, the accent, or all of the above—Texans do stand out!

After my service in the USMC and a tour in Vietnam, I came back to West Texas and went into the family business of architectural woodwork manufacturing. My dad started the business in 1946, I became the president in about 1980, and, in 1986, I bought the business from the rest of the family. Today, my son is a third generation Terrill to run a family-owned business that has been providing employment for from fifty to one hundred fifty workers for over fifty years. Texas proud, YES!

Values run deep in West Texas: God, family, country, "Texas." We wave to one another when we meet on the highway; we pray when the need arises and when we choose. We respect the flags—United States and Texas—and other's opinions, and the right of freedom of choices.

Last July Fourth we celebrated a little different. Because of dry weather conditions fireworks were out of the question. We still had our traditional Fourth of July meal of fajitas and all the trimmings and at sundown we had a flag-lowering ceremony with everyone saying the Pledge of Allegiance. With the younger children and with each other we shared our stories of what independence was all about and the struggles others had endured and the sacrifices they had made for the sake of freedom. Included among our friends and family who gathered together that evening were veterans representing World War II, the Korean Conflict, and Vietnam. Interestingly enough, as different as they are alike, each of those Texas veterans gathered that day are independent thinkers and self-sufficient men, each having their own independent businesses, each taking their place, each making a positive difference in this land.

Texas—the land of opportunity and unconditional friendship, the land of neighbors helping neighbors. My roots are as deep in West Texas as are the mesquite tree that grows here!

Captain BURL TERRILL is a lifetime rancher and businessman, and the owner and chairman of the board of directors at Terrill Manufacturing Company. He and his wife Jan and their two dogs Wrangler and Levi live west of San Angelo, Texas, where they enjoy the company of family, friends, sunrise and sunset, good sippin' whiskey when the occasion calls for it, and always a few good riding horses.

No Drugstore Cowboys

BY JAMES "DOC" BLAKELY

☆ Ab Blocker was a legendary pioneer in the cattle business, the original foreman for the huge XIT ranch in West Texas, and a trail boss who probably pointed more cows north than any other man. And he was a personal friend of my family.

My father is now 94, a living link with the past. When I was just a child of five or six, about 1939, I can remember clearly how my father tried to impress upon me the importance of this legendary, crusty old character who was, as I recall, close to ninety when I first saw him.

My father prepared us all morning for the arrival of a "real old-time cowboy." About noon Ab finally arrived at our place on his way from the ranch where he lived in Duval County, Texas, to the nearby town of Freer to get a few groceries. He was horseback, as always, never learned to drive a car or truck and took great pride in resisting the temptation. He would, however, ride with someone he felt was properly trained and trustworthy.

My father was one of the few who met his strict requirements of having "good enough sense" to drive "one of them contraptions."

The reason for Ab's visit was to coordinate a trip to the most important event in the Brush Country of South Texas: the Fourth of July rodeo in Cotulla.

I'll never forget the image of Ab Blocker that day. In time, I would learn that his appearance was always the same. He rode a bay mare, long of tooth, gentle of disposition. As he drew rein in front of our house, I looked up to see a large man riding a creaking saddle of very old style, narrow wooden stirrups, a hemp rope coiled neatly on the right side. A large empty mesh sack, previously containing oranges, hung from the saddle horn. This would be the container for groceries he would buy in town. Hanging from his right wrist by a leather thong was a Mexican style, hand-braided, leather quirt with a brass handle painstakingly carved with an intricate design. I never saw him take the quirt off his wrist even when not mounted. His big white hat had a rolled brim with a Chisholm crease, sometimes called a Tom Horn crease. His hair was snow-white, as was his handlebar moustache. He wore a white shirt, buttoned all the way to the top, but with no tie, bolo, or bandana. He

Ab Blocker.
PHOTO COURTESY OF DOC BLAKELY.

also wore a wool sweater, no matter the season. It, too, was always buttoned, but only at the top button, the sweater forming an upside down "V" over his white shirt. His belt was simple and the buckle modest and functional, not like the large buckles so popular today. His pants were always Levi's jeans, tucked inside handmade cowboy boots with steep-sloped and very high heels. His spurs were the awesome, Mexican-style, large-rowled type that dragged the ground in front of our house when he dismounted and walked the few steps to sit on our porch. They made a beautiful ringing sound that sing in my ear to this day.

After this first meeting, Ab began making monthly visits to our house to make plans for the rodeo. After sitting a spell in a rocking chair provided especially for him on our porch, Ab would again go over the details of the big day when we would all go to Cotulla on the Fourth of July. Then he'd promise to be prompt and arrive " 'bout daylight" so we could make the long drive. He always called me "Sonny" as he did all male children he came in contact with, but referred to my father by his given name of Jim, as my father had requested. My mother was always "Ma'am."

Finally, the Fourth of July came. At dawn, we loaded into our 1938 Chevy sedan and headed for Cotulla. Arriving hours later, we parked the car in a dusty field with what seemed like hordes of others but probably amounted to 1,500 or so, still very impressive by our standards. Bulldozers had dug trenches for mesquite log fires, hog wire was stretched over the coals and beeves of half and quarter sides were being barbecued on the wire, turned by pitchforks, thick red sauce being applied with brand-new regulation-size house mops.

My dad, a machinist and welder by trade, always tried to impress Ab with modern technology and tried to get him to admit that things were bigger and better as compared to the old days.

"How about that, Ab?" he asked, pointing to the action at the huge barbecue pits, "ever see anything like that on the trail?"

"Humphh," Ab replied, "wouldn't make a wart on a camp cook's behind."

After eating our fill of barbeque and all the fixin's, we found a good seat in the stands. Ab allowed me to sit in his lap through much of the show. I even took a nap during the duller parts. But when it came time for the bronc busting, my father pulled me off Ab's lap and told the both of us to pay strict attention because the horses brought in for this event were mean, ornery, and some had never been ridden . . . ever. I watched Ab for some sign of emotion. He sat ramrod straight, hat pulled down low over his eyes, arms folded across the "V" of his wool sweater.

The horses that day were awesome. They jumped, fishtailed, doubled back, fell over backward, kicked, and tried to bite the riders even while they were bucking. When the dust cleared and the last cowboy had ridden, many of them successfully to high scores, the crowd went wild with applause, appreciation, and a standing ovation.

My dad, trying to get a compliment from Ab for our modern-day buckeroos, asked, "What'cha think about that, Ab? They'd give the guys on your drives a run for their money, wouldn't they?"

Without a hint of a smile, Ab said, "Humphh, damn drugstore cowboys."

For the next few years, the trip to the Fourth of July Rodeo at Cotulla became an annual event for my family, and Ab. I learned to look forward to each monthly visit, and each rodeo, and although I didn't appreciate it fully at the time I realize now that I am privileged to have shared a link with a legendary time and a legendary man.

When Ab Blocker died in 1943, at the age eighty-seven, he left his entire estate to my father. It consisted of a saddle, rope, bridle, quirt, spurs, and assorted tack which fit neatly into a mesh orange sack. My father, wiser than most of his day, donated it all to the Witte Traildrivers Museum in San Antonio, Texas. It hardly filled the trunk of our car but it represented an epic time in American history when bold and daring men risked life and limb for a chance to live the dream. They were men who would lay down their lives for one another—wranglers, bronc busters, swing riders, ramrods, trail bosses, night-herders, chuckwagon cooks—men with titles of every sort, except one. At trail's end there were no "drugstore cowboys."

JAMES "DOC" BLAKELY, owner of The Broken B Ranch, in Wharton, Texas, is the great grandson of Fred C. Blakely who drove the largest herd of cattle up the Chisholm Trail. Doc has been a professional speaker/musician/entertainer for thirty years and performs nationwide with his son, Mike, a western novelist/musician.

On Coming to Texas

BY WALTER CRONKITE

⭐ I became a Houstonian in 1927 at the age of ten. The city's population, probably including all suburbs worth counting, was not much over 100,000 as I recall. But it didn't take a wild imagination to foresee the huge and rapid growth ahead. The ship channel was fairly new and the Conroe oil field had just burst into glory. The old-timers—those who talked of cotton and sugar and timber—still hung out in the chairs under the canopy in front of the Milby Hotel. Main Street ran on south but to no major purpose beyond McGowan.

I arrived with my mother and father by train from our previous home in Kansas City. The departure from the Katy station was a terrible disappointment. There were no horses tethered to a rail outside. There were no cowboys—at least not recognizable from the movie version—in the streets. And there were no ocean-going ships tied up to Main street docks.

But I was a mighty fortunate kid. My folks early on were introduced to a chap named Bassett Blakely and he invited us to his ranch a distance out of town. And there were, indeed, the cowboys I missed in downtown Houston, and herds of cattle, and a genuine bunkhouse out a way from the Blakely home.

As I grew a little older and could drive—and that was "just a little older" for Texas didn't have drivers' licenses then—I drove out to the Blakely ranch on weekends and helped work the cattle with the cowboys. There was a small town down the dirt road a piece—its name I've long since forgotten—whose general store actually had a hitching post outside. It was a Saturday gathering place for the cowboys—and their sycophantic charge.

The Blakely ranch once was one of the centers of a Texas dream that long has been buried in cobwebs. It was a vision of Texas as the center of the new motion picture industry. Two major pictures starring Richard Dix, an early hero of the Silent Screen, had been filmed there and outside one of the barns were still remnants of a couple of sets. Hollywood, of course, ended up being in Hollywood.

It was a long drive on shell and dirt roads out to the Blakely ranch. You drove out what was Westheimer Road for the first couple of miles. It sort of disappeared somewhere just west of Shepherd Drive. I'm not sure now just where the gates to the ranch were, but they couldn't have been much farther than where the Galleria is now.

The ranch weekends beat all hollow the weekday, after-school activity of a youth armed with a BB gun in (fruitless) hunt for wild game through the mesquite forest that stretched from Hazard all the way to Shepherd.

Ah, those were the days.

Born in St. Joseph, Missouri, in November 1916, longtime CBS news anchorman WALTER CRONKITE *was raised in Houston, Texas. He went to Houston's San Jacinto High School. In 1933 he became a student at the University of Texas.*

Cronkite got his training in broadcast journalism at Midwestern radio stations, and during World War II he covered the European theater for United Press. After the war, he served as chief United Press correspondent at the Nuremberg trials.

He joined CBS News in 1950, worked on a variety of programs, and covered national political conventions and elections from 1952–1981. He was one of the original creators of the CBS Evening News *in 1962, and anchored that broadcast until his 1981 retirement. The public's perception of him as honest, objective, and levelheaded led to his popular title as "the most trusted man in America." His nightly sign-off, "and that's the way it is," was his trademark.*

Walter Cronkite.
PHOTO COURTESY OF WALTER CRONKITE.

100%

BY TOM C. FROST

⭐ My life has been 100% Texan. Every day I go to work two blocks from my birthplace—Santa Rosa Hospital, whose founding physician, 130-plus years ago, was my maternal great, great-grandfather—a German immigrant.

My job is with a 132-year-old firm founded by my great-grandfather on my father's side who came to Texas in 1854 as an assistant professor at our then *only* institution of higher learning, Austin College.

All of my life the traditions and values of my Texas family have formed the backbone of my teachings, both from family and the primary and secondary schools who taught my ancestors.

The pride of being so privileged and the incentive this has provided has stimulated me to add all that I can to what has been given me. My daily efforts are to pass these values and pride in our community and our state to my children and grandchildren with the faith that they, too, will add positively to our Texas in the future.

TOM C. FROST is the senior chairman at Frost National Bank, San Antonio, Texas. The Frost family has had a strong and meaningful presence in Texas for well over a century and the personal and economic contributions the family has made towards the development of the state of Texas has been significant.

"I'll Always Be a Texan"

BY GALE STORM

☆ No matter where I am, in my heart I'll always be a Texan. From the time my grandfather held me on his lap and told me stories about how our family first came to Texas as one of seven families with Stephen F. Austin, I've felt that Texas pride! When I learned that my great, great uncle George Washington Cottle died in the Alamo, my pride was abundantly enhanced! Although the only memento on display in the Alamo to commemorate him is his cheese box, his name is on that beautiful bronze plaque! Every time I have visited the Alamo and heard the guide tell it's famous story, I never fail to tear up!

I have such fond memories of growing up in Houston, attending Longfellow Elementary School, Albert Sidney Johnston Junior High, and San Jacinto High School. Two of my teachers at San Jacinto—Miss Rona Collier and Miss Mary Ellen Oatman—were responsible for urging me to enter "The Gateway to Hollywood" contest which took me to Hollywood and started me on a career which has changed and blessed my life! I will be eternally grateful to them and love them forever! They had the kind of strength and inspiration that belongs to Texas!

Note: George Washington Cottle to whom Ms. Storm refers was the son of Jonathan and Margaret Cottle of Missouri and came to DeWitt's Colony, Texas, with his family on July 6, 1829. In 1835, he was granted title to one league of land on the Tejocotes Creek and La Vaca River, twenty-eight miles from Gonzales. He had three children—a daughter, Melzinia, and twin sons, born after Cottle's death at the Alamo.

During the fight for the Gonzales cannon, in late September 1835, George Cottle served as a courier to rally reinforcements to Gonzales. *He fought in the actual skirmish for the cannon, on October 2, 1835, in which the Mexican force was driven back toward Bexar. Cottle went to the Alamo as part of the relief force from Gonzales, arriving there on March 1, 1836. He was killed in battle on March 6, 1836. He was twenty-five years old.*

Once known as Texas's Li'l Darling, GALE STORM *has appeared in many western films and was the star of the popular television series* My Little Margie. *Today she lives in California and remains active with family and friends.*

Gale Storm.

Short and Sweet

"I never met a Texan woman I didn't like"
—Buck Owens

Buck Owens.

Alvis Edgar Owens, Jr. was born on August 12, 1929, near Sherman, Texas. Buck took his name from a mule on the Owens's farm. Beginning in the late 1950s, and for the following decade, he and his band, The Buckaroos, took country music to its zenith. In 1996 he was awarded country music's highest honor when he was inducted into the Country Music Hall of Fame. Throughout his career this legendary gentleman has never forgotten his humble beginnings and never forgotten to recognize and honor his fans.

On Family Values

BY GOVERNOR GEORGE W. BUSH

☆ "... while the world may be changing dramatically, remember that families are the backbone of our society. Families must endure forever. In our families we find love and we learn the compassionate values essential to make us good citizens of the world. When the time comes for you to start your own families, I hope each and every one of you will strive to build not just a house, but a home. It takes hard work and dedication—just ask your parents. But home is where our hearts find peace, and home is where our dreams take wing.

"I have learned that, no matter how old you are or what you do, you can never escape your mother. I learned that one weekend in Fredericksburg, Texas.

"Mother and Dad joined me on stage for a fiftieth anniversary celebration of America's World War II victory in the Pacific. The day was sunny and beautiful, and more than thirty thousand people lined the streets for the parade. It was a wonderful opportunity for me to say thank you on behalf of the sons and daughters of my generation to the moms and dads of my parents' generation for the sacrifices they made for our freedom.

"I walked up to the podium, turned to Dad and said, 'Mr. President,' and everybody gave him a nice round of applause. Then I said, 'Mother,' and the crowd went wild. I said, 'Mother, it is clear they still love you.' And there was more cheering and applause.

"I said, 'Mother, I love you, too. But after forty-nine years, you are still telling me what to do.' And some guy in a huge cowboy hat on the front row yelled out, 'And you better listen to her, too, boy!'

"I do listen to her, and one of the things she has taught me is the *final* and most important fixed star: God exists today, and God will exist forever. I am convinced that to truly change America, we need a renewal of spirit in this country, a return to selfless concern for others, for duty, and for country. We must let faith be the fire within us.

"Government can hand out money, but it cannot put hope in our hearts or a sense of purpose in our lives. A successful career can put a fancy car in the driveway, but it cannot fill the spiritual well from which we draw strength every day. Only faith can do that."

GEORGE W. BUSH was born in New Haven, Connecticut, moved to Texas with his parents as a toddler, and grew up in Midland and Houston. He was an F-102 Fighter Pilot in the Texas Air National Guard from 1968 to 1973. On November 8, 1994, he was elected Governor of Texas. In a historic re-election victory, he became the first Texas govenor to be elected to consecutive four-year terms. Now in his second term, Govenor Bush has earned a reputation as a compassionate conservative who shapes policy based on the principles of limited govenment, personnal responsibilty, strong families, and local control.

Governor George W. Bush.

TEXAN BY CHOICE

BY MAYOR LEE P. BROWN

☆ Why Texas? My connection to Texas does not stem from deep-rooted ancestry or a fortune made in the oil fields. I came to Texas by chance, but I remain a Texan by choice.

I was born in the small town of Wewoka, Oklahoma. My parents did not have access to a doctor or a hospital, so my aunt delivered me. When I was five, my family loaded all of our belongings on the back of an old truck and drove to California in search of a better way of life. We ultimately made our home in and around Fowler, California, earning a living by picking cotton, cutting grapes, and working in the other agricultural crops in the San Joaquin Valley. Who could have imagined then what promise the future held for me?

My family survived the tough times, and I earned a fine education that prepared me for a career in law enforcement. I quickly rose through the ranks, first in San Jose, California, then Portland, Oregon, and eventually as Commissioner of Public Safety in Atlanta. But when my career landed me in Texas, I knew I was home.

My family and I came to Houston in 1982 when I was hired by then-Mayor Kathryn Whitmire to serve as the city's chief of police. Soon after my arrival, the city faced difficult times in the wake of a severe downturn in the oil industry. Weaker cities would have crumbled, but the people of Houston refused to run from adversity. They pulled together to brave the storm, and today Houston is a multicultural, multilingual city, a reflection of America's future.

The chance Houston's first-ever female mayor took in appointing the city's first-ever black police chief did not go unnoticed. The eight years I served in that position opened up wonderful opportunities in other parts of the nation. I served as police commissioner in New York and as a cabinet member in the White House. These experiences were highlights of my career, but throughout that time, I looked forward to returning to my adopted home of Texas.

I have lived all over the nation, and I have traveled the world, but the spirit of the people have always drawn me back to Texas. The earliest Texans were pioneers, people who came to the frontier with a dream in their heads and a will to succeed. They left behind not only the foundation for a great state, but also a legacy of individual achievement that is unparalleled. My story is not about the history of this proud state, but about the future that it promises its citizens.

I believe Texas is still a land of opportunity, where men and women of all different backgrounds can come to realize their dreams. After all, that boy with the humble roots of a poor family from American's heartland today serves as Mayor of Houston, in the great state of Texas.

Mayor LEE P. BROWN lives in Houston, Texas, with his wife, Frances. He has four children and eleven grandchildren. Among his many awards Mayor Brown was selected Father of the Year in 1991 by the National Fathers Day Committee.

Lee P. Brown, mayor of Houston.
PHOTO COURTESY OF LEE P. BROWN

MY TEXAS HERO

BY JOHN CORNYN III

He was as much a hero as Bowie, Travis, and Crockett. Or Sam Houston and Stephen F. Austin. At least he was for me. Actually, he was even a little bit more. He was my dad.

The history books aren't filled with anecdotes of the man from Milford, Texas, which my mom (Gale) described as "one of the wide places in the road" where Dad lived long before he met her.

John Cornyn, Jr. retired from the Air Force a full colonel and then enjoyed a distinguished teaching career at the University of Texas Health Science Center in San Antonio. Still, there is a larger story to be told about Dad.

I was aware, of course, that he flew B-17s in World War II. What I wasn't aware of—until his death in 1989—was that he was shot down over Mannheim, Germany on his thirteenth mission. And that for five months, he was held in a German prison camp.

Going through his personal items after he died, I couldn't believe that he had this experience . . .

More than that, I couldn't believe he *never* told Olivia, Mark (my sister and brother), or me about his time in the prison camp. There were narratives of his experiences that listed all the traumatic things he was exposed to in those months in captivity. I remember asking my mom why he never shared this with us. She just said it wasn't his way.

Even after reading all the harrowing tales in his personal articles, I guess it didn't fully hit me until I saw the movie *Memphis Belle*. Seeing that group of bomber pilots. Seeing how young they all were. Seeing the danger that they faced. All of it gave me yet another reason to admire Dad.

He always had my respect. I knew the work he put in, going to Delmar College in Corpus Christi on the GI Bill. Then going to dental school and opting for the study of oral pathology . . . which was a pretty narrow specialty. But it was something he loved and did until his retirement in 1971, when I was a sophomore at Trinity University in San Antonio.

Dad embodied what I always have believed a Texan is: an independent thinker, never shy about expressing what was on his mind.

On occasion, he would embarrass us because of that independent streak. He would speak up . . . and even walk out of a situation, instead of just letting it ride. But by doing this, he taught me the importance of having the courage of your convictions. My dad defined character as how someone acted when they knew no one was looking. Another trait which also is very much a part of being a Texan.

John Cornyn, Jr.
PHOTO COURTESY OF JOHN CORNYN III.

Actually, Dad showed me everything I ever needed to know about courage in the way that he handled his imprisonment . . . even as such a young man. He never used the frightening episode as an excuse for problems he might have or as a crutch.

There have been times—in some quiet moments—since I learned of what happened to my dad on that fateful mission that I wondered, how in the world could he have lived through that? How in the world could anyone live through that? But he did. That's why he embodies what a Texan is. That's why he's my hero. That's why . . . I'm glad he was my dad.

JOHN CORNYN III was born in Houston, Texas, and raised in Texas and Maryland. He graduated from high school in Japan where his father was stationed as a United States Air Force officer. He is a graduate of Trinity University (1973) and St. Mary's School of Law (1977), both in San Antonio. Before his election as Attorney General, he served as a distinguished member of the Texas judiciary for thirteen years and as a private lawyer for seven. In 1990, he was elected to the Texas Supreme Court.

John Cornyn was elected in 1998 as the forty-nineth Attorney General of Texas. As Attorney General, he is committed to serving Texans by elevating professionalism over politics and the rule of law over political expediency.

A Texas Legacy

BY JAMES A. BAKER III

⭐ As a native Texan, the Lone Star State has played an important role in my life. Texas has always been my home.

Since 1852, when my great-grandfather Judge James A. Baker moved to Huntsville, the State of Texas has been an important part of my family history. One example is my grandfather, Captain James A. Baker, who made a number of significant contributions throughout his life to the state.

Captain Baker was born in Huntsville, Texas, in 1857, and moved to Houston when his father joined the law firm that would later become Baker & Botts. After attending Austin College and Texas Military Academy, Captain Baker also joined Baker & Botts in 1877.

Captain Baker's legal career in Houston spanned more than fifty years, during which time he helped transform Baker & Botts into one of the leading law firms in the world. He left his distinct mark on the emerging banks and businesses of Houston, and played a prominent role in the establishment of Rice University, of which he was the first Chairman of the Board of Trustees, a capacity in which he served for fifty years.

Captain Baker also played an important role in the sensational trial that followed the murder of William Marsh Rice, the founder of the university. It was my grandfather who suspected Albert Patrick, Mr. Rice's New York City attorney who had forged a will that would have left the entire Rice fortune to Mr. Patrick. Captain Baker exposed the murder plot, and successfully had Patrick prosecuted. If it had not been for my grandfather, Houston might never have been home to such a fine university!

Today, Rice University is home to the James A. Baker III

Institute for Public Policy, where we have had the honor of welcoming many world leaders to Texas.

I am very proud of my Texas heritage and the influence which Texas has had on me and my family. I hope that in the future I will continue to be able to make a positive contribution to the Lone Star State.

JAMES A. BAKER III has served in senior government positions under three United States presidents. He served as the nation's sixty-first Secretary of State from January 1989 through August 1992 under President George Bush. During his tenure at the State Department, Mr. Baker traveled to ninety foreign countries as the United States confronted the unprecedented challenges and opportunities of the post–Cold War era. In 1995, Mr. Baker published The Politics of Diplomacy, *his reflections on those years of revolution, war, and peace.*

Mr. Baker served as the sixty-seventh Secretary of the Treasury from 1985 to 1988 under President Ronald Reagan. As Treasury Secretary, he was also chairman of the President's Economic Policy Council. From 1981 to 1985, he served as White House Chief of Staff to President Reagan. Mr. Baker's record of public service began in 1975 as Under Secretary of Commerce to President Gerald Ford. It concluded with his service as White House Chief of Staff and Senior Counselor to President Bush.

Today he is a senior partner in the law firm of Baker & Botts and senior counselor to The Carlyle Group a merchant banking firm in Washington, D.C. He is honorary chairman of the James A. Baker III Institute for Public Policy at Rice University and serves on the boards of Rice University, Princeton University, the Woodrow Wilson International Center for Scholars at the Smithsonian, and the Howard Hughes Medical Institute.

James A. Baker.

HOUSTON'S INAUGURAL ADDRESS

BY SAM HOUSTON

☆ "MR. SPEAKER AND GENTLEMEN: Deeply impressed with a sense of the responsibility devolving on me, I cannot, in justice to myself, repress the emotion of my heart, or restrain the feelings which my sense of obligation to my fellow-citizens has inspired. Their suffrage was gratuitously bestowed. Preferred to others, not unlikely superior in merit to myself, called to the most important station among mankind by the voice of a free people, it is utterly impossible not to feel impressed with the deepest sensations of delicacy in my present position before the world. It is not here alone, but our present attitude before all nations has rendered my position, and that of my country, one of peculiar interest.

"A spot of earth almost unknown to the geography of the age, destitute of all available resources, few in numbers, we remonstrated against oppression, and, when invaded by a numerous host, we dared to proclaim our independence and to strike for freedom on the breast of the oppressor. As yet our course is onward. We are only in the outset of the campaign of liberty. Futurity has locked up the destiny which awaits our people. Who can contemplate with apathy a situation so imposing in the moral and physical world? No one. The relations among ourselves are peculiarly delicate and important; for no matter what zeal or fidelity I may possess in the discharge of my official duties, if I do not obtain cooperation and an honest support from the coordinate departments of the government, wreck and ruin must be the inevitable consequences of my administration. If, then, in the discharge of my duty, my competency should fail in the attainment of the great objects in view, it would become your sacred duty to correct my errors and sustain me by your superior wisdom. This much I anticipate—this much I demand. I am perfectly aware of the difficulties that surround me, and the convulsive throes through which our country must pass. I have never been emulous of the civic wreath—when merited, it crowns a happy destiny. A country situated like ours is environed with difficulties, its administration is fraught with perplexities. Had it been my destiny, I would infinitely have preferred the toils, privations, and perils of a soldier, to the duties of my present station. Nothing but zeal, stimulated by the holy spirit of patriotism, and guided by philosophy and reason, can give that impetus to our energies necessary to surmount the difficulties that obstruct our political progress. By the aid of your intelligence, I trust all impediments in our advancement will be removed; that all wounds in the body politic will be healed, and the Constitution of the Republic derive strength and vigor equal to any emergency. I shall confidently anticipate the establishment of Constitutional liberty. In the attainment of this object, we must regard our relative situation to other countries.

"A subject of no small importance is the situation of an extensive frontier, bordered by Indians, and open to their depredation. Treaties of peace and amity, and the maintenance of good faith with the Indians, seem to me the most rational means for winning their friendship. Let us abstain from aggression, establish commerce with the different tribes, supply their useful and necessary wants, maintain even-handed justice with them, and natural reason will teach them the utility of our friendship.

"Admonished by the past, we cannot, in justice, disregard our national enemies. Vigilance will apprise us of their approach, a disciplined and valiant army will insure their discomfiture. Without discrimination and system, how unavailing would all the resources of an old and overflowing treasury prove to us. It would be as unprofitable to us in our present situation as the rich diamond locked in the bosom of the adamant. We cannot hope that the bosom of our beautiful prairies will soon be visited by the healing breezes of peace. We may again look for the day when their verdure will be converted into dyes of crimson. We must keep all our energies alive, our army organized, disciplined, and increased to our present emergencies. With these preparations we can meet and vanquish despotic thousands. This is the attitude we at present must regard as our own. We are battling for human liberty; reason and firmness must characterize our acts.

"The course our enemies have pursued has been opposed to every principle of civilized warfare—bad faith, inhumanity, and devastation marked their path of invasion. We were a little band, contending for liberty—they were thousands, well appointed, munitioned, and provisioned, seeking to rivet chains upon us, or extirpate us from the earth. Their cruelties have incurred the universal denunciation of Christendom. They will not pass from their nation during the present generation. The contrast of our conduct is manifest; we were hunted down as the felon wolf, our little band driven from fastness to fastness, exasperated to the last extreme; while the blood of our kindred and our friends invoking the vengeance of an offended God was smoking to high heaven, we met our enemy and vanquished them. They fell in battle, or suppliantly kneeled and were spared. We offered up our vengeance at the shrine of humanity, while Christianity rejoiced at the act and looked with pride on the sacrifice. The civilized world contemplated with proud emotions conduct which reflected so much glory on the Anglo-Saxon race. The moral effect has done more towards our liberation than the defeat of the army of veterans. Where our cause has been presented to our friends in the land of our origin, they have embraced it with their warmest sympathies. They have rendered us manly and efficient aids. They have rallied to our standard, they have fought side by side with our warriors. They have bled, and their dust is mingling with the ashes of our heroes. At this moment I discern numbers around me who battled in the field of San Jacinto, and whose chivalry and valor have identified them with the glory of the country, its name, its soil, and its liberty. There sits a gentleman within my view whose personal and political services to Texas have been invaluable. He was the first in the United States to respond to our cause. His purse was ever open to our necessities. His hand was extended in our aid. His presence among us and his return to the embraces of our friends will inspire new efforts in behalf of our cause. [The attention of the Speaker and that of Congress, was directed to Wm. Christy, Esq., of New Orleans, who sat by invitation within the bar.] A circumstance of the highest import will claim the attention of the court at Washington. In our recent election the important subject of annexation to the United States of America was submitted to the consideration of the people. They have expressed their feelings and their wishes on that momentous subject. They have, with a unanimity unparalleled, declared that they will be reunited to the great Republican family of the North. The appeal is made by a willing people. Will our friends disregard it? They have already bestowed upon us their warmest sympathies. Their manly and generous feelings have been enlisted on our behalf. We are cheered by the hope that they will receive us to participate in their civil, political, and religious rights, and hail us welcome into the great family of freemen. Our misfortunes have been their misfortunes—our sorrows, too, have been theirs, and their joy at our success has been irrepressible.

"A thousand considerations press upon me, each claims my attention. But the shortness of the notice of this emergency (for the speaker had only four hours notice of the inauguration, and all this time was spent in conversation) will not enable me to do justice to those subjects, and will necessarily induce their postponement for the present. [Here the President, says the reporter, paused for a few seconds and disengaged his sword.] It now, sir, becomes my duty to make a presentation of this sword—this emblem of my past office. [The President was unable to proceed further; but having firmly clenched it with both hands, as if with a farewell grasp, a tide of varied associations rushed upon him in the moment, his countenance bespoke the workings of the strongest emotions, his soul seemed to dwell momentarily on the glistening blade, and the greater part of the auditory gave outward proof of their congeniality of feeling. It was in reality a moment of deep and painful interest. After this pause, more eloquently impressive than the deepest pathos conveyed in language, the President proceeded.] I have worn it with some humble pretensions in defense of my country—and should the danger of my country again call for my services, I expect to resume it, and respond to that call, if needful, with my blood and my life."

My Trip to Texas

BY BRIGITTA HERFORT

☆ Growing up in Germany during WWII and graduating from optometry school in Berlin, I had found employment with a firm in the Lichtenberg district of the city. When, in the summer of 1952, the boss took his family on vacation, he left me in charge of bookkeeping, payroll, deposits, etc. While sitting at this desk one day, pushing paperwork around, I accidentally knocked down a low-hanging picture and smashed it to bits and pieces. What to do? And who was this stranger in the black-and-white photo anyway? An older employee explained that this was one of the few existing pictures of the boss's younger brother who'd emigrated to the United States some years before the war and had not been heard from in a long while. Fortunately, the same old-timer remembered a previous address; and so I sat down to write and explain to this person in Texas about my mishap, asking politely if he could send another picture, please?

Well, within ten days I received an impressive new photo to replace the out-dated one over the desk. It showed a dark-haired, friendly face above an open-collared white shirt—rather a handsome man, I thought. Of course, I sent a thank-you note in reply and, you guessed it, we began corresponding on a regular basis. This turned into a real long-distance romance and, within a few months, he asked me to marry him. How flattering! But I had the good sense to suggest that we really ought to meet in person before I gave my answer. And so, on a cold after-Christmas day in 1952, the boss and I were standing at Tempelhof Airport to wait for his brother's arrival.

He turned out to be the one without an overcoat, sporting

instead a cowboy hat and cowboy boots. Never in my life had I seen such getup, especially the pointed toes and elevated heels looked outrageously outlandish to me. Nevertheless, we liked each other in person so well that we became engaged on New Year's Eve and got married a week later. Nothing slow-pokey about this Texan. He had to rush back to his business, of course, while I waited for immigration officials to let me depart from Germany. Finally, in April of that year, I left my homeland and flew to Houston, Texas, to begin a new life.

Originally, my husband's first name had been Johannes, but upon becoming an American citizen, he'd changed it to John, and that's what everybody called him in Fort Bend County. In the early 1940s he had settled in Rosenberg, a small town southwest of Houston. Here he had started a tiny jewelry store on the strength of his excellence as a master watchmaker (a craft learned from his father), selling watches, jewelry, china, crystal, and silverware.

From the beginning, I helped out in the business by doing paperwork. The first time I took a deposit to the downtown bank, he asked me who had waited on me, whereupon I answered "Mr. Teller"—and simply couldn't understand why he burst out laughing. I was sure that this name had been prominently displayed at the bank teller's window . . . until I looked it up in the dictionary: meaning cashier. And I thought I knew English! But I soon found out that my high school English was not only unlike the English spoken in England, but also quite different from Texas English. To this day, whenever a Lady Bird Johnson interview is aired, I am reminded of the soft, friendly, neighborly voice of local Texans I met almost half a century ago. Though I gradually became more familiar and comfortable with the Texas talk, I never quite lost my German accent.

There were still other challenges to be met, for instance the difference in weights and measures. My decimal-system trained mind had to adjust to miles, yards, inches, pounds, quarts, gal-

lons—as well as read temperatures in Fahrenheit instead of the
comfortable Celsius scale. And, I wondered when counting
money, what meant two bits?

But people here seemed to like me, they never looked down
on me or made fun of my speech. In fact, they turned out to
be the most generous, helpful, affectionate, and warm-hearted
folks I ever met. It seemed to go with the territory, the wide-
open spaces, the vast gulf coast, the huge hill country, the endless miles of highways across the countryside. There was a
grandness of spirit about them that was proud and down-to-
earth at the same time. Everything in Texas was bigger than
anyplace else, so people thought and acted on a larger scale,
too. Even my native land, Germany, seemed to easily fit into
one of those huge counties under the endless Texas sky. It took
me some time to get used to the long months of summer heat,
and an unpredictable hurricane could be rather frightening, but
on the whole, it was a welcome experience, this huge place
called Texas.

I never felt like a foreigner, nor did I get homesick. It helped,
of course, that we started our own family here. Over the years,
we became the proud parents of four healthy children who,
eventually, gave us a total of ten grandchildren. All of them
native-born Texans! A pretty good accomplishment for a pair
of immigrants from humble beginnings . . .

For years, we worked side by side, John and I, in this small
business he had founded by sheer determination and boundless
energy. Long hours of plain hard work had made him a successful businessman, taking proper care of his customers was
his pride and reward. When the original site became too small,
we constructed a two-story building just down the street to
accommodate the growing business. He had by then specialized
into the complete manufacture of fine jewelry, drawing customers' attention from far and wide. He was the one who dreamed
the big dream and turned it into a Texas-sized reality.

When John passed away some years ago, he left the company
to me, and I still tend to business as I've always done, but now

I'm ably assisted by our grown children. It's been a fascinating life.

I have been a Texas resident now for nearly half a century, still speaking with a German accent, but feeling completely at ease here. Starting a new tradition, I have been taking my grandchildren, one at a time, on annual vacation trips to Europe with me. I want them to experience the Old World and know where their German grandmother came from. And every time we return from overseas and land in Houston, I look around and feel truly glad to be back home in Texas. . . .

BRIGITTA HERFORT lives in Rosenberg, Texas, where she continues to be a strong and positve influence with her family both in business and personally.

The Little German Girl

BY CAROLINE VON HINUEBER

☆ When my father came to Texas I was a child of eleven or twelve years. My father's name was Frederick Ernst. He was by profession a bookkeeper, and emigrated from the duchy of Oldenburg. Shortly after landing in New York he fell in with Mr. Fordtran, a tanner and a countryman of his. A book by a Mr. Duhde, setting forth the advantages of the new State of Missouri, had come into their hands, and they determined to settle in that state. While in New Orleans, they heard that every settler who came to Texas with his family would receive a league and labor of land from the Mexican government. This information induced them to abandon their first intention. We set sail for Texas in the schooner *Saltillo*. Just as we were ready to start a flatboat with a party of Kentuckians and their dogs was hitched to our vessel, the Kentuckians coming aboard and leaving their dogs behind on the flatboat.

We were almost as uncomfortable as the dogs. The boat was jammed with passengers and their luggage so that you could hardly find a place on the floor to lie down at night. I firmly believe that a strong wind would have drowned us all. We landed at Harrisburg, which consisted at that time of about five or six log houses, on the third of April, 1831. Captain Harris had a sawmill, and there was a store or two, I believe. Here we remained five weeks, while Fordtran went ahead of us and selected a league of land, where now stands the town of Industry.

While on our way to our new home, we stayed in San Felipe for several days at Whiteside's Tavern. The courthouse was about a mile out of town, and here R. M. Williamson, who was then the alcalde, had his office. I saw him several times while I was here, and remember how I wondered at his crutch and wooden leg. S. F. Austin was in Mexico at the time, and Sam Williams, his private secretary, gave my father a title to land which he had originally picked out for himself. My father had to kiss the Bible and promise, as soon as the priest should arrive, to become a Catholic. People were married by the alcalde also, on the promise that they would have themselves reunited on the arrival of the priest. But no one ever became Catholic, though the priest, Father Muldoon, arrived promptly.

My father was the first German to come to Texas with his family. He wrote a letter to a friend, a Mr. Schwarz, in Oldenburg, which was published in the local newspaper. This brought a number of Germans, with their families, to Texas in 1834.

After we had lived on Fordtran's place for six months, we moved into our own house. This was a miserable little hut, covered with straw and having six sides, which were made out of moss. The roof was by no means waterproof, and we often held an umbrella over our bed when it rained at night, while cows came and ate the moss. Of course we suffered a great deal in winter. My father had tried to build a chimney and fireplace out of logs and clay, but we were afraid to light a fire because of the extreme combustibility of our dwelling. So we had to shiver.

Our shoes gave out, and we had to go barefoot in winter, for we did not know how to make moccasins. Our supply of clothes was also insufficient, and we had no spinning wheel, nor did we know how to spin and weave like the Americans. It was twenty-eight miles to San Felipe, and, besides, we had no money. When we could buy things, my first calico dress cost fifty cents per yard.

No one can imagine what a degree of want there was of the merest necessities of life, and it is difficult for me now to understand how we managed to live and get along under the circumstances. Yet we did so in some way. We were really better supplied than our neighbors with household and farm utensils, but they knew better how to help themselves. Sutherland used his razor for cutting kindling, killing pigs, and cutting leather for moccasins. My mother was once called to a neighbor's house, five miles from us, because one of the little children was very sick. My mother slept on a deerskin, without a pillow, on the floor. In the morning, the lady of the house poured water over my mother's hands and told her to dry her face on her bonnet.

At first we had very little to eat. We ate nothing but corn-bread at first. Later we began to raise cow-peas, and afterward my father made a fine vegetable garden. At first we grated our corn, until Father hollowed out a log and we ground it as in a mortar. We had no cooking stove, of course, and baked our bread in the only skillet we possessed. The ripe corn was boiled until it was soft, then grated and baked. The nearest mill was thirty miles off.

The country was very thinly settled. Our three neighbors, Burnett, Dougherty, and Sutherland, lived in a radius of seven miles. San Felipe was twenty-eight miles off, and there were about two houses on the road thither. In consequence, there was no market for anything you could raise, except for cigars and tobacco, which my father was the first in Texas to put on the market. We raised barely what we needed, and we kept it. Around San Felipe, certainly, it was different, and there were some beautiful farms in the vicinity.

Before the war there was a school in Washington, taught by Miss Trest, where the Doughertys sent their daughter, boarding her in the city. Of course we did not patronize it.

We lived in our doorless and windowless six-cornered pa-vilion about three years.

Immigrating from Germany with her family, young CAROLINE VON HINUEBER *was an early Texas settler.*

CAPTAIN LAFITTE

WRITER UNKNOWN (1819)

To the captain's hail, "Is Commodore Lafitte in the harbor?" a tall, good-looking person in a palmetto hat, with bushy whiskers and mustaches, answered in good English, "*Captain,* Lafitte [with a marked emphasis on the "captain"] is."

"I wish to see him."

"You'll find him on board that brig yonder."

We pulled to the brig—she was full of men.

All sorts of faces, white, yellow, black, and dingy, reconnoitered us from the bulwarks, and seemed to look with little love at the cocked hat and epaulettes of the regular man-of-war.

"Is Captain Lafitte on board?"

"No, Señor," a hardy-looking, gray-headed old fellow answered, taking his cigarette from his mouth and proceeding to light a fresh one. He gave us some directions in Spanish, which I did not understand; the amount of which, however, was that "El Capitan" [the captain] might be found on board the schooner. And to the schooner we accordingly rowed. To our inquiry, Captain Lafitte answered himself, with an invitation to come on board.

My description of this renowned chieftain, to correspond with the original, will shock the preconceived notions of many who have hitherto pictured him as the hero of a novel or a melodrama. I am compelled by truth to introduce him as a stout, rather gentlemanly personage, some five feet ten inches in height, dressed very simply in a foraging cap and blue frock of a most villainous fit. His complexion, like most creoles, was olive; his countenance full, mild, and rather impressive but for a small black eye which now and then, as he grew animated in conversation, would flash in a way which impressed me with a notion that "El Capitan" might be, when roused, a very "ugly customer."

His demeanor toward us was exceedingly courteous, and upon learning Captain Kearny's mission, he invited us below, and tendered "the hospitalities of the vessel."

"I am making my arrangements," Lafitte observed, "to leave the bay. The ballast of the brig has been shifted. As soon as we can get her over the bar we sail."

"We supposed that your flotilla was larger," Captain Kearny remarked.

"I have men on shore," said Lafitte—not apparently noticing the remark—"who are destroying the fort, and preparing some spars for the brig. Will you go to shore and look at what I am doing?"

We returned to the deck, and Lafitte pointed us to the preparations which had been made on board the brig for getting her to sea. The schooner on which we were, mounted a long gun amidships and six nine-pounders a side. There were, I should think, fifteen or twenty men on deck, apparently of all nations; and below I could see there were a great many more. There was no appearance of any uniform among them, nor, to the eyes of a man-of-war's man, much discipline. The officers, or those who appeared such, were in plain clothes, and Lafitte himself was without any distinguishing mark of his rank.

On the shore we passed a long shed under which a party was at work, and around which junk, cordage, sails, and all sorts of heterogeneous matters were scattered in confusion. Beyond this we came across a four-gun fort. It had been advantageously located, and was a substantial-looking affair, but now was nearly dismantled, and a gang was completing the work of destruction.

"You see, Captain, I am getting ready to leave. I am friendly to your country. Ah, they call me a pirate. But I am not a pirate. You see there?" said he, pointing suddenly toward the point of the beach.

"I see," said our skipper, "what does that mean?"

The object to which our attention was thus directed was the dead body of a man dangling from a rude gibbet erected on the beach.

"That is my justice. That *vaurien* [good-for-nothing] plundered an American schooner. The captain complained to me of him, and he was found guilty and hung. Will you go on board my brig?"

On this vessel there was evidently a greater attention paid to discipline. Lafitte led the way into his cabin, where preparation had already been made for dinner, to partake of which we were invited. Sea air and exercise are proverbial persuaders of the appetite; and Mr. Lafitte's display of good stew, dried fish, and wild turkey was more tempting than prize money. Under the influence of the most generous and racy wines he became quite sociable. Lafitte was evidently educated and gifted with no common talent for conversation.

"I should like very much to hear your life, Captain," I remarked.

He smiled and shrugged his shoulders. "It is nothing extraordinary," he said. "I can tell it in a very few words. But there was a time"—and he drew a long breath—"when I could not tell it without cocking both pistols.

"Eighteen years ago I was a merchant in San Domingo. My father before me was a merchant. I had become rich. I had married me a wife. I determined to go to Europe, and I wound up all my affairs in the West Indies. I sold my property there. I bought a ship and loaded her, besides which, I had on board a large amount of speçie—all that I was worth, in short. Well, sir, when the vessel that I was on had been a week at sea we were overhauled by a Spanish man-of-war. The Spaniards captured us. They took everything—goods, specie, even my wife's jewels. They set us on shore on a barren sand key, with just provisions enough to keep us alive—a few days. An American schooner took us off, and landed us in New Orleans. I did not care what became of me. I was a beggar. My wife took the fever from exposure and hardship, and died in three days after my arrival. I met some daring fellows who were as poor as I was. We bought a schooner, and declared against Spain eternal war. Fifteen years I have carried on a war against Spain. So long as I live I am at war with Spain, but no other nation. I am at peace with the world, except Spain. Although they call me a pirate, I am not guilty of attacking any vessel of the English or French. I showed you the place where my own people have been punished for plundering American property."

Ninnie L. Baird, a Texas Legend

BY MEMBERS OF BAIRD FAMILY

☆ Ninnie and her husband, William Baird, moved to Fort Worth, Texas, with their young family in 1901. William was in the restaurant business in Tennessee and had intentions of starting a new business in Texas—he wanted to introduce Fort Worth to its first steam popcorn machine. Shortly after making a trip to Fort Worth on his own to prospect for business, William brought his wife and four small children to Texas by train.

Once they settled in, William set up his popcorn business at the corner of Seventh and Main in downtown Fort Worth. The bright red machine with its brass fittings and steam whistle attracted a lot of attention and within eight months, Mr. Baird purchased another one and put it at Fifth and Main. His oldest son, Dewey, who was only eight years old at the time, ran the new machine.

Shortly after, a restaurant in town was put up for sale and William decided to get back into the restaurant business. He sold the popcorn machines and bought the restaurant. Things went so well with the restaurant that William decided he could support his family by buying "run down" restaurants, fixing them up, running them, and then selling them. So, in 1905, he sold the restaurant and bought another one.

It wasn't long after this that William became ill with diabetes (an untreatable disease in those days). Despite his deteriorating health, he continued to work in his restaurant with the help of both his sons Dewey and Hoyt. Dewey, who was about ten years old at the time, quit school so he could help at home. While working with his father, Dewey learned how to cook and bake for the restaurant. Clayton Baird, Sr., Dewey's son, recalls his father telling him about how he helped out. "Dad said his father is the one who taught him how to bake," says Clayton. "He told me they would bake nickel pies in the morning and then they'd take them out to the packing houses in Fort Worth. They would sell the pies there and then bring them to the lunch wagons. This is when Dad really became the 'man' of the house." At the same time, Ninnie was home with the children and she would keep house and bake for the family. In those days, baking was no small task. Like everyone else in the early 1900s, Ninnie did all her baking in a wood-fired stove. Not only was it hot during the summer (a roaring fire had to be kept constantly to keep the oven temperature as even as possible) but it was also hard work. Wood needed to be chopped by hand and then loaded into the stove. Starting the fire was also a challenge. The stove's damper was small and didn't create much draft to get the fire started or to keep it going.

Ninnie had her work cut out for her. Despite the lack of modern conveniences, she was an excellent baker. She'd bake enough loaves of bread, cakes, and pies for her family and give away the extras to her neighbors. Ninnie always had a generous spirit that was evident her entire life. Because she shared her baked goods with her neighbors, her baking talents were quickly recognized and it didn't take long for everyone to start asking about Mrs. Baird's delicious bread.

She recognized fairly quickly that she could make a living by selling her bread. And, because her husband's health was deteriorating and it was getting harder for him to work regularly, she needed to support her family. So, in 1908 Mrs. Baird's Bread was born. Shortly after, in 1911, William died.

Ninnie had no choice but to continue the business she began. She and her four boys, Dewey, Hoyt, Roland, and C.B., worked together to bake and deliver the bread as it came fresh out of the oven.

Everyone helped in one way or another. The boys helped bake and deliver the bread and the girls took care of the smaller children and did other chores around the house. One of the daughters, Bess, worked outside of the house to help bring in extra money as the business was still getting off the ground. Eda Whitehead, Bess's daughter, recalls that her mother quit school in the tenth grade so that she could work as a secretary. Even from the start, Mrs Baird's was a family effort with everyone working together to make the business work.

At first, Ninnie did all of her baking in her small wood-fired stove that baked only four loaves at a time. Each day, Ninnie had to fire up the stove and keep the fire hot enough to bake all the bread and cakes that were needed to meet the demand. All deliveries were made on foot—the boys would carry baskets full of fresh bread to houses throughout the neighborhood. They went door-to-door selling bread, cakes, and pies. As sales grew, so did the area to which they delivered. Soon, the boys traded in their walking shoes for bicycles.

Around 1915, as demand for Mrs Baird's Bread continued to grow, baking multiple loaves each day became too difficult in the small wood burning stove. So, the family purchased its first commercial oven from a local hotel—the Old Metropolitan Hotel in Fort Worth. The oven cost $75. Ninnie didn't get a loan from the bank, but, instead, did some creative financing—$25 down in cash and the balance was paid out in bread and rolls. The new oven was able to bake forty loaves of bread at a time and helped Ninnie keep up with the growing demand for her products. The business also expanded in another way; the baking moved outside of the house to a small wooden building in the backyard.

With the arrival of the new oven, the boys could no longer handle the delivery load by riding their bicycles. The family buggy was converted into a sales wagon and Ned, the family horse, was at the helm. The family hired a man named Mr. Lipps to drive the wagon. Whenever he was ill, thirteen-year-old Hoyt replaced him. Within the year, Hoyt was the regular driver. Hoyt and his mother would often drive the route together. Ninnie would help get new customers while Hoyt served the regulars. She would also check the ledgers to make sure they were being kept properly. The ledgers kept track of charge sales and each week the customers would pay their bills. Customers could buy twenty-four tickets for one dollar—each ticket was good for a one-pound loaf of bread.

Other than the notebook carried on the wagon, the family didn't do any bookkeeping for the business. If at the end of each month they had money left over, they figured they made a profit. Carroll Baird, Hoyt's son, recalls some stories his dad would tell about delivering bread to the neighborhood.

"I remember my dad talking about when he was a kid and had to deliver the bread from door-to-door," recalls Carroll. "He would talk about one woman who had a goose in the yard and how it would come out flapping its wings all around him. The lady also had a pet bulldog and it was always yipping at his heels and biting him. She would tell him, 'Oh no, he's not going to bite you.' And, he would say, 'He's already bit me three times!' "

Although driving a horse and wagon made the deliveries a little easier, Carroll still heard plenty of stories. Hoyt would tell his kids about how Ned, the horse, would eat the grass at each stop and the ladies to whom he was delivering bread weren't pleased that Ned had chosen to dine in their yards. He also recalled how Ned knew the route so well that after each stop he would start trotting down the street towards the next stop before Hoyt could jump back into the wagon.

There were times when Hoyt would be off the route for a day or two and someone else would fill in. When he came back, Ned might suddenly stop in front of a strange house and no matter how much urging Hoyt did, Ned wouldn't budge. Later, Hoyt would learn that the house had been added to the route while he was gone.

Hoyt continued to serve customers by horse and wagon until 1917 when the family bought a Ford car. A panel body was built for it, the passenger seats were taken out, and the truck was painted a cream color. The words, "Eat More Mrs. Baird's Bread" were written on each side. During this time, the Baird's took on three wholesale accounts: the Telephone Exchange at Rosedale and Jennings, which bought only pies; the Telephone Exchange at Lamar and 10th, which bought only pies; and the Sandegard Grocery at 10th and Houston.

Sandegard's proved to be a lucrative account for Mrs Baird's. It was a large store that also had a delicatessen. At first the store only bought cakes which it prominently displayed in a case. Later, bread was added to its order and in time, the small store grew to fifteen stores. Sandegard continued to carry Mrs. Baird's products in each of its stores across Fort Worth.

In September of 1918, Hoyt entered the army and the sales route had no driver. The family decided to discontinue the retail route and go wholesale. The Baird's hired Charlie Longguth, the bakery's iceman, to operate the new wholesale route. The new demands on the business stretched its limits and soon the bakery needed to expand to keep up with customer requests.

Also in 1918, Mrs Baird's new headquarters moved to 6th and Terrell. The new facility was thirty feet wide and seventy-two feet long and in later years, was enlarged and improved until it became one of the largest baking plants in Texas.

Shortly after the new bakery opened for operation, the family bought a second truck for the sales route. Within a matter of months the two sales routes increased to four, and then five covering the entire city of Fort Worth. As route sales grew, so did the bakery itself. From 1918 to 1928, the new bakery was enlarged nine times to keep up with the production demand.

In those early years there were nine wholesale bakeries in Fort Worth with which Mrs Baird's was in competition. Allen Baird, Hoyt's son, remembers his dad talking about them.

"I can remember Dad talking about all of them, but I especially recall him talking about Walker's Big Dandy Bread. Bruno Reich ran the bakery for Walker and there would be times when Dad would have to go to Bruno to buy bread to fill an order for a customer," recalls Allen. "It would make Dad so made because Bruno would give him a hard time about coming to him for bread. So it became a fixation with Dad that we were going to make better bread than anyone ever thought of and we were going to be better than anyone else in town. It was a matter of pride and it was a challenge that came up every day."

The move to the new facility on 6th and Terrell created other challenges as well. There were more jobs to be filled and there was a greater capacity for production. Bess Hornbeck, a former employee who can recall when Hoyt would deliver bread to her mother by horse and buggy, remembers what it was like working at the new bakery.

"When I started working there it was very rugged compared to what it's like today," recalls Bess. "I started working in the early '20s at the plant on 6th and Terrell. I could walk to work because we lived just around the corner. I remember that everything was done by hand. I can recall icing cakes with a big spatula—we held the cakes in our hands and put the icing on and in the summer time it was very hot and sticky!"

Despite the comparatively modern facilities offered at the new location, running a bakery during the 1920s required a lot of work. The building was not air-conditioned and quite a bit was still done by hand. During the hot Texas summers temperatures inside the bakery would soar to the century mark or more and it could be even hotter next to the ovens that ran constantly.

A fleet of route trucks in 1920.
Today there are over 1,000 trucks in the fleet.
PHOTO COURTESY OF BYRON BAIRD.

The business continued to grow, but by 1929 things began to change. In the fall of 1929, the stock market crashed marking the beginning of the Great Depression. As the Depression deepened, millions of investors lost their life savings, business houses closed their doors, factories shut down, banks failed, and millions of unemployed walked the streets in a hopeless search for work.

"I can remember when the banks were all closed," recalls Bess. "I know I was cashier at the bakery then and I think at one time we had a million dollars in the vault at the plant. You couldn't put it in the bank and neither could anybody else. The different grocery stories around town would come to the bakery to get money—we sort of became an unofficial bank."

Bess also recalls that the Depression caused cutbacks at the bakery in the early thirties as well. "During that time business really fell off and they cut everybody's salary. I don't think any of us ever suffered. I know we always had bread if we didn't have anything else."

By 1938 business was doing well and Mrs Baird's expanded again. The two new bakeries also had a feature the other bakeries didn't have—plate glass windows. The windows were installed so customers could watch the baking process. Passersby not only delighted in watching all the activity at the bakery but they enjoyed the wonderful aroma as well. In fact, Mrs Baird's once won an award for the best aroma in Fort Worth!

In December of 1941, with the bombing of Pearl Harbor, the United States found itself in the middle of World War II. The war brought many changes—and challenges—to the bakery. Sugar and other ingredients were in short supply, as were human resources. As the men went off to war, many women came into the workforce. Because of the various shortages, Mrs Baird's found itself cutting back on the number of varieties it produced and limited itself to using the valuable ingredients to produce what became its core business—white and wheat breads, as well as hamburger and hot dog buns.

Mrs Baird's may have had to reduce the number of varieties

it produced; however, it never compromised on the quality of its products. "Quality, freshness, service—those things were inbred in us," explains Allen. "My dad, Dewey, Roland, and C.B.—I can remember them talking about the value of quality and that didn't change during the war."

The war ended and somehow the bakery again had weathered turbulent times, and by 1949 was ready to expand again.

"I can remember when we opened the Abilene plant," recalls Byron Baird, son of C.B. "It wasn't too long after WWII and there were balloons and other things that we hadn't seen in a long time—like Fleer's Double Bubble Gum. It was nice to see all of those things at the time."

While the Korean Conflict didn't have the same impact on the bakery as did WWII, American businesses did feel some effects.

"Help was a little hard to find," explains Clayton. "I was working at the Houston plant and had been in the navy. Dad said he needed help with the family business, so when I came home I went to work for the bakery full time. I can remember we spent quite a bit of hours hiring people and trying to keep people. We started to get a lot of women, and there were a lot of people working for us with hearing disabilities. I had to learn how to speak with sign language. I found it a pretty good way to communicate because down in the shop with all the noise I could tell someone across the shop what I wanted to say with my hands."

During all this time, as the bakery grew and flourished, Ninnie Baird continued to be a part of the business. Throughout the years, her boys began taking more control in the day-to-day affairs, but she still kept an office at the Fort Worth plant and kept a controlling interest as chairman of the board.

However, by the 1950s, Ninnie's health began to decline. She was now in her eighties and spent most of her time at home. "She always maintained that interest throughout her life," explains Clayton. "I can remember when she finally started having problems getting around. We held board meetings at her house. She was still chairman and my dad was president at the time. She would ask us questions about what was going on at each plant. She always wanted to keep up with the business."

Byron has similar memories of his grandmother's role in the bakery. "Dad and the other three boys always had to go to Grandmother with the big decisions. She no longer dealt with the day-to-day operations but she wanted to be in on major decisions, such as building a new plant."

"I don't think the focus has ever been on getting bigger," adds Allen. "The focus has always been on being better, and as a result, the business has grown. Our first responsibility was to produce the best loaf of bread that we could and put it into the hands of the consumer as quickly as we could. And that way we knew that people were going to come back and buy a second time."

This work ethic and commitment to quality weren't the only things passed on from generation to generation. Ninnie Baird also stressed the importance of family, a Christian upbringing, and looking out for others in the community. Until the day she died, Ninnie reached out to the community and shared what she had with others. Mrs Baird's continues that tradition today by its involvement with numerous charities and local organizations through her legacy The Ninnie L. Baird Foundation supporting children and families through family preservation, education, and nutrition. "I also remember Great-grandmother being very particular about things," says Scott D. Baird, grandson of Dewey. "She was a very kind and generous woman, but she definitely liked things to be done a certain way. I can recall her saying, 'Cleanliness is next to Godliness.' We even put a sign up at the Dallas bakery when it was opened in the fifties. I remember wheeling her around in her wheelchair and when she saw that sign it made her laugh. She believed that if you were going to do something you had to do it right, no matter what it was."

On June 3, 1961, Ninnie L. Baird died at the age of ninety-two. The minister at her funeral described her as "an ideal woman in the eyes of God." He said she had fulfilled the highest traditions of American life but in all the fullness of her work she had always been a devoted mother and family woman.

Minnie L. Baird.
PHOTO COURTESY OF BYRON BAIRD.

From Havana to Silicon Hills

BY ROGER J. PINEIRO

☆ It all started with a bang. The date was April 17, 1961. The place was Havana, Cuba. I was born as bullets and mortar shells zoomed overhead during the failed CIA-backed invasion at Bay of Pigs. In the middle of my cesarean delivery, while the distant sound of artillery rounds rattled the hospital windows, Castro's militia burst inside the operating room and arrested the surgeon on treason charges—never mind that he had still not completed the procedure, leaving my fate—and my mother's—in the hands of nurses.

I guess in retrospect that shouldn't have been too surprising. Though I didn't know it then, I had just been born into a family of fighters, men and women with fire in their hearts and steel in their fists. My exciting delivery fit right in with my family's tradition.

Take my dad, for starters, a young engineer with a beautiful wife and an infant son, trying to get us out of the country while Castro still allowed one daily "freedom" flight to Miami for *gusanos*—the worms opposing his revolution. But Castro wasn't letting professionals out, *gusanos* or not. He wanted to hang on to the doctors, the industrialists, the scientists, forcing my dad to resort to desperate measures: sneaking into the university at night—at the risk of getting five years in prison—and stealing his school records. "I burned them," he once told me. "So no one would know that I was an engineer." For him, as for so many other Cubans, the choices were clear: *libertad o muerte* (freedom or death). His trick worked. Six agonizing months later he boarded a plane to Miami, but without my mother and I. That was another one of Castros's ploys to deter *gusanos* from fleeing his regime: not letting families leave together. Undaunted by this threat, determined to live by his own rules, my dad chose to call Castro's bluff and left anyway. High gamble paid off: my mother and I joined him six weeks later. Of course, we all reached freedom with nothing but the clothes we wore. If Castro's militia caught you trying to smuggle anything out of the country; even your own wedding band, they would take your children away from you to be raised by the Communist system—a risk neither of my parents was willing to take.

But that episode wasn't nearly as exciting as my dad's youngest sister's saga to leave Cuba. The freedom flights were canceled before my aunt's turn came up. Three months pregnant at the time, she was forced into a more radical approach: together with her husband and a friend, they hijacked a Cuban airliner and forced the pilot to fly to Miami at gunpoint. Unfortunately, none of them knew much about navigation. The pilot tricked them by circling over the ocean for twenty minutes before doubling back to the island, landing at a nearby airport, where local officials had stretched a banner reading, WELCOME TO MIAMI. Somehow the pilot had managed to notify the authorities and they sprung this spontaneous trap. All three were arrested as they ran away from the plane thinking that they had reached freedom. Instead they were all sentenced to thirty years in prison. My aunt served seven years (she gave birth in her cell) before being paroled. She then managed to get a temporary visa to visit Nicaragua, and from there she fled north, by foot, through Central America and Mexico, crossing the Rio Grande and obtaining political asylum in the United States.

Fire in our hearts and steel in our fists.

Someone once told me that good judgment comes from experience. The problem is that experience often comes from bad judgment. In hindsight, one could argue that my father used poor judgment when he opted to move to Argentina instead of remaining in Florida. But at the time he needed a job (he was into plastics in those days) and his only immediate prospect was in Buenos Aires. So off we went, with my mother already pregnant with my twin sisters, to a land that soon fell into the economic depression of the Peron years—and the rapidly devaluating peso that made my father's savings worthless. We only lasted two years down there, before starting our slow migration back north, with a supposedly six-month pit stop in El Salvador, Central America, where the chance to launch a new plastics factory presented my dad with a unique short-term opportunity. Back in 1965 El Salvador was quite the tropical paradise with plenty of growth opportunity—so much that we stayed there for sixteen years. And I think my parents would have settled there permanently had it not been for the unrest that precluded that country's twelve-year-long civil war.

Having lived through the Cuban revolution, my dad saw it coming again in El Salvador and started making preparations to come to the United States. This time around he would not leave with just the shirt on his back.

In my years growing up in El Salvador I saw my fair share of death and destruction that so often comes with living in Third World countries, and more so as the nation spiraled into a bloody civil war between Marxist rebels and the right-wing government. Civilians, of course, are always caught in the middle in such conflicts. Rebels would often stop traffic to collect donations for their cause. They smiled as they produced an empty can and asked for your pocket change. They continued to smile while patting their AK-47 assault rifles hanging from their shoulders. Later on government forces would question those caught supporting the rebels and label them as Communist sympathizers. You were really stuck between a rock and a hard place, destined sooner or later to become a victim of either the right-wing death squads, or the leftist rebels. It was really time to pack it up and head north.

But we couldn't all leave at once. Many preparations needed to be done before leaving, so I volunteered to come up first. I'd always wanted to move to the U.S. and saw the unrest in El Salvador as my chance to start living life by my own rules, just like my father had. I'd known for some time that I would come here for college, so why not do it a little sooner and finish high school in the States? So I did, coming to this country (Florida of all places) in 1977 at the age of sixteen to start my new life, alone, and in a country in which I didn't speak the language. But I adapted quickly, and within one year I had not only mastered the English language, but was one of the highest-ranking students in my high school, plus I had earned my private pilot's license by my seventeenth birthday. I guess some of that fire and steel did live within me after all.

By 1979, civil war finally erupted in El Salvador, and my parents and sisters could no longer remain there, so they joined me in Baton Rouge, where I had just begun attending college at Louisiana State University.

I always tell people that two good things came out of the four years I spent at LSU: my computer engineering degree, and my wife, Lory Anne, with whom I'll be celebrating my seventeenth wedding anniversary soon, in the company of our ten-year-old son, Cameron.

Joining the emerging high-tech industry in Austin seemed like the next logical step after LSU. In hindsight it turned out to be one of the best decisions I've ever made. When I began my career at Advanced Micro Devices in 1983, the personal computer was a little more than a novelty and the Internet was a pipe dream. But it was here that our battle began in the growing field of microprocessors, the heart of the personal computer. As I write this, seventeen years later, I realize just how blessed I've been to have participated in this incredible revolution in speed and performance—a revolution equal to the birth and development of twentieth-century aviation. Those old eight-bit, first-generation microprocessors that I worked on as a young engineer, and which powered the original IBM PCs at frequencies of 2 MHz, were the fragile contraptions flown by the Wright brothers at Kitty Hawk—good concepts with little immediate practical application, but with a lot of potential. By contrast, today's 64-bit, eighth-generation, gigahertz microprocessors can be equaled to the latest airliners. But while it took forty years for air transportation to become a practical reality, it only took half that time for computers to change the world. But the change didn't come without extreme personal sacrifice. There are tens of thousands of unsung heroes in this high-tech race, the brave men and women fighting daily battles at places with names like AMD, Motorola, IBM, and Gateway. These are the unknown warriors, the faceless teams that invent the technology of our times, paving the way for the future, oftentimes at the cost of failed marriages and deteriorating health. They are the ones who created Silicon Valley, as well as its recent sibling in Austin, Texas, Silicon Hills.

There is also another aspect of my life that I've failed to mention. While my love for technology propelled me into a career in engineering, I also discovered another passion ten years ago: writing. I began writing fiction almost overnight, from the heart, finishing my first novel in six months. Getting published, however, turned out to be the single most challenging thing I've ever done. But some of the old family determination that flows through my veins kept me going, chipping away at each road-block, until my writing career finally took wing.

From Havana to Silicon Hills. At times I think of all the forces that got me to Texas, of all of the sacrifices my parents made to give us a better life. This is indeed a wonderful land—and blessed state—whose virtues are often overlooked by those focusing on petty things. They should be kissing the ground they walk on. I know I do it every day.

ROGER J. PINEIRO is a computer engineer working on leading-edge microprocessors at Advance Micro Devices. He is the author of several thrillers, including Ultimatum, Breakthrough, and Shutdown as well as the millenium thrillers, 01-1-00 and Y2K. He lives in Austin, Texas, with his wife Lory Anne and his son Cameron.

WHY HE CAME TO TEXAS

BY ALEX E. SWEET

A good many years ago, when Austin was a very small town, quite a number of prominent citizens went out on a hunting expedition. One night when they were all gathered around the camp fire, one of the party suggested that each man should give the time and reason for his leaving his native state and coming to Texas, whereupon each one in turn told his experience. Judge Blank had killed a man in self-defense, and Arkansaw. Gen. Soandso had forged another man's signature to a check, while another came to Texas on account of his having two wives. The only man who did not make any disclosures was a sanctimonious-looking old man, who, although a professional gambler, was usually called "Parson."

"Well, Parson, why did you leave Kentucky?"

"I don't care to say anything about it. Besides, it was only a trifle. None of you would believe me anyhow."

"Out with it! Did you shoot somebody?"

"No, gentlemen, I did not. But since you want to know so bad, I'll tell you. I left Kentucky because I did not build a church."

Deep silence fell on the group. No such excuse for coming to Texas ever had been heard before. There was evidently an unexplained mystery at the bottom of it. The "Parson" was called on to furnish more light.

"Well, gentlemen, you see a Methodist congregation raised $3,000 and turned it over to me to build a church—and I didn't build the church. That's all."

ALEX E. SWEET was an Austin, Texas, satirist and humorist.

Building Texas Railroads

BY RICHARD RUSSACK

☆ As civilization was taking root in Texas in the mid-nineteenth century, men like Colonel Warren H. H. Lawrence and Greenville M. Dodge saw great opportunity for railroads in the Southwest. They recognized the value of a Texas railroad to the Rocky Mountain region of the United States, a link that would establish a thriving route.

President Abraham Lincoln appointed Dr. John Evans, another visionary, territorial governor of Colorado in 1862. At the time of his appointment, Colorado was as isolated as the territory was difficult to colonize. In the 1870s, the Rio Grande, the Santa Fe, and the Union Pacific built rail lines into the territory. Dr. Evans believed an alternate rail outlet to eastern markets was a necessity for Colorado. His idea was to build a line to the Gulf of Mexico, where steamers would connect and move traffic to the Atlantic seaboard.

Thus, the stories of the Fort Worth and Denver City and the Colorado and Southern railroads began similarly and ended with the same final chapter, becoming predecessors of today's Burlington Northern and Santa Fe Railway Company.

Among the reasons that encouraged the creation of the Santa Fe, which became the nation's second transcontinental rail line, was the rush to California following the discovery of gold there in the mid-1800s, prosperous cattle drives from Texas to Kansas City, and the booming population of Kansas, where "sodbusters" had produce and crops that needed to be moved to markets.

In Texas, with its tremendous undeveloped resources, there were opportunities everywhere for rail transportation. Texas's first railroad began operations in 1853 and by early 1870, a

700-mile rail network had emerged. Construction moved northwest from the Gulf Coast and by 1873, Fort Worth was just thirty-five miles from the Gulf-Kansas City main line. Colonel Lawrence moved to Fort Worth in 1868. His vision was also a Gulf-to-Rockies route. He had introduced a bill to the Texas Legislature encouraging a connection with any Colorado railroad. Though the bill was vetoed, Lawrence continued pursuit of his vision.

Working with other leading citizens, he drew up a charter for the Fort Worth and Denver City Railway Company (FW&D), and it became effective May 26, 1873. The charter specified that the FW&D would build and operate a line at or near Fort Worth, where it would form a junction with the Texas and Pacific Railway, and then head northwesterly in the direction of Denver. As a result of the "Panic of '73," the line's construction was delayed.

Grading for the FW&D began in 1881 at Hodge, near Fort Worth, under the guidance of General Greenville M. Dodge, a civil engineer who had built several major rail lines. Shortly thereafter, with the coming of the Texas and Pacific Railway, the beginnings of Fort Worth as a railhead took shape. In 1880, the frontier town of Fort Worth had a population of nine thousand people.

The first step in Dr. Evans's vision was in 1881 when he organized a railroad to run southward from Denver. The railroad was called the Denver and New Orleans Railroad (DNO) and it was planned to connect with the Texas Central, which would provide access to the Gulf of Mexico at Galveston. The DNO would cross the Santa Fe Railway at La Junta, Colorado, providing access to the Gulf of California, and connect with the Missouri, Kansas, and Texas at or near Fort Worth, where the rails of the Texas and Pacific Railway would lead to New Orleans.

The early 1880s saw the St. Louis & San Francisco Railway Company (the Frisco) head south from Monett, Missouri, with a line through the Boston Mountains of Arkansas to Fort

Smith, through the Choctaw Nation to Paris, Texas, and a connection with the Santa Fe's line to Dallas and Fort Worth. Somehow, Evans had overlooked the FW&D developments in the 1870s. But in 1881, General Dodge and Dr. Evans negotiated an agreement that would have their two roads meet at the Canadian River in the Texas Panhandle. However, Dodge and the FW&D remained cautious by not extending their line without certainty that Evans's road was financially stable.

FW&D's caution was well founded. Evans faced much opposition from other railroads and his enterprise suffered losses and floundered, causing him to reorganize his railroad in 1885 as the Denver, Texas, and Gulf Railroad Company.

In 1887, Santa Fe wanted an independent entrance into Denver and explored buying Evans's railway or building one. Evans used Santa Fe's offer as a bargaining point with Dodge. Following negotiations, Evans and Dodge finally reached an agreement, signed February 15, 1887. The agreement would close the 481-mile gap between Pueblo, Colorado, and Quanah, Texas, the current FW&D railhead. In addition, the agreement would provide for an independent operation of the entire Gulf-to-Rockies route.

Under the guidance of both Evans and Dodge, a new company was designed—the Denver, Texas, and Fort Worth, which was incorporated in Colorado on April 12, 1887. This company operated a railroad from Pueblo to the Texas–New Mexico border and acquired control of both the Denver, Texas and Gulf, and the FW&D. By March 14, 1888, the FW&D physically connected with the Denver, Texas, and Fort Worth Railroad, which would later be known as the Colorado and Southern, at Union Park, near Folsom, New Mexico. This "Panhandle Route" would complete the through route from Denver to Texas. On December 17, 1898, the Colorado and Southern was incorporated. It comprised nearly thirty railroad companies, combined 1,085 miles and held a controlling stock interest in the FW&D. At the same time, the Santa Fe was continuing to actively settle developing territories including Texas and New Mexico.

The Frisco completed its own line to the Dallas/Fort Worth area in 1901, through construction south from Sapulpa, Oklahoma to Denison, Texas, and the purchase of a fifty-eight-mile line from Sherman to Carrollton, Texas, near Fort Worth.

In 1908, both the C&S and the FW&D became a part of the Chicago, Burlington, and Quincy (CB&Q) railroad. The CB&Q system and the Frisco, along with another 330 railroads are now a part of the Burlington Northern and Santa Fe Railway Company, a subsidiary of Burlington Northern Santa Fe Corporation, headquartered in Fort Worth, Texas.

In 1911, Santa Fe began operating the DeLuxe, weekly extra-fare train service between Chicago and Los Angeles, which was limited to sixty people. The rich heritage of Santa Fe's passenger train service included such landmark trains as the Texas Chief, El Capitan, the Grand Canyon, the Kansas Cityan, the Chicagoan, the Scout San Diegans, and the San Francisco Chief.

RICHARD RUSSACK is vice president of Corporate Relations for Burlington Northern Santa Fe Corporation. He has lived in Fort Worth since 1991 and is active in a variety of community activities including the Arts Council of Fort Worth and Tarrant County, the United Way of Metropolitan Tarrant County, and the National Conference for Community and Justice.

Forth Worth & Denver yard engine #31, Wichita Falls, Texas, 1890.
PHOTO COURTESY OF THE BURLINGTON NORTHERN AND SANTA FE RAILWAY.

Santa Fe's "Texas Chief" operating between Chicago, Illinois,
and Dallas, Texas.
PHOTO COURTESY OF THE BURLINGTON NORTHERN AND SANTA FE RAILWAY.